HIGHER

A Family Devotional

Written by
Fountainview Academy Students

Fountainview Academy
Box 500, Lillooet, BC, V0K-1V0
Canada

Fountainview Academy
P.O. Box 500
Lillooet, British Columbia V0K 1V0
CANADA

Web Address: www.fountainview.ca
E-mail: info@fountainviewacademy.ca
Copyright © 2010 by
Fountainview Academy
All rights reserved

This book was
Edited by Mike Lemon, Cara Dewsberry, Anneliese Wahlman, and Matthew West
Dedication written by Valerie Jacobson
Cover Design by Robert Richards, Daniel Glassford, and Jerick Arceo
Cover Photo by Seth Dixon of Jonathan Sharley, Jourdain Smith, and Benjamin Jenkins
Authors' Pages by Georgina Holdal, Daniel Glassford, and Jerick Arceo
Electronic Makeup by D. Luke Gonzalez and Matthew West
Typeset: 9/10/12/32 Liberation Sans, 11 Liberation Serif

PRINTED IN U.S.A.

ISBN 10: 0692009817
ISBN 13: 9780692009819

Introduction

"Higher than the highest human thought can reach is God's ideal for His children. Godliness—godlikeness—is the goal to be reached" (*Education*, pg. 18). If the ultimate goal of our development is godlikeness, and Jesus came to show us what God is like by descending from Heaven to Earth, then to go HIGHER, we must first go lower. You see, Jesus gave us the formula for reaching HIGHER when He said, "If any man desire to be first, the same shall be…servant of all" (Mark 9:35 KJV).

Clearly, the way up is through descent, and success comes through sacrifice. Jesus left the highest heights of Heaven to descend to the fallen lowlands of our sinful planet. He cast aside the privileges of deity and chose to be a humble servant of sinners. He wasn't finished yet; He descended lower still and became obedient unto death, even to the extent of dying the most shameful of deaths on a rough, wooden cross. Because of His great sacrifice, God lifted Him high and honored Him far above and beyond anyone or anything in all of God's creation (Philippians 2:5-11).

So how high is HIGHER? HIGHER means to keep climbing until you reach Jesus. And that's much HIGHER than you can get climbing the world's highest mountain!

The Fountainview Academy, Grade 11 English class (Graduating Class of 2011), wrote this FAMILY DEVOTIONAL, HIGHER. Their assignment was to read the book *Education*, by Ellen G. White, and then to write twenty-three devotional readings each, based off Bible verses or quotes from *Education*. After marking and editing their work, I had the assistance of four students: Cara Dewsberry, Anneliese Wahlman, Luke Gonzalez, and Matthew West. They helped me to format, to organize the order of the devotional readings, to do the electronic makeup of the book, and to make corrections to the book prior to publication. Through the strength of Christ's Spirit, we were always inspired to aim HIGHER!

Mike Lemon
English Teacher
Fountainview
Academy
British Columbia,
CANADA

The authors would like to dedicate this devotional book to:

Charles Smith,
who believed in the principles laid out in the book "Education," and
who, in mentoring and encouraging the future leaders of
Fountainview Academy, left a legacy that sparked a fire in their
hearts;

Scott Richards,
one of those "future leaders," now the President of Fountainview
Academy, who, fanning the flame, put forth the effort to make these
principles a reality—principles that are clearly evident in his own life
and have shaped this school to become what it is today;

and the Youth of Our Generation,
who are called to keep the fire burning, and whose duty can be
summed up in one word: Higher.

About
the
Authors

Sarah Chang, 17
California, USA
Interests/Goals: design, the arts, scuba
diving, public speaking; to follow God with all
my heart, inspire others, lead by example, &
perform at Carnegie Hall with Sarah Chang.

Kevin Corrigan, 17
British Columbia, Canada
Interests/Goals: bird watching, music,
creative design, photography, hiking; to
get an all-around education and be used
wherever God calls me.

Valdis Cuvaldin, 17
Bucharest, Romania
Interests/Goals: human behavior, traveling,
reading; to become a dentist or psychologist.

Wesley Donesky, 18
Tennessee, USA
Interests/Goals: airplanes, engineering, music,
culinary arts, sports, cello; to be an engineer or
mission pilot. But more than anything, to follow
God's will and bless others.

Elisa Eliasdottir, 17 Visiting Student
Iceland
Interests/Goals: God, music, photography,
eating good food, seeing new places,
learning new things, reading, nutrition & health;
to reflect Christ's character.

Anna Fink, 17
Montana, USA
Interests/Goals: backpacking,
skiing/snowboarding, swimming, math,
music, recycling paper; travel, go on a
mission trip, and to be a Christ-like example.

Daniel Glassford, 17
Arizona, USA
Interests/Goals: God, guitar, engineering,
electronics, snowboarding; to be a balanced
person, make the most of my opportunities,
do something in the medical field.

Cyrus Guccione, 16
California, USA
Interests/Goals: photography, travel, guitar,
running, snowboarding, reading, swimming;
grow a full beard, be a part of the 144,000,
and live a life of service.

Jessica Hall, 16
British Columbia, Canada
Interests/Goals: crocheting, gymnastics,
working out, baking/cooking, music, spending time with family, friends, & God; become
a physical therapist, eventually own a cafe.

Carmen Hartwell, 16
British Columbia, Canada
Interests/Goals: sleeping, writing,
drawing, climbing trees, cooking, bungee-
skiing; become a clear channel for God to
shine through, go into the dental field.

Jo Holdal, 16
British Columbia, Canada
Interests/Goals: skiing, reading, backpacking, all season camping, cooking/ baking;
travel, be a missionary, become a radio-
logical technician, and possibly a mother.

Valerie Jacobson, 16
British Columbia, Canada
Interests/Goals: violin, music, having fun with
friends, running sports; taking engineering &
music in university, play at Carnegie Hall if
that's God's will.

Sarah- Kate Lingerfelt, 17
Tennessee, USA
Interests/Goals: art, individuality, politics &
history, cutting hair, cooking; work for ADRA
possibly at an orphanage, start a restaurant.

Wesley Mayes, 17
Tennessee, USA
Interests/Goals: snowboarding, back-
packing, guitar; get a hippie van, back-pack
Europe, go to college, go to Heaven, gain
the ability to fly, write a book.

Megan Metcalf, 17
North Carolina, USA
Interests/Goals: family & friends, music,
adventure, outdoor activities, cooking,
English, photography, reading; use medical
aid to serve God, learn to play guitar.

Rachel Petrello, 17
Washington, USA
Interests/Goals: violin, writing, marine
biology, painting, photography, camping,
cooking; build doll houses.

Danielle Schafer, 17
British Columbia, Canada
Interests/Goals: photography, double bass, poetry, music, doodling; become a graphic designer, travel, learn a new language, go to school overseas.

Sophia Simard, 17
British Columbia, Canada
Interests/Goals: reading, skiing, whitewater kayaking; have fun, travel, be either a brain surgeon or lawyer.

Yannika Stafford, 17
Washington, USA
Interests/Goals: piano, brushing my teeth, listening to music, going to symphonies, hanging out with friends; go into dentistry, travel the world.

Laelle Teranski, 18
Ontario, Canada
Interests/Goals: photography, camping, dirtbiking, listening to music; become a good nurse, have a closer relationship with God, and become a missionary.

Anneliese Wahlman, 17
Colorado, USA
Interests/Goals: knitting, photography, writing, gymnastics; travel Europe, become good at photography, make Jesus my Best Friend.

Bristi Waid, 18
Washington, USA
Interests/Goals: cooking, reading, cutting hair, Indian art, traveling; to daily grow closer to God, become a nurse, work in an orphanage in Bangladesh.

Victoria West, 17
Washington, USA
Interests/Goals: violin, gymnastics, dogs, swimming, math, nutrition, skiing; travel Europe, become a radiologist, lead a Pathfinder club.

Laura Williams, 18
Washington, USA
Interests/Goals: flying, singing, photography, web design, camping; be a mission pilot and be involved in music ministry.

Cara Dewsberry, Senior Student/ Editor, 18
California, USA
Interests/Goals: reading, music, traveling,
daydreaming, hanging out with friends; get my
driver's license, learn a foreign language,
become better friends with God.

D. Luke Gonzalez, Senior Student/ Book Compiler, 18
California, USA
Interests/Goals: theology, teaching, learning, cooking,
eating, computers; to become a professor, and to
become a loving husband and father.

Matthew West, Sophomore Student/ Editor, 16
Washington, USA
Interests/Goals: snowskiing, frisbee, computer
programming, violin, hiking/backpacking;
to follow God's plan for my life.

Mike Lemon, English Teacher
British Columbia, Canada
Interests/Goals: Jesus, my wife & children,
teaching, preaching, reading, writing,
horseback riding, gardening, learning new
things, and getting lost in the mountains.

Higher

There is need of a broader scope, a higher aim. True education means more than the pursual of a certain course of study... In Him "are hid all the treasures of wisdom." - Education, pg. 13

What exactly is learning? Is it just a preliminary gaining of knowledge before entering the "real" world? Or is it something deeper and more elevated?

As a student, I sometimes feel that I am being drowned in knowledge. Tests and deadlines are constantly coming around to gauge the amount of information I have learned, and I'm just trying to keep my head above water and get a good grade. Now don't get me wrong, schooling is very important, and it shouldn't be taken lightly. But there is more to knowledge than just book learning. There is something higher, something mysterious. This is called the knowledge of God.

I know this may seem a little cliche, but think about it. Where do we get most of our knowledge? Well, we know that a student learns from his teachers, teachers learn from scientists or professors, and scientists and professors learn from others or by studying for themselves. But, where did the knowledge itself come from? All the knowledge that we have now has always been there; we have just had to learn it. This information had to have a source, a creator.

Job 12:13 says: "With Him is wisdom and strength, He hath counsel and understanding" (KJV). The only way to truly learn is to get to know your Creator, the same Creator who designed the immense galaxies and formed the minute atoms. How do you get to know Him? The same way you got to know your best friend. Interact with Him. Read His Word, talk to Him, have faith in His promises. And, unlike your earthly friends, He will never fail you. Trust me, He wants to get to know you, too.

~ Wesley Mayes

Heaven or Snails?

True education means more than the pursual of a certain course of study... It has to do with the whole being, and with the whole period of existence possible to man. - Education, pg. 13

There is an old legend of a swan and a crane. The beautiful swan alighted by the banks of a pond in which a crane was wading around looking for snails. For a few moments, the crane gazed upon the swan in stupefied wonder and then inquired:

"Where do you come from?"
"I come from heaven!" replied the swan.
"And where is heaven?" asked the crane.

"Heaven!" exclaimed the swan, "Have you never heard of heaven?" Then the swan began to describe the wondrous glories of heaven. She told of the streets of gold and the gates and walls of precious stones, of the pure River of Life and the Tree of Life that shades its banks. In eloquent terms, the swan sought to describe the hosts who live in that other world; but none of this aroused the slightest interest in the crane.

Finally, the crane asked, "Are there any snails in heaven?"
"Snails!" repeated the swan, "No, of course there are no snails."
"Then," said the crane, as it continued its search along the slimy banks of the pool, "You can have your heaven. I want snails!"

Sometimes we treat education as the crane treated heaven. We are happy and comfortable with what we already have learned and totally ignore the fact that there is something better. Education is not merely the study of facts and information, but it is the lifetime work of perfecting our characters. How much more fulfilling life will be when we take this view of education... heaven instead of snails!

~ Anna Fink

Learning from the Best

The world has had its great teachers, men of giant intellect and extensive research, men whose utterances have stimulated thought and opened to view vast fields of knowledge; and these men have been honored as guides and benefactors of their race; but there is One who stands higher than they. - Education, pg. 13

Sir Isaac Newton had just finished making his solar system machine when his friend, an atheistic scientist, came by for a visit. His friend saw the new machine and exclaimed, "How wonderful!" Then he hastily walked over and started cranking the strong wooden handle.

As the man continued cranking, he asked, "Who made this?"

Sir Isaac stopped writing and said, "Nobody did." Then he continued writing.

"You didn't hear me," the scientist friend retorted, "Who made the machine?"

"I told you, nobody did." Isaac replied.

"Now listen, Isaac, this machine must have been made by somebody. Don't just keep saying that nobody made it."

At this point, Isaac stopped writing and turned to his atheist friend with a smile. "Now isn't it amazing, I tell you nobody made a simple toy like that, and you don't believe me. Yet, you gaze out into the solar system—the intricate, marvelous machine that is around you—and you dare say to me that no one made that. I don't believe it."

When the scientist left Sir Isaac Newton that day, he was no longer an atheist. He became converted to the belief that God was the One who had created the laws found in nature.

Sir Isaac Newton is often regarded as the most influential scientist in history. He was a mathematician, physicist, astronomer, alchemist, inventor, and natural philosopher. But even Sir Isaac Newton understood that God was the One who had come before him, and that He was the One who in the beginning flung the stars into the heavens and made each planet unique in the universe. Learning from God's Word and all that He has created is such a privilege for us. We truly get to learn from the Best!

~ Jessica Hall

Be the Moon

As the moon and the stars of our solar system shine by the reflected light of the sun, so, as far as their teaching is true, do the world's great thinkers reflect the rays of the Sun of Righteousness.
- Education, pg. 14

The day I met my good friend Luke Gonzalez, I noticed he was wearing a strange article of clothing. He had on a black T-shirt with a picture of the moon on the front. Across the top in white letters was written, "Be the Moon." At first, I was puzzled about the meaning of the shirt. Be the moon? What was it about the moon that the shirt was implying I should be like? Big? Round? Bumpy? In outer space? Later that day, I saw the back of the shirt when Luke took off his jacket. "Oh!" I thought, "Now it all makes sense!" Written on the back were the words, "Reflect the Son."

When Jesus was just a child, He knew the focus of His work. One day when His family was traveling back home from Jerusalem, His parents realized He was missing. After frantically looking all over for Him, they finally found Jesus in the temple with the rabbis. With a frustrated sigh of relief, His parents asked, "Son, why have You done this to us? Look, Your father and I have sought You anxiously." Surprised, Jesus looked up and replied, "Why did you seek Me? Did you not know that I must be about My Father's business?" (Matthew 2:48,49 NKJV).

Jesus was only twelve, but already He had figured out His life's purpose: to spread the Light which was given to Him by His Father. All knowledge comes from God, the Great Teacher. But are we, as students and teachers, reflecting the Light that God has given us? Just as Jesus lived to reflect God's glory, so it is our responsibility and privilege to be Christ's representatives. Search your heart and ask God today to help you "be the moon" and reflect His light of love.

~ Rachel Petrello

Communing with the Infinite

The mind of man is brought into communion with the mind of God, the finite with the Infinite... In this communion is found the highest education... "Acquaint now thyself with Him," is His message to mankind. - Education, pg. 14

Just a few weeks before my Social Studies 11 Provincial Exam, my grade was the lowest "A" possible. So, I had high hopes of getting 100% on my next test to raise my grade before the Provincial Exam. I prayed over and over, "Lord, please help me to get 100% on this test." I even asked others to pray this same prayer for me. I also studied very hard. Finally, the morning of the test came. I felt fairly confident after having taken it. Then, on the following day, I got my test back—83%. I was devastated and began to cry. My expectations for my own achievement had been too high. That night at worship, I made the decision to stop relying on my own power and give my academic life over to God. It wasn't easy. I had to constantly remind myself, "I'm only doing this through God's power and for His glory." Soon we had another Socials test. This time, though I was still praying for 100%, I also prayed for God's will to be done with my grades. And I didn't let my expectations get too high. "I'm leaving this in God's hands," I told myself. The next day, Mr. Lemon handed me my test. I was ecstatic to see the numbers "1-0-0" scrawled at the top of my paper in red ink. "Thank you, God!" I cried.

When I was in communion with God, He gave me success. Communion is defined as being "an intimate relationship with deep understanding." I made God my priority and kept studying my Bible and praying regularly, and He blessed me.

I would encourage you to enjoy communion with God, starting today. Make Him your priority. Spend time with your Maker in Bible study and prayer, pouring out to Him your heart's desires and sorrows. Devote your life completely to God, and He will bless you.

Let's finish with a word of prayer. "Dear Father in Heaven, I want to devote every portion of my life to you today. Please give me sweet communion with You and help me to trust You with my life. In Jesus' name, Amen."

~ Victoria West

Simply Talk

Face-to-face, heart-to-heart communion with his Maker was his high privilege. - Education, pg. 15

"When I said, 'Let there be light,' there was light. It was so beautiful, Adam!" God exclaimed.

"Oh Lord, thank You for doing that just for me. The morning sun brings me so much joy!" Adam replied.

"Adam, I have made everything just for you! I want you to learn from it all, so that your life may be enriched, and you may understand my love for you even more. The water, land, plants, animals, trees, and flowers—everything is all for you! Oh, and I want you to name the animals. Will you do that for me, Adam?"

"I would love to do that; it will be such a privilege! Thank You, Lord, my God!"

Adam had such an amazing opportunity to be able to talk with God anytime, anywhere. I imagine God and Adam must have talked as best friends.

How do you talk with your best friend? Do you say the same things to them each time you see them? Probably not. I know each time I talk to my best friends, I'm eager to tell them all that happened in my day. And I'm just as excited to hear about what is going on in their lives.

Did you know that God desires to talk with you? He longs to have heart-to-heart communication with you, just as He had with Adam. He wants to be your Best Friend. He wants to know what's going on in your life. God tells us in John 15:15, "I have called you friends" (KJV). Like a friend, God wants to talk to and comfort you.

Only in heaven will we see God face-to-face, but we can have heart-to-heart communication with Him right now. Let's simply talk to Him today, since having intimate communion with our Maker is our highest privilege.

~ Jessica Hall

Seeing God

Face-to-face, heart-to-heart communion with his Maker was his [Adam's] high privilege. Had he remained loyal to God, all this would have been his forever. - Education, pg. 15

Before I came to Fountainview, I lived at home with my parents and brother in Ontario, Canada. I was able to talk to them without anything between us. But, now that I'm at Fountainview, there is a whole country between us. The only way I can communicate with my family is over the phone, through e-mail, or by snail-mail. I am no longer able to see them unless they come and visit me. However, despite the distance, I know that they still love me.

When Adam was first created, it was God's plan for him to be able to communicate with his Creator as with the best of friends. But after Adam sinned, he could no longer talk directly to his Maker. There was a barrier, called sin, that separated them. God made it possible for them to still be friends, but they weren't able to talk to each other like they had before. Adam, with his sinful nature, could no longer see God clearly. God's countenance was too glorious and perfect. If Adam had looked upon his Creator, he would have been overwhelmed by the brightness of God's purity.

Sin has come between God and us. We are no longer able to communicate with our Maker face-to-face. If we had not sinned in the beginning, we would still have first-hand communion with God. But, fortunately, this is not the end of the story. God loves us so much that He sent His Son to die on the cross to take that barrier away, so that someday soon, we will once again see our Creator and speak with Him face-to-face.

~ Laelle Teranski

Restored in Full

Man's physical powers were weakened, his mental capacity was lessened, his spiritual vision dimmed. He had become subject to death. Yet the race was not left without hope. By infinite love and mercy the plan of salvation had been devised, and a life of probation was granted. To restore in man the image of his Maker, to bring him back to the perfection in which he was created, to promote the development of body, mind, and soul...this was to be the work of redemption. - Education, pp. 15, 16

Can you think of one attribute that you are known for? Now, try to envision that special characteristic being taken away from you, without you being able to do anything about it.

This is precisely what happened to my friend Tina. Tina was like any other girl her age, except for one thing: her hair. She had beautiful waste-length auburn locks. But a couple of months after her 24th birthday, Tina was diagnosed with cancer. At first, it was not too severe, but as time passed, and the cancer progressed, she was sent to the hospital where she started chemotherapy. Little by little, she lost her most treasured possession as her silky hair fell out of her scalp.

Tina kept growing weaker and weaker. Her family and loved ones were by her bedside praying over her day after day. Then one early August morning, their prayers were answered. Tina started to recover from her chemotherapy! This was a miraculous answer to prayer because the doctor had given her no hope of ever getting better. Then, about two months after that phenomenal August morning, her doctor informed her that she was cancer free. Another couple of months later, her hair started growing back, and gradually, Tina was returned to her former beauty. Now, two years later, Tina has more hair than she had before she was diagnosed with cancer. God more than fully restored her hair.

"For the Son of man came to seek and to save what was lost" (Luke 19:10 NIV). Christ wants to restore each of us to His image. He is ready to restore your life. Will you let Him?

~ Bristi Waid

Caring Cards

The law of love calls for the devotion of body, mind, and soul to the service of God and our fellow men. And this service, while making us a blessing to others, brings the greatest blessing to ourselves.
- Education, pg. 16

I was having a bad day. Classes had been hard, work was stressful, and my friends seemed oblivious to how I was feeling. Have you ever felt this way? I have had many days like this. How can you get yourself out of a bad mood? What can you do to lift your spirits? Do you think dancing or listening to music will make you happy? These may temporarily mask the symptoms of life's problems, but when the thrill wears off, the pain is still there.

No, I know a better way to get rid of loneliness and bad moods: do something for someone else. I'm serious. It works! During that bad day I was having, I saw a girl who looked like she felt worse than I did. I gave her a card and something sweet to cheer her up. After leaving the card in the lobby, I asked a dean to call the girl to get it. She was so excited! I felt so happy to have made her day, that I wrote more cards for other friends! It was amazing to see the change in my attitude after finishing my card-making spree. I was happy and full of excitement to see how I had personally brightened someone's day by doing a secret deed for them! The contentment I gained was much more lasting than any song or dance.

So, when you feel down or depressed, don't think inward; think outward and find something special to do for someone else. It doesn't have to be much, just a note, candy, stickers, or even a smile. What you give isn't as important as what you do for others. It will brighten their day and yours! Try it!

~ Yannika Stafford

True Love

The law of love calls for the devotion of body, mind, and soul to the service of God and our fellow men. And this service, while making us a blessing to others, brings the greatest blessing to ourselves. Unselfishness underlies all true development. - Education, pg. 16

I love my friends. However, some of my friendships seem weak. Why is this? Sometimes, I find that I have made certain friends only for the purpose of getting their attention, sharing their popularity, feeling accepted, or for some other selfish reason. Much of the time, it's all about me, and if I don't get what I want from a friendship, it falls apart. So, how do I make strong friendships that last? How do I love my friends no matter how they treat me? God loves us so infinitely and deeply that He sent His Son to die for us. He died for the people who killed Him. Would I be willing to die for those whom I claim to love?

About two months ago, I began reading 1 Corinthians 13, the "Love Chapter" of the Bible, every day. In verses four through seven, more than twelve characteristics of love are listed. I discovered that if I replaced the word "love" with "God," every phrase was true. But when I tried putting my own name in place of the word "love," it dawned on me that I was far from being like God in character. I asked God to help me devote my whole self to Him, my friends, and my family. Now, by God's grace, I find myself more willing to be of service to others. I am so thankful to be blessed with ever-strengthening friendships.

God's commandments are summed up in these two great commandments: "Love the Lord thy God with all thy heart, and with all thy soul, and with all thy mind" and "Love thy neighbour as thyself" (Matthew 22:37, 39 KJV). I have experienced the joy of service to others and am growing closer to God each day because of His love working in me. Don't you want a similar experience? All it takes is a simple, honest prayer, and in giving your whole self to God each day, everything will change as you are filled with His true love.

~ Valerie Jacobson

To Move or Not to Move

Unselfishness underlies all true development. - Education, pg. 16

The day dawned bright and clear, the sun rising warm and golden between the rolling hills. The green grass was speckled with hundreds of cattle, and herdsmen were already heading out to the fields to watch over the great number of animals. This sizable herd was actually two separate herds belonging to a man named Abraham and his nephew, Lot. The Lord had blessed these two men, and their cattle were multiplying quickly. The quiet hills were becoming crowded and over-grazed, and the herdsmen were becoming desperate for equal pasture space for their respective herds. Some minor scuffles had even broken out between the lead herdsmen.

Abraham realized that something needed to be done about the land issue. He took Lot up to a high hill where they could gaze out over their adjoined pastures to the city of Sodom beyond. There they discussed the situation and came to the conclusion that one of them would have to move toward the city in order for each of them to have the necessary space. Abraham gave Lot the choice whether to stay or to move closer to Sodom. Whichever one Lot chose, Abraham would simply do the opposite. The land surrounding the city was luscious and filled with all sorts of fruit trees and fertile fields. As Lot gazed upon the city, his mind began whirling with all the opportunities of urban life. The choice was obvious to him. With but a few moments of contemplation, he informed Abraham of his choice, and within a few weeks, Lot, his family, his herdsmen, and all his cattle had been packed up and moved to the plains of Sodom.

We all know how the story ends. Lot's selfish choice brought him much grief in the long run. But God blessed Abraham where he was. Abraham's herds and riches were increased by the Lord's hand in reward for his unselfishness. It truly is better to give than to receive.

~ Carmen Hartwell

The Golden Rule

Unselfishness underlies all true development. Through unselfish service we receive the highest culture of every faculty. More and more fully do we become partakers of the divine nature. We are fitted for Heaven, for we receive Heaven into our hearts. - Education, pg. 16

It seems that the predominant mentality in our world today is "me first and others last." Almost every time, self-gratification takes first place over the well-being of others. Everyone is in a mad rush to have the most money, the biggest house, or the fastest car. Even in the smaller areas of life, the general attitude is "I only want what makes me comfortable and happy."

God has set aside his people to be a peculiar people, to stand out from the crowd. The mark of a peculiar people is doing right when the popular trend is to do wrong. The way we dress, what we eat, and how we speak are all important ways of showing that we are Christ's. However, these things must be connected with unselfish love and a desire to serve. In first Corinthians 13:1 Paul says, "Though I speak with the tongues of men and of angels, but have not love, I have become sounding brass or a clanging cymbal" (NKJV).

Jesus said it best when He gave us the golden rule: "Do to others what you would have them do to you" (Luke 6:31 NIV). Just imagine how different our world would be today if we all lived by this rule.

I believe that one of the best ways to share God's love to the world is by making our motto "others first, myself last." People really notice someone who is serving those around them with genuine and unselfish love. Today, let's each start to show Christ's love to our little corner of the world.

~ Laura Williams

January 13

When I Consulted God

...God is the source of all true knowledge... - Education, pg. 16

Today, we have so much knowledge. It seems that every day a new fact is discovered, a new theory proved, an advance in technology made. But science, striving to achieve remarkable goals, often fails when operated under human wisdom alone. It is necessary for man to consult a Higher Power, the One who imparts all knowledge this world has ever obtained. No being can ever hope to understand a single precept without being taught by the Creator Himself.

Recently, I was feverishly studying for an important Social Studies exam and was limited on my time for studying a large amount of material. I decided that I would rely fully upon God to teach me and to guide me to the information I needed to study the most. On the morning of the exam, I studied for close to an hour, carefully reviewing my notes one chapter at a time. On the exam I was to take that afternoon, there would be two essays that could be on any topic from the textbook. In the last ten minutes of my studying time, I closed my eyes and whispered a prayer to God to please impress upon my mind what I should study for my exam essays. Immediately, I felt deeply impressed to review the Cold War section one last time. I did so and then packed up my books to head for class. After opening the exam, I turned directly to the back section where the two essay questions were listed. In amazement, I stared at the essay topic at the top of the page: *Canada's Role in the Cold War*. How good God is! Truly, He will teach all things to those who ask in His name and petition Him for knowledge and understanding.

God is ready and eager to guide us into all truth. If we only ask according to His will, we shall receive. In this new year, start today to consult God at every opportunity that arises, no matter how big or small it may be. Who better to ask than He who knows all and created all, the Author of all wisdom?

~ Megan Metcalf

Tuning In

Upon every page of the great volume of His created works may still be traced His handwriting. - Education, pg. 17

Growing up as a black person during the prejudice of the 1800s was not easy, especially for young George. He yearned to be educated, but sadly, was not allowed to attend school due to the color of his skin. This, however, didn't stop a very curious George, who instead delved into the natural world. He had a great fascination for plants and even planted his own garden where he studied various plant species and discovered different uses for them.

Years later, George Washington Carver found himself at the Tuskegee Institute in Alabama, educating African American students about the scientific wonders of the agricultural world. He invented more than 300 different uses for the peanut and 180 for the sweet potato. He also devoted much of his time to helping former slaves and teaching poor southern farmers how to revitalize their nitrogen-depleted soil. Carver believed that his faith in Jesus was the only tool by which he could pursue and perform the art of science. He once said, "I love to think of nature as an unlimited broadcasting station, through which God speaks to us every hour, if we will only tune in."

There is a whole world out there teaming with ways in which we can learn the life lessons God wants to teach us. However, it is our duty to "tune in."

~ Sarah-Kate Lingerfelt

Brain Power

Every human being, created in the image of God, is endowed with a power akin to that of the Creator–individuality, power to think and to do. - Education, pg. 17

Green smoothies are healthy for you—SUPER healthy. They are made from oranges, bananas, apples, flax, and lettuce, which makes it green. Some people get really creative and put kale, spinach, garlic, and other crazy things into their smoothies.

At school, green smoothies were really popular for a while. Many students would drink a green smoothie with every meal. So, wanting to be healthy, I decided to have a green drink for lunch one Friday. I poured a bunch of the green stuff into a jar and drank it. However, there was still some smoothie clinging to the sides and bottom of the jar. Since I was at the dorm, I left the jar in my room and conveniently kept "forgetting" to take it to the cafeteria to be washed. Eventually, the smoothie wasn't a pretty green color anymore; it looked like something very disgusting. Curious, I opened the lid and smelled the smoothie. Let's just say my nose wasn't very happy.

Our brains are like my green smoothie. If we just let them sit around and don't challenge them to learn everything possible, they will decay and become dysfunctional or deranged. Instead, we should seize the opportunity we have to develop our minds with "a power akin to that of the Creator." Then we will possess "individuality" and "power to think and to do."

~ Sarah Chang

Fully Able to Do

Instead of educated weaklings, institutions of learning may send forth men strong to think and to act, men who are masters and not slaves of circumstances, men who possess breadth of mind, clearness of thought, and the courage of their convictions. - Education, pg. 18

Mastery—being fully able to do something—is the kind of education God wants us to obtain. Man was not created to merely soak up others' ideas and then spit them back out on command. Created in the image of God, man was endowed with high mental capabilities, that he might think for himself and become skilled in a wide range of fields.

On the first day of 9th grade health class, the students entered the classroom and saw a blackboard covered with the names and locations of the major bones and muscles of the human body. This diagram stayed on the board throughout the term, although the teacher never referred to it. On the day of the final exam, the students came to class to find that the board had been wiped clean. The sole test question was, "Name and locate every bone and muscle in the human body."

"We never studied that!" the class protested in unison.

"That's no excuse," replied the teacher. "The information was there for months."

After they struggled with the test for a while, the teacher collected the papers and tore them up.

"Always remember," he told them, "that education is more than just learning what you are told."

The truest and highest education is not found in the teachings of man. His insight is marred and blighted with sin. The fullest education can only be found in the words of Christ recorded in the Bible and in the nature that He has created. Christ, the Great Teacher, is offering free daily lessons; all you have to do is pay attention.

~ Carmen Hartwell

Bitter or Better

...Men who are masters and not slaves of circumstances... - Education, pg. 18

"So, you and dad are getting divorced?" I asked my mother numbly.

"Yes, we are getting divorced," she replied. My mom, grandma, younger siblings, and I were sitting in our living room. My mom and dad had discussed their relationship for a while. Now, she was telling us the decision they had come to.

I don't even remember most of what she said. I just remember asking that blunt question and getting that blunt answer. I felt as though I had been slapped or run into a brick wall. Not so much because I was feeling the hurt of what those words meant, but because it was so strange to actually hear them coming out of my mom's mouth. I never expected to hear those words.

This is the starting of a new year. Because we live in a crazy world, bad things will happen, things you might never have seen coming. Maybe it's not as extreme as a broken relationship; maybe it's just struggling to keep up with school or having your best friend move away. But whatever the situation, you have two options: you can let these situations make you bitter or better. You can let yourself become angry and upset, choosing not to work through your problems. Or you can strive to master your circumstances by gaining what you can from the situation and not continuing the same mistakes. It's a struggle, and that's why it is imperative that we pray. It is only by God's power that we become masters and not slaves. I struggle with myself to see it all from a better and not a bitter perspective. I can't help that my parents did get a divorce, but I can choose how I handle it.

God wants to make you a conqueror. When life tries to beat you down into slavery to your circumstances, choose instead to be master of those circumstances through Christ.

~ Anneliese Wahlman

God's Scholarship

Higher than the highest human thought can reach is God's ideal for His children. Godliness—godlikeness—is the goal to be reached. Before the student there is opened a path of continual progress. He has an object to achieve, a standard to attain, that includes everything good, and pure, and noble. He will advance as fast and as far as possible in every branch of true knowledge. - Education, pg. 18

If a well-known and prestigious college offered you a complete scholarship with no strings attached, what would you do? After jumping up and down and running around your house (possibly knocking over some lamps or chairs), you would probably accept the offer. And once you started taking classes at the college, you would probably work hard to learn and get good grades because you know that college will prepare you for a better life filled with great opportunities and improved abilities.

This is just how we should act toward our loving Savior's offer of a better education, a better life, and a better reason for living. He is offering each of us a scholarship at the most prestigious school in the universe. At this heavenly school, He wants us to learn about His love and saving power by reading His textbook, the Bible. God's Word is the source of all knowledge and wisdom. Its inspired pages, will prepare us for life in the *real* real world. And they will enable us to enjoy all the blessings of trusting in Him completely. There is no reason to reject this offer; so why not accept God's scholarship today?

~ Wesley Donesky

Me? Like God?

Godliness—godlikeness—is the goal to be reached. - Education, pg. 18

Ever since I was little, I wanted to have a perfect character. Every January, I saw an exciting new beginning ahead of me. I always made resolutions and promised myself that I would perfect my character that new year. But, as soon as the rubber met the road, I forgot about the improvements I wanted to make in my life. Often, I became discouraged and felt powerless to change. My mom frequently advised me to pray to God, but I felt that it was pointless to pray to Someone whose perfection I would never be able to reach. At the same time, I knew that it was impossible to change in my own strength. I had tried, and it didn't work. So, I decided to try my mom's suggestion and trust God. At first, I didn't notice any changes, but a month later I could see some significant improvements had taken place. Still, I was not *perfect*. Do you ever find yourself in my situation?

Recently, I discovered that the way I see perfection is totally different from how God sees it. He views Christianity as a walk, not a leap. Imagine for a moment that you are a first-grade student trying to write the word *cat* for the first time. You work your hardest and finally come up with a scribbled draft of *cat*. Later, you show your dad what you have written. He looks over it and smiles, "That is just perfect!" Sure, your writing is not as good as a twelfth-grade student's, but for that stage of your learning process, it is perfect.

If you feel today that you cannot achieve perfection, ask God to help you. He will not only be there for you, but will also encourage and strengthen you to achieve a more Christ-like character. You might not take very big steps in your "perfection process," but if you are willing to daily open your life to Christ by spending time with Him, you will ultimately achieve your goal: godliness. Never give up on Jesus because He will always be there for you.

~ Valdis Cuvaldin

Precious Jewels

His thoughts toward them were "thoughts of peace, and not of evil."
His every purpose was their highest good. - Education, pg. 21

Deep within a mine, far under the ground, a small gem is found by a miner. However, this gem has no resemblance to anything beautiful or valuable. But the miner knows that beneath the covering of stone and dirt is a beautiful jewel, one that will shine with dazzling color when held up to the light. The gem is subjected to a great deal of polishing and refining until all the rough edges are finally removed. It then becomes a valuable jewel to be sold for a great price. The process can be intense and even overwhelming, yet the finished product is something to admire and cherish.

God also sees within us something of great worth. When God looks at His children, He sees a precious gem in each of us that He wishes to polish into a gorgeous jewel. But, before we can shine brightly for Him, He must allow trials and circumstances to refine our rough edges until our characters are perfected. The moment we pray for a Christlike character, we must expect hardships to come because this is the only way our rough edges can be smoothed.

Praise God for the hard times and let Him draw you closer to Himself, for His strength is sufficient to carry you through. He will always be there for you, to impart courage and strength. Lean on Him and ask Him to use the trial to fashion you into a finer picture of His image. Always remember 1 Peter 4:12, 13, which says, "Beloved, think it not strange concerning the fiery trial which is to try you, as though some strange thing happened unto you: But rejoice, inasmuch as ye are partakers of Christ's sufferings; that, when His glory shall be revealed, ye may be glad also with exceeding joy" (KJV).

~ Megan Metcalf

Developing Character

...They were not to be idle. Useful occupation was appointed them as a blessing, to strengthen the body, to expand the mind, and to develop the character. - Education, pg. 21

A man named Ron worked for a Scottish shoemaker named Dan Mackay. Ron's job was to pound leather for shoe soles. A piece of cowhide would be cut to size and soaked in water. Then, using a flat piece of iron over his knees and a hammer, Ron would pound the soles until they were hard and dry. It seemed like an endless process to him.

Now, there was another cobbler's shop just a block away. Ron would often look in the window as he passed by, and he noticed that this cobbler never pounded the soles for his shoes. Instead, he took them from the water and nailed them on wet, with the water splashing from them as he drove each nail in. Yet somehow, this cobbler's shop seemed to thrive, possibly to a greater extent than Dan Mackay's shop. One day, Ron ventured inside the competitor's shop. Timidly, he inquired, "I noticed you put the soles on while still wet. Are they just as good as if they were pounded?" The cobbler shot Ron a wicked, sneering glance as he answered, "They come back all the quicker this way."

Later, Ron related the experience to his boss and suggested that he was possibly wasting time in drying out the leather so carefully. Dan stopped his work and opened his Bible to the passage, "...Whatsoever ye do, do all to the glory of God" (1 Corinthians 10:31 KJV). "Ron," he said, "I am doing this work for the glory of God. I expect to see every shoe I have ever made or repaired in a big pile at the judgment seat of Christ, and I do not want the Lord to say to me in that day, 'Dan, this was a poor job. You did not do your best here.' I want Him to be able to say, 'Well done, good and faithful servant.'"

While on this earth, Christ did His best at whatever task He was given. Even at the lowliest of jobs, He was faithful in His duties. Labor expanded His mind and developed His character. So, in all things, we are to follow His example of faithful, honest service.

~ Bristi Waid

The New Earth

Useful occupation was appointed them [Adam and Eve] as a blessing, to strengthen the body, to expand the mind, and to develop the character. - Education, pg. 21

Have you ever wondered what we will do throughout eternity on the New Earth? We are told that we will eat at God's table and join the heavenly choir, and I can't wait to do those things. But somehow, I feel there would be something missing if all we ever did was celebrate. In Eden, the first couple found joy in accomplishment as they worked at a useful occupation, and it will be the same in Eden restored.

My family had welcomed some special guests into our home. The first day was as good a vacation as any. We told our friends about the wall my grandfather helped me build for my new room, the recent paint job we did on our house, and many other things that had happened since we were last together. On the second day, we took our friends exploring over the rocky hills, covered in sagebrush and sturdy pines, that surround our home. On the third day, our guests were sore from the previous day's exploration and were, not surprisingly, happy to spend some of their vacation relaxing in the house. At first, I did not mind, but soon, time really began to drag. I needed something to do. I was glad to have the company of our guests, but vacationing was starting to get old. So, while our friends relaxed their sore muscles, I found some household chores to keep me busy.

Now, imagine vacationing for eternity. I know there will be plenty of new sights and wonderful places to go, but don't forget, we have FOREVER! I am relieved to read in *The Adventist Home* that God will give us useful occupations to do on the New Earth. We will build our own houses in the country and tend our own gardens (pg. 549). Can you imagine? We will have our own houses and properties besides mansions in the Holy City! It will be wonderful. I can hardly wait to find out what other exciting plans God has for us to carry out! Oh yes, and would you please meet me at my property and give me some tips on building my house? I know you won't be offended, though, if I give Jesus' suggestions top priority.

~ Kevin Corrigan

January 23

Whining or Working

Useful occupation was appointed them as a blessing, to strengthen the body, to expand the mind, and to develop the character. - Education, pg. 21

Oh no, I thought as I scanned the work list posted in the cafeteria. *Today, I'm working at the carrot farm...again!* My positive attitude of a few seconds before plummeted to the level of my sandals. I plodded up to my locker to change into work clothes, griping inwardly all the way. As I was striding purposefully towards the barn where the harvested carrots were washed, I realized my attitude needed a serious adjustment! The Holy Spirit prompted, "If God gave Adam and Eve, his perfectly created beings, work to do, shouldn't you be happy to follow their example?"

God knew we would not be happy if we sat around with nothing to do. Work, especially outdoors, refreshes both the body and mind. I have found studying and learning much easier after I have had physical exertion. In the garden of Eden, God did not give Adam and Eve work because it was necessary for the garden, but because it was necessary for their characters.

That day, as I walked to work, the Lord showed me that the purpose of the work was not only to get the job done, but to be a benefit to me as well. I have come to look forward to the days when I can work outside. It's all a matter of the way you look at it. God, in His infinite knowledge, knew that we would be the happiest when we have a "useful occupation" to do. So, let's stop whining and start working!

~ Anna Fink

Be Still

The book of nature, which spread its living lessons before them, afforded an exhaustless source of instruction and delight. On every leaf of the forest and stone of the mountains, in every shining star, in earth and sea and sky, God's name was written. - Education, pg. 21

God often uses nature to teach us lessons. One day, when I was feeling sad and depressed, we took a walk during PE class. Going at a slow pace, I fell behind the rest of the group and soon found myself walking alone. Trying to relax, I looked around at the beautiful reds, oranges, and golds of the autumn forest. A small stream was flowing beside the road, and I listened for the sound of the gurgling water, but I couldn't hear it! I slowed down, but still couldn't hear. Finally, I stopped and stood perfectly motionless. Then, ever so faintly, I heard the gentle babbling of the brook.

This experience reminded me of the verse that says, "Be still, and know that I am God..." (Psalm 46:10 KJV). Often, in the hectic events of everyday life, we fail to receive the cooling refreshment given to us in God's Word. The blessings are always there, just as the stream in the woods was constantly flowing. But, we cannot fully receive those blessings unless we take the time to be still and listen.

"And in the morning, rising up a great while before day, He...departed into a solitary place, and there prayed" (Mark 1:35 KJV). Every morning, Christ spent time with His Father out in nature, and it is our privilege to do the same. Set aside some time each day which you can spend outdoors. As you look at the beautiful creation around you, be still and listen to what God has to say.

~ Rachel Petrello

Moonstruck

On every leaf of the forest and stone of the mountains, in every shining star, in earth and sea and sky, God's name was written. - Education, pg. 21

It was a captivating night. The moon's gentle glow beamed through my dorm-room window as I prayed beside my bed. I felt very discouraged and was pouring out to God my frustrations, problems with my friends, and the struggles I was having in my spiritual walk. When I finished my venting, I didn't feel as though I had really gained any consolation from it. I had laid my problems on the table before God, but none of them had been solved. Still discouraged, I sat on my bed. Before crawling under the covers, I looked out the window at the moon and was astonished at what I saw! The beams of light shining from the moon formed a cross, with the moon in the center. God had sent a sign of encouragement just for me!

The cross is the ultimate sign of God's love. I felt as though this sign in the sky was softening my stony heart, so I could actually feel that love. It was as if God was telling me, "Allie, My love is still here in the night. Whether you are awake to see it or not. It will always be here. No matter what you are going through."

God's love is always there for you, too, even in life's darkest nights, whether you feel far from it or not. Every day He is trying to show you how much He loves you; He's crazy about you! Many times though, we are too focused on ourselves, and we don't see how much He loves us. Why don't you ask God to open your eyes, so you can see the signs of His love?

~ Anneliese Wahlman

God's Signature

On every leaf of the forest and stone of the mountains, in every shining star, in earth and sea and sky, God's name is written. - Education, pg. 21

If there is one thing in nature I love more than anything else, it would have to be the sky. Every time I look up, it's as if God put it there just for me. Its constant change fascinates me. Each cloud floating by is shaped uniquely. Each evening, the sun sets more fantastically than the night before. And to think, God did it all just for you and me.

When you see a painting done with a certain style, you don't even need to look at the signature before you know exactly who the artist is. Likewise, God's name is written all throughout nature, so that as soon as we see a mountain or a meadow, we can right away think of the Creator of all things, Jesus.

He has put thought and creativity into everything He has made. All too often, I think that we forget to thank God for His awesome creations and praise Him for His wonderful works. We don't give Him the acknowledgment He truly deserves. Sometimes, we even forget that it was He who made it all.

Don't let yourself get caught up with man-made materials that will one day cease to exist. Instead, put your thoughts and time into what the Lord has made, and you will find yourself to be so much more satisfied.

Next time you get a chance, spend some time in nature and thank God for all the wonderful things He has made for us to enjoy.

~ Danielle Schafer

Thoughts for Life

Therefore He gave them the power of choice—the power to yield or to withhold obedience. And before they could receive in fullness the blessings He desired to impart, their love and loyalty must be tested.
- Education, pg. 23

All around me, I experience pressures to follow the usual customs and standards upheld by the world. Each day, my faith is tested to show whether my devotion is to God or to Satan.

There is a common pattern which I follow that determines the direction my life will take. Everything begins with my thoughts. If I keep thinking about something, my human nature will automatically end up acting out these thoughts. My actions are then repeated until they become ingrained habits. The habits I have created then begin to form my character, and my character determines my final destiny. To think that the smallest thought, whether good or evil, will determine the outcome of my life is a deep matter. Each thought proves where my faithfulness lies and shapes the person who I am. Is it easy for me to change my thoughts? No. However, God can do it for me. No human being can change his thoughts and character without God's help.

When a wrong thought enters my mind, I immediately surrender it to God. As time goes on, I look back and wonder why I haven't thought of such things for a while. I see the power of the Holy Spirit working in my life to change my character into the perfect image of Christ. It is a long process, yes, but thought by thought, true Christ-likeness will be achieved through God's grace. And each time I practice changing my thought patterns, it becomes easier until my actions and habits begin to show the change. Just as sin began with a single thought, Godliness can also be achieved through my thoughts.

Try lifting your thoughts to higher and nobler things, to God's love, heaven, and the needs of humanity around us. You will find true happiness and fulfillment that will surpass anything this world has to offer.

~ Megan Metcalf

For Your Own Good

The knowledge of good had been freely given them; but the knowledge of evil,—of sin and its results, of wearing toil, of anxious care, of disappointment and grief, of pain and death,—this was in love withheld. - Education, pg. 23

"It's for your own good...You'll understand when you're older." Parents often say this to their children as they're growing up, and I myself remember my parents telling me the same thing. Now as a teenager, I can remember being a young child and wanting something so desperately, and not seeing the wisdom in my parents' decision to withhold it from me. Little did I know that the thing I wanted so badly would not have been in my best interest. My parents, in their wisdom and abounding love for me, would not grant me my every desire because they could foresee consequences that I didn't even think about.

Recently, my school went to film the last part of our latest Christmas DVD. We were going to a place where there was about a foot of snow on the ground, and we were really hoping to film in falling snow. As we were leaving campus, we all prayed for falling snow, and it wasn't ten minutes down the road before the snow began to fall! Naturally, we were all very excited at the answer to our prayer. But later, when we were nearing our film site, it stopped snowing, and the sky became clear and blue. We were all very confused as to why God had granted our request for snow, then taken it away. But we realized that God must have a greater plan. He had granted our request for a little while simply to show us that He had the power to do it, but falling snow was not His will for us at the time. Personally, this strengthened my faith just as much as it would have had the snow continued to fall.

God has infinite wisdom, far more than any earthly parent. He encourages us to ask Him for what we want, for He loves to grant our requests. Yet, our insight is shallow and earthly, and often we ask for things that would not be in our best interest to have. God would go against His nature to grant us those things that He knows would be harmful or would not benefit us in the long run. So, next time you ask something of God, and He in His wisdom withholds it, praise Him, because He knows what is best.

~ Carmen Hartwell

28

January 29

Counterfeit Knowledge

*Satan desired to make it appear that this knowledge of good mingled with evil would be a blessing, and that in forbidding them to take of the fruit of the tree, God was withholding great good... Eve, infatuated, flattered, beguiled, did not discern the deception. *
- Education, pg. 24

On August 15, 2002, nine men were convicted by Philadelphia police of creating counterfeit one-hundred-dollar bills. The bills were created by bleaching genuine one-dollar and five-dollar bills and then photocopying the well-known pictures of Benjamin Franklin and Independence Hall onto the crisp white pieces of cotton paper. Soon after the counterfeit bills were distributed, the police quickly located and arrested the men who were responsible. The store owners who had accepted the counterfeit money thought it was genuine. They were either too busy to notice the suspicious looking bills or too deceived by its immediate appearance to look closely.

If you have ever seen a counterfeit dollar bill, you probably realize how difficult it is to tell counterfeit money from genuine money. If you didn't know the subtle differences between counterfeit and real money, you probably wouldn't be able to tell them apart. However, even though counterfeit money might appear newer and even more valuable than real money, it is still worthless paper. Purchasing items with counterfeit money only results in a guilty conscience or a prison term.

Whenever we try to gain knowledge in our daily lives, we have to watch out for the counterfeit knowledge that Satan is trying to teach us. In the Garden of Eden, Satan made the knowledge of evil appear beneficial and desirable. But eventually it would cause only pain, suffering, and death. By Satan's lies and deceptions, Eve was led to distrust God and eat the forbidden fruit. Each day, we face the decision to either seek God's genuine knowledge of good or Satan's corrupt and counterfeit knowledge of evil. I want to encourage you to pray that God will give you both the ability to see and choose the truth.

~ Wesley Donesky

Dangerous Beauty

She coveted what God had forbidden; she distrusted His wisdom.
- Education, pg. 24

There is a tropical sea creature called the Blue-ringed Octopus that lives in the Pacific Ocean. This octopus is alluringly beautiful, with many iridescent blue rings shimmering on its body. However, if provoked, the octopus will bite, injecting a paralyzing venom that can kill an adult within minutes. Children who play in the ocean are warned not to disturb or touch the octopus, but nevertheless, they often ignore the warning and are bitten.

It was the same in the garden of Eden. Eden was perfect, yet God still placed the Tree of the Knowledge of Good and Evil in the garden, not only to give Adam and Eve the power of choice, but to test their love and loyalty to Him.

At first, Eve heeded God's command to stay away from the tree. However, curiosity got the better of her. Like the children in the tropics, Eve disregarded God's warning and ventured too near the tree, falling into Satan's trap. If Eve had stayed away from the tree at all times, Satan would never have had the opportunity to tempt her.

How often do we, like the children that are mesmerized by the blue rings of the octopus, or like Eve who was deceived by the smooth words of the serpent, inch as close to evil as possible, excusing ourselves by saying, "Oh, I have time," or, "It's all right. I'll repent eventually"? Let's not make the same mistake that Eve made. Let's stay as close to God as possible.

~ Sarah Chang

The Key of Faith

...[Eve] distrusted His wisdom. She cast away faith, the key of knowledge. - Education, pg. 24

What is faith? I usually think of faith as trusting in something or someone without seeing all the evidence. In fact, faith is dependent on trust because you can't have faith in someone without trusting him to the utmost. Do you trust God enough to have true faith in Him? Do you know God enough to trust Him? It seems that faith depends on knowledge, but faith can unlock knowledge as well.

Have you ever struggled with an issue in your life, whether it be family, friends, school, or work, and knew that you just couldn't handle it alone? Perhaps it came to mind that you should ask God for help, but you did it almost as a mere afterthought or a matter of routine. Maybe you actually did want to surrender the problem to God, but even as you did so, you stubbornly grasped the wheel, saying, "God, I need some help here, but I think I'll handle most of the driving myself. Can you just give me a hand when I feel like it?" I've gone through similar experiences, and it's only when I crashed again that I realized I wasn't depending on God completely. I wasn't finding answers or peace, and I didn't know how to move on because I didn't have enough faith to truly surrender every aspect of the problem to God.

If I trust God's wisdom and believe that His will is best, God will continue to open my eyes to the plan He has for my life. He won't reveal more of His plan to me if I refuse to trust Him now with the instruction and promises He has already given. Through faith in Him, I can discover more of His will; I can gain more reasons to trust Him; I can learn more of His love and the peace that He gives, and I can hold His hand through any trials I face. Faith is the key to knowing God ever deeper; it is the key to knowing all He longs for us to experience.

~ Valerie Jacobson

The Key to Knowledge

She [Eve] cast away faith, the key of knowledge. - Education, pg. 24

It was a summer day in late June, and I was mowing the lawn with the old, green John Deer mower. I had mowed row after row of grass in between the trees in the orchards, when I looked up and realized that my work supervisor was staring at me. He called me over, and suddenly, it hit me that I had forgotten to lower the lever that brings the blade into contact with the ground. All that time, I had been riding on the mower, but not cutting any grass. I felt so stupid, and to top it off, my work supervisor had seen me. I was so embarrassed that I didn't even remember to stop before I slammed the mower into park. My supervisor had a little chat with me, mentioning that by not remembering to stop before I parked, I could have jammed the gears. When he was finished talking, he walked away.

As soon as he was out of sight, I tried to take the lever out of park, but it wouldn't budge! I called my friend over, and we prayed, but I realized that I didn't have faith that God would free the gears. So, we prayed again, and God impressed me to put the tractor into third gear at the same time that I tried to get it out of park. Instantly, the mower slid into drive! We thanked God, and I carefully finished the last row. Then, of course, I had to redo the areas I had missed earlier. But I will never forget that day, because it taught me that faith in God is the key to knowledge.

Eve lacked faith, and this led her to make the unwise choice of picking the forbidden fruit. The only way we can make wise decisions is to have faith in God, to listen for His guidance, and follow His will for our lives.

~ Daniel Glassford

February 2

With Him

Acquaint now thyself with Him... - Job 22:21 KJV

The other day, I was out filming with my school in the beautiful mountains of British Columbia. We were filming by a quaint little stream that meandered its way through a lovely snow-filled meadow. As I was waiting to start singing a song, I peered at the ground and saw a tiny black bug walking around on the cold snow. Curious to see if he would crawl onto my warm finger, I placed it in front of him. I thought he would climb right onto my finger, but he did the opposite: he quickly turned away. I put my finger into his path a second time, and again he turned away, but this time he was less cautious. As I continued doing this, the bug shied away less and less. Eventually, after a bit more coaxing, I had him on the end of my finger.

I found this interesting. My finger was so warm and inviting; however, compared to that little bug, I was all powerful, and if I had wanted to, I could have easily crushed him. Perhaps he knew that, so stayed away. When he finally warmed up to me, it seemed he had figured out that he could trust me. Each time I encouraged him to climb onto my finger, he got more and more used to the idea of being closer to me.

This reminds me of how God draws us closer to Him. Even though we may reject Him, God is persistent. He loves us so much that when we turn away, He follows and is ready to pick us up and gently draw us close to Himself. God tells us to acquaint ourselves with Him, and He makes that easier for us by being there when we are ready to accept Him. In Matthew 28:20 Jesus promises: "...I am with you alway, even unto the end of the world" (KJV).

~ Jessica Hall

Unlocking Knowledge

...Faith, the key of knowledge. - Education, pg. 24

Have you ever thought of faith as being something that unlocks knowledge? Until recently, I'd never connected faith with gaining know-ledge in everyday life. However, I've been finding that when I trust God to guide me in even my smallest affairs, He gives me His wisdom, and I accomplish much more than I expect to.

For example, when I was younger, I would pray about something others might think was insignificant. I would be in the midst of a complex Lego creation, and after extensive searching in a mountain of Legos, I still could not produce the right piece. I would pray, asking God to help me find it, and without fail, I would find the needed Lego piece almost immediately. Soon, my faith began to grow. I stopped waiting until I had scoured every possible place three times and began asking God for help as soon as I couldn't find the piece I needed. He always led me to speedily discover the elusive part.

More recently, I've been asking for God's help on different projects. I've been amazed to see Him guide my hands while I pound a nail that I just could not keep from bending over, or give me just the idea I needed to finish a project that seemed riddled with endless problems. Sometimes I just need the courage to stick with it and figure it out.

I've found through experience that God wants to help us. He is just waiting for us to ask, so that our faith can grow when He answers. Try asking God to be your Partner, to do everything with you. Yes, He's always with us, but you'll find it surprising how much He does when we specifically ask for His help. God invites, "Ask, and it shall be given you" (Luke 11:9 KJV).

~ Kevin Corrigan

February 4

The Beginning of Sin

When Eve saw "that the tree was good for food, and that it was pleasant to the eyes, and a tree to be desired to make one wise, she took of the fruit thereof, and did eat." - Education, pg. 25

When I read in the Bible of how Eve believed the Devil and ate from the tree of the knowledge of good and evil, my first thought is, *How could she have been so stupid? Why did she even go near the tree when she knew she shouldn't?* God had specifically told Eve not to eat that fruit, and she should have known that the best way for her to avoid temptation would have been to stay away from the tree altogether.

However, when I think about it, I realize that if I had been in Eve's place, I would have done just as she did. Really, how can I think I would have done any better when I repeat the same mistake every day? Just as Eve put herself in the way of temptation, I often don't stay away from temptation when I could. I'm perfectly able to say no; but sometimes I don't because, at the moment, I feel rebellious, or it's just easier to say yes.

How often do we walk straight into a temptation, knowing our danger, but thinking we have the strength to resist? Usually, we realize too late that we aren't strong enough, and we end up saying or doing something wrong. Every time this happens, we practically walk up to the tree of the knowledge of good and evil and pick its fruit again.

Do you want to know one of the best ways you can help yourself resist temptation? Avoid, as much as you can, the things that tempt you. As Proverbs 4:14, 15 says, "Enter not into the path of the wicked...Avoid it, pass not by it, turn from it, and pass away" (KJV).

~ Sophia Simard

In the Wilderness

Yea, forty years didst thou sustain them in the wilderness, so that they lacked nothing; their clothes waxed not old, and their feet swelled not... - Nehemiah 9:21, KJV

Sometimes the landscape of my life seems like a dead desert with not a creature in sight. Friends seem foreign, sandstorms of confusion whirl around me, and hope appears as a distant mirage.

At times like this, it is easy to identify with the Israelites and their wayward mistakes. They wandered without a permanent home for forty years. At times, they were hungry, thirsty, and afraid, lost in a vast wilderness. They had never seen the place that was to be their future home. Sometimes with lips parched, faces burnt, and skin dry, they must have wondered if the promised land would be worth it.

As they marched, they would come to an oasis God had prepared for them. A shout of joy would go up as they viewed God's blessing. I often ask myself why the Israelites weren't frequently jubilant over God's evident love for them. After all, they were healthy, manna fell without fail, and the special cloud by day and pillar of fire by night never left them. Had they chosen to focus on their blessings and listen to God's reassuring voice as they gazed on the majestic mountains that clearly demonstrated His power, or the simple desert creatures that God cares for every day, they would have arrived at Canaan more quickly. The same discouraging circumstances would still have existed, but with a change in focus, everything would have appeared in a new light.

When you are tempted to be discouraged, remember the Israelites. They wandered forty years in a wasteland, seeming to gain nothing, but at last arriving at the promised land. God allowed them to go through trials so that when prosperously situated in Canaan, they could look back to how He helped them when they were in need and choose not to forsake Him later when things were easier. In the same way, God will use your trials to be a blessing in your life if you meekly follow Him and choose to dwell on the blessings, not the hardships.

~ Kevin Corrigan

The First Bite

It was distrust of God's goodness, disbelief of His word, and rejection of His authority, that made our first parents transgressors, and that brought into the world a knowledge of evil. - Education, pg. 25

"Eve."

I turn and look towards the melodious voice. *How did I get so close to the Tree?* Something urges me to leave and find Adam, but the brilliant winged serpent is captivating, and the luscious fruit hanging from every green branch keeps me staring in wonder. I ask myself, *Why is God prohibiting me from eating or touching it?*

"Did God really say that you can't eat fruit from every tree in the garden?"

Curious that a serpent would be speaking, I reply, "We can eat from all the trees, except the one in the middle of the garden. God said, 'Don't eat from it or touch it, or you will die.'"

"You won't die! You've eaten from the Tree of Life. God knows that if you eat this fruit, your eyes will be opened, and you will become like gods, knowing both good and evil. I received the power of speech after eating this delicious, exhilarating fruit."

Somewhat taken aback by this foreign, direct contradiction to God's word, questions begin to form in my mind. *Could I not die? Is God keeping me from gaining more wisdom and knowledge? The serpent is the only animal now capable of speech! What more could this fruit do for me, since I can already think and speak? I want to be equal to God. It's time to make my own decisions. Reaching out, I take the fruit from the serpent and eat the first bite.*

When we read this infamous story, we usually think that we would have resisted Satan. Who would believe a talking serpent over God? Yet all of us, like Eve, are guilty of the same sin. I've never eaten forbidden fruit, but more than once I've distrusted God's plan for my life. In doing so, I have indirectly disbelieved the promises in His word. You and I must submit to God's authority every day. If we don't make that firm decision to trust, believe, and obey God, we will find ourselves taking more bites of sin and discovering a deeper knowledge of evil that He never intended for us to know.

~ Valerie Jacobson

Opened Eyes?

Their [Adam and Eve's] eyes were indeed opened; but how sad the opening! The knowledge of evil, the curse of sin, was all that the transgressors gained. - Education, pg. 25

There it sat, a perfect, luscious-looking orange just waiting to be eaten. My mouth watered as I reached for it and began to peel it. The orange broke off into beautiful sections, sitting in neat, soldier-like rows on the counter. As I popped the first slice into my mouth and bit down, I expected an explosion of succulent flavors. But, to my surprise, the orange I had thought would be so good was dry and tasteless!

Sin is like that orange. It can look so good from the outside, but when you get to the heart of the matter, it's really as distasteful as an unripe orange. Satan is a master at making sin look pleasant on the outside, but when you get through all the "pretty packaging" you can see the naked truth.

Adam and Eve, our first parents, wanted something they thought would be better than what God had already given them. "Ye shall not surely die," Satan lied, "for God doth know that in the day ye eat thereof, then your eyes shall be opened, and ye shall be as gods, knowing good and evil" (Genesis 3:5 KJV). Adam and Eve's lack of faith in God's wisdom ended up causing an infinite amount of pain and suffering. God says, "For I know the thoughts that I think toward you...thoughts of peace, and not of evil, to give you an expected end" (Jeremiah 29:11 KJV). God knows the end from the beginning and graciously tries to withhold things from us that would not be for our good.

~ Anna Fink

Are You Cooking?

By the mingling of evil with good, his [man's] mind had become confused, his mental and spiritual powers benumbed. No longer could he appreciate the good that God had so freely bestowed. - Education, pg. 25

Frogs are equipped with tiny temperature sensors in their skin to alert them of sudden changes in temperature. If you put a frog in boiling water, the frog immediately reacts and tries to escape. However, if you place a frog in cold water and slowly heat it up, the frog will become numb to the slow increase in temperature and will eventually get cooked. Similarly, sin can slowly creep into our lives. At first, we are completely appalled by sin, but gradually we become numb to it and are unaware of our fatal danger until we boil to death.

Movies and TV shows affect us in this very same way. Popular, thrilling story lines provide a way to escape the realities of life. On the surface, a movie may appear to have a good moral value, but when taking a closer look, we find the characters telling lies, disrespecting their families, or using a cuss word every now and then. We continue to watch these displays and assume that we can leave unaffected. But sin always leaves its mark; the more times we are subjected to it, the less harmful it seems.

It is so important to keep your mind as pure and free from sin as possible. Your eyes will then be able to behold God's love and goodness towards you. Greater happiness and joy will be found in following the Bible's guideline in Philippians 4:8: "Finally, brethren, whatever things are true, whatever things are noble, whatever things are just, whatever things are pure, whatever things are lovely, whatever things are of good report, if there is any virtue and if there is anything praiseworthy—meditate on these things" (NKJV).

~ Megan Metcalf

Evergreens and Redemption

Although the earth was blighted with the curse, nature was still to be man's lesson book. It could not now represent goodness only; for evil was everywhere present, marring earth and sea and air with its defiling touch. - Education, pg. 26

Once, there was a small evergreen tree that sprouted and began to grow in the forest. As it grew and matured, it became friends with the other trees around it. The months passed by, and the weather became colder. The young tree began to notice that the leaves on the other trees were becoming brown and wilted. Soon, snow began to fall, and many of the tree's friends became listless and silent. Believing that his friends were dead, the small tree began to cry. An older, wiser evergreen who saw the little tree crying said, "Don't worry. Your friends aren't dead. They are only sleeping. In the spring, they will awake and grow new leaves." The small tree waited while the months crept by. Spring finally came, and the forest trees awoke with new leaves on their branches. The young evergreen tree never forgot about his first year in the forest. And even in the darkest days of winter, he knew that spring was not far away.

Throughout nature, the results of sin are evident. Everywhere on earth, we see the marks of decay and death. Even the air we breath is often polluted and poisonous. But despite all this deterioration, you can still see God's redeeming power at work. The trees that lose their leaves in the fall bear the promise of new leaves and new life in the spring. Wilting flowers leave their seeds to spring up next year. Whatever Satan defiles or destroys, God wants to cleanse and renew. I encourage you to pray that He will change your heart and give you new life every day.

~ Wesley Donesky

Breathe

Even the air, upon which their life depended, bore the seeds of death.
- Education, pg. 26

Have you ever noticed how invigorating country air is? I always love it when I can escape the city and head out to the mountains. The air feels so much fresher, cleaner, and sweeter. It seems to clear the cobwebs that clutter my mind. Yet, this air that seems so wonderful bears the seeds of death.

It's hard to believe, but everywhere the air is polluted, even in the country. This malignant form of poisoning reaches across the globe to affect those farthest from its source. Because of air pollution, over 50,000 people die annually in the U.S., and in India the numbers are around 527,700! Incredible isn't it? What we do here and now has an affect on those who live far away and on those who will live years after us. The air pollution from the U.S. and other developed countries impacts the respiratory health of those in developing countries and contributes to asthma, pneumonia, and other respiratory illnesses. If we will choose to control the amount of toxins we use and release into the air, we can help those who otherwise have little hope of a healthy life.

But, there is more than just chemical pollution in this world. Satan has worked his way into everything good and mixed evil with it. He has done his best to make sure that no matter what, we will be polluted by sin. We must, therefore, be certain that we keep in close communion with Christ. He is the Great Physician who can and will heal us of all our diseases, both physical and spiritual.

~ Jo Holdal

Forgiveness

But man was not abandoned to the results of the evil he had chosen...
All that had been lost by yielding to Satan could be regained through
Christ. - Education, pg. 27

While Clay and his sister, Lucy, were visiting their grandparents, Clay was given his first slingshot. One day, he went out to the woods to practice shooting, but he could never hit his target. As he was walking back to the house, he spied Grandma's pet duck. Out of curiosity, he pulled his slingshot out of his pocket and took aim. The stone hit, and the poor duck fell dead. Clay panicked and hid the duck in the woodpile. But as he looked up, he saw that his sister was watching. Lucy had seen it all, but she said nothing.

After lunch, Grandma asked Lucy, "Would you wash the dishes?"
But Lucy replied, "Clay told me he wanted to help in the kitchen today. Didn't you, Clay?" And she whispered in his ear, "Remember the duck!" So Clay did the dishes.
Later that day, Grandpa inquired if the children wanted to go fishing. Grandma replied, "I'm sorry, but I need Lucy to help me make supper."
Lucy smiled and said, "That's all taken care of. Clay wants to do it." Again she whispered in his ear, "Remember the duck." So Clay stayed to make supper, and Lucy went fishing.

After several days of doing both his and Lucy's chores, Clay couldn't take it anymore. He went and confessed to Grandma that he had killed her duck.
"I know, Clay," she said. "I was standing at the kitchen window and saw the whole thing. I forgave you, but I was wondering how long you would let Lucy make a slave of you."

In this story, Lucy is like Satan, and Clay represents you and me. Satan often makes our sin appear like a big cliff that's about fall and crush us. Because we are afraid to confess to God, we go along with Satan's lies, and let our sin keep hanging over our heads. But God is ready and willing to forgive us. When we realize the ridiculousness of our situation and ask for forgiveness, we will experience complete freedom.

~ Laelle Teranski

Growing Back

All that had been lost by yielding to Satan could be regained through Christ. - Education, pg. 27

I have a plant a friend of mine gave to me as a going-away present. It grows in a white plastic pot on my counter. When the plant was first given to me it was full of curling stems and luscious green leaves. But, that all changed when I went home for summer break. I forgot to ask the dean to water my plant while I was gone. When I returned to school in the fall, the plant looked almost dead. The leaves were brown and shriveled. The soil looked about as dry as a hundred-year-old skeleton. I thought about throwing it away, but never got around to taking my withered plant to the big trash bin outside. I watered it, even though I figured it was probably a lost cause. One day, I pulled out my green-handled scissors and cut off all the dead, brown leaves. My plant looked stubby and naked. But I kept watering it. Surprisingly, it began to grow back, and green spiraled shoots gradually appeared.

I have a sinful, fallen nature. I'm like my plant: my leaves are brown and shriveled, and my soil is dry. I look dead and appear to contain no spiritual moisture. But there is hope. Through Christ I can have the assurance that I am being redeemed, that my sinful nature is being changed. Through everyday experiences, He is watering me, trimming off my dead leaves, and helping me grow. My plant didn't grow back overnight; neither will my sinful nature be changed overnight. However, I do have the assurance that Christ has redeemed me because He has promised, and Jesus never breaks His promises.

"But now thus saith the Lord that created thee... Fear not: for I have redeemed thee, I have called thee by thy name; thou art mine" (Isaiah 43:1 KJV).

~ Anneliese Wahlman

Ants

All that had been lost by yielding to Satan could be regained through Christ. - Education, pg. 27

In the book *Bruchko,* Bruce Olson used the following story to explain the gospel to the Motilone Indians. There once was a young Indian warrior, and one day, while walking through the forest, he stooped to watch some ants build their home. "If only they knew how to build a home like my people build," he said to himself. So, he decided to help them. He crouched down and started to scoop the dirt into a mound, like his house, but the ants didn't realize that he was trying to help them. They scattered and hid. "How am I going to help them?" he wondered.

Suddenly, as if by a miracle, he turned into an ant. He looked like an ant, thought like an ant, and talked like an ant. Slowly, he gained the confidence of the other ants and joined their clan. One day as he was working, he decided to tell them about when he was an Indian.

"What?" the other ants scoffed, "That was you?" And then they burst out laughing because they didn't believe him. Then, just as quickly as he had turned into an ant, he turned back into an Indian. Only then did the ants realize who he truly was and allow him to help them build their home.

We chose to follow Satan by disobeying God. The penalty for sin is death, and that is what all of us deserve. But God didn't want to lose us; so, just like the Indian, He became one of us. He wanted to help us, to save us from our sin, so that we could become His best friends and live with Him for eternity. He came down to this puny planet and lived and died for us on Calvary. His free gift of salvation is offered to everyone; He's just waiting for you to accept it. Why don't you ask Him into your life today?

~ Wesley Mayes

February 14

From Your Valentine

The life and the death of Christ, the price of our redemption...
- Education, pg. 28

Legend has it that Valentine was a third century priest in Rome, who specialized in preparing couples for marriage, despite the Emperor's orders that certain young men were not allowed to get married. When the Emperor found out that Valentine was still conducting "illegal" marriage ceremonies, he had Valentine arrested. While he was in jail, Valentine fell in love with the jailer's blind daughter and healed her blindness in the name of Jesus Christ. He was going to be released on the condition that he would renounce his faith. But, since he would not abandon his faith or mission, he was martyred. Before he died, Valentine sent a final note to his love. In this note, he talked about his passion and love for Christ and how he wanted to be faithful to Him, even if it meant death. He signed the letter "From your Valentine."

Jesus Christ was here on earth two thousand years ago. He specialized in preparing the world for its marriage union with Himself, despite the opposition of the priests and Pharisees. When the Jewish leaders realized that, no matter what they said, Jesus was going to continue wooing lost souls to Himself, they had Jesus arrested. After being brought to Pilate, then to Herod, and back to Pilate, Jesus was sentenced to death. Through His life and death on the cross, Jesus sent a beautiful note to every human being. In this letter, God wrote how much He loved and adored us and explained why He sent His Son to earth to die for our sins. He signed the letter "From your Valentine."

"For God so lo**V**ed the world
That He g**A**ve
His on**L**y
Begott**E**n
So**N**,
Tha**T** whoever
Believes **I**n Him
Should **N**ot perish
But have ev**E**rlasting life" (John 3:16 NKJV).

~ Jessica Hall

45

His Great Faithfulness

Though the earth bears testimony to the curse in the evident signs of decay, it is still rich and beautiful in the tokens of life-giving power. The trees cast off their leaves, only to be robed with fresher verdure;the flowers die, to spring forth in new beauty...Thus the very objects and operations of nature that bring so vividly to mind our great loss become to us the messengers of hope. - Education, pg. 27

"British Columbia is the most beautiful place on earth." That statement may sound a little arrogant to an outsider, but having lived there all my life, I must say I tend to agree. I love mountains and maple trees, which are British Columbia's trademarks. At home, we have a huge maple tree on our front lawn. Every season brings a change of scenery through our front window as the tree changes its outfit.

Imagine what nature would be like if it bore no signs of sin at all. Every flower and blade of grass would shine with the glory of God. Then imagine seeing death—the falling of a single leaf—for the first time, and realizing that your sin caused it. When the first leaf fell, Adam sobbed with heart-wrenching sorrow at the realization of the consequences of his sin.

Although sin has marred some of the beauty of nature, God still reveals Himself to us by taking our breath away with a magnificent sunset or an intricate spiderweb laced with dew. Every fall and winter things wither and die, but then God envelops them in a gentle blanket of snow. Every season is different and distinct, and God places something beautiful in them all.

Summer and winter, and spring-time and harvest,
Sun, moon, and stars in their courses above,
Join with all nature in manifold witness,
To Thy great faithfulness, mercy, and love.
                - by Thomas Chisholm

~ Carmen Hartwell

February 16

Four Seasons

Though the earth bears testimony to the curse in the evident signs of decay, it is still rich and beautiful in the tokens of life-giving power. The trees cast off their leaves, only to be robed with fresher verdure; the flowers die, to spring forth in new beauty; and in every manifestation of creative power is held out the assurance that we may be created anew in "righteousness and holiness of truth." Thus the very objects and operations of nature that bring so vividly to mind our great loss become to us the messengers of hope. - Education, pg. 27

Which of the four seasons is your favorite? My favorite season is summer. Everything is alive, and the air is warm. I can enjoy keeping cool in lakes and rivers, getting a tan, and eating popsicles! There are things we can learn from every season. Though nature is marred by sin and death, we can still see evidence of hope through the amazing things God has designed.

Now, fall is not my favorite season. The trees lose their leaves, and while that is pretty for a few weeks, the leaves soon begin rotting, the weather gets colder, and the color in the world changes from living green to darker earth tones. The fall season came into existence ages ago. Inspiration tells us that when Adam and Eve saw the first leaf die, they wept. Even the name "fall" reminds us of the first fall in heaven. Yet even in this dreary season, we can see hope!

God doesn't leave our world in a fallen state. He brings us winter with beautiful, purifying snow that covers the miserable, dead landscape, turning it into a miraculous wonderland full of a whole new beauty. It reminds me of the purifying qualities of God's love and how He cleanses us from our sins and makes us as white as snow. Our sins are nasty and gray, muddy and gross, and yet, when we ask God to forgive and cleanse us from them, He takes them away and makes our hearts as beautiful as freshly fallen snow. I'm reminded of Isaiah 1:18, which is God's invitation to all of us: "Come now, and let us reason together, saith the LORD: though your sins be as scarlet, they shall be as white as snow..." (KJV).

~ Yannika Stafford

47

Once upon a Time

By sin man was shut out from God... Sin not only shuts us away from God, but destroys in the human soul both the desire and the capacity for knowing Him. - Education, pp. 28, 29

Setting: The Garden of Eden, before the fall of man.

Eve: That fruit looks so good! Maybe I should try just one bite! It won't hurt anybody. Besides, that snake told me that if I eat it, my eyes will be opened, and I will be like God. I know that the Father said not even to get close to this tree, but it won't be the end of the world. Or maybe...maybe I should go and see if Adam needs my help in the garden. But wait—the fruit! Okay, Eve, this is it—now or never. Make up your mind!

A few minutes later...
Adam: This fruit is really delicious!
Eve: I told you! And, I have started seeing things differently!
Adam: [Big silence] Eve... WE ARE NAKED! We need to cover ourselves. How are we going to talk with God like this?
God: Adam? Eve? Where are you?
Adam: Quick! The fig leaves.

In choosing to sin, Adam and Eve didn't think about the consequences of their selfish actions. One of the most obvious results was their loss of the ability to see God face to face. Sin also brought them pain, suffering throughout the generations, and ultimately death. Adam and Eve's biggest regret was refusing to listen to the God who created them and loved them the most, and instead, listening to their venomous enemy, Satan.

Every time we sin, our desire to spend time with God lessens. Sin also affects our judgment, and in turn, the decisions we make. How senseless it is to trade such a loving God who gave His life for us for our degraded desires! Even though it sounds ridiculous, we make this decision every day. When, today, you are tempted to sin, think about the consequences of that action. Is it worth allowing sin to destroy everything you have?

~ Valdis Cuvaldin

February 18

Let There Be Light

Christ is the "Light, which lighteth every man that cometh into the world." - Education, pg. 29

When I walk between the school building and the dorm, I sometimes take a steep path called The Shortcut. This dear little trail has taught me many lessons.

Probably the most meaningful experience I've had on this trail occurred during the winter. In the winter, the sun does not rise until late in the morning, and it disappears before suppertime. So, I always walk to and from school in the dark. I distinctly remember looking outside one night and cringing because I didn't want to walk in the dark by myself. The wind was howling, and as I walked away from the school building, darkness enveloped me, until I couldn't see three feet in front of me. I walked in the direction of the the trail. I took one step, then another. I thought that I was on the trail, but the path felt unfamiliar. Should I keep going? Then, I heard a car coming up the road below. The headlights pierced the darkness around me, and I realized that I wasn't even on the trail; I was bushwhacking up the side of the mountain. In those few moments of light, I was able to get safely on the trail while whispering my thanks to God. In the darkness, I would have blindly kept making my way, not even realizing that I was on the wrong path and probably would have ended up in some trouble.

After that incident, I really did not like walking in the dark. But, I am glad that I was able to learn a valuable lesson. This world is filled with darkness. It pervades every aspect of our lives and clogs our sight, so that we come to the point where we can hardly see a foot in front of us. However, if we let Christ's love come into our lives, it will shine forth from us and illuminate the darkness. "When the world's darkness is deepest, that is when God's light shines brightest." Don't you want to be that light?

~ Sarah Chang

Bent

Not only intellectual but spiritual power, a perception of right, a desire for goodness, exists in every heart. But against these principles there is struggling an antagonistic power...There is in his [man's] nature a bent to evil, a force which, unaided, he cannot resist...He can find help in but one power. That power is Christ. - Education, pg. 29

As we grow, circumstances around us shape our characters and define who we will be. But even before we can walk or talk, we have certain characteristics already built into our personalities. Now, these can be good things, such as a good sense of humor or a positive attitude. But, they can also be bad, such as a tendency towards selfishness and greed. Where do these character traits come from? How can we be born with something that we have never experienced?

Before the fall, we had no knowledge of evil. We lived in perfect harmony with Christ and His creation. Our characters were modeled after Christ's, and we only grew in a knowledge of God. But after disobeying God, our human natures became warped and gained a knowledge of evil. Because of this, I was born, not only with a knowledge of good, but also with a knowledge of evil. And every human is born with natural tendencies to evil.

However, I do not have to stay this way. I can choose to starve the evil and feed the good. How is this possible? Without the help of Christ it isn't possible; I cannot starve evil on my own. When I try, it feels as if I am trying to swim against the current. Although I may be pointed in the right direction, I cannot swim upstream. I must remember that I have a Savior who can walk on water. Only He can take my hand and lift me above the waves of sin that are drowning me.

~ Wesley Mayes

February 20

Just Ask

The result of the eating of the tree of knowledge of good and evil is manifest in every man's experience. There is in his nature a bent to evil, a force which, unaided, he cannot resist. To withstand this force...he can find help in but one power. That power is Christ. Co-operation with that power is man's greatest need. - Education, pg. 29

Have you ever attempted to work on a project or fix a problem, only to find that you needed to ask for help in order to finish it?

I am the type of person who likes to try every possibility in order to accomplish my goal before asking for help. I enjoy the satisfaction of finishing a project by myself. I remember many occasions when I would attempt to open a tightly sealed jar, struggling with it for a long time.

My dad would patiently stand beside me and occasionally ask, "Would you like my help?"
"No," I would answer. "I can do it by myself."

I would continue my struggle until I either opened the jar or gave up in frustration. My dad would then proceed to open the jar with a simple twist of the lid. Why did it always look so easy when he did it?

In our Christian life, we often try to change our hearts on our own. We struggle to reform our habits in our own way and strength, while, all the time, Jesus is standing by our side asking gently, "Would you like My help?"

Christ is ever ready to help you if you will just ask Him. All you have to do is pray, "Create in me a clean heart, O God; and renew a right spirit within me" (Psalm 51:10 KJV). He alone can do that for you. Why not ask Him?

~ Laura Williams

Conquer in Christ

There is in his nature a bent to evil, a force which, unaided, he cannot resist. To withstand this force...he can find help in but one power. That power is Christ. - Education, pg. 29

Ever since the fall of man, sin has been bred into his very nature. The longer Satan has had to reveal his character, the more the knowledge of evil has increased. A falling leaf once brought tears of grief to Adam and Eve, but now we have grown callous to scenes of war and death. Sin has polluted minds and bodies throughout the generations, and the image of God, in which He originally created us, has been distorted and degraded.

This "bent to evil" that we have inherited makes us easily prone to temptation. Even the smallest temptations can cause problems in our friendships, our work, and our family life. Ultimately, they can affect our relationship with God. For instance, I used to be obsessed with reading books. I read all the time: I read at school and while I ate; I read at home when I should have been practicing violin or doing homework, and sometimes I read late into the night. The books weren't necessarily bad, but they caused me to neglect the more important aspects of my life. I still managed to spend some time in God's Word, but I was hurried and less focused, as I would quickly do my Christian duty so I could move on to "more interesting" books.

Since then, I have realized how important it is for my focus to remain on Christ. I knew that my obsession was unhealthy and that I needed help. But, it wasn't until I truly submitted to Christ and believed in His power to work through me that I was able to overcome the temptation. The temptation is still there, but it has no power when I depend on Christ's strength. Still, I can't say, "Christ has helped me overcome once, now I'll never fall again." There is no power within you or me that will cause us to win the victory over sin. It is only a continual surrender to Christ, every single day, that will fortify us to meet Satan's temptations and conquer in Christ.

~ Valerie Jacobson

Synergy

There is in his [man's] nature a bent to evil, a force which, unaided, he cannot resist. To withstand this force...he can find help in but one power. That power is Christ. Co-operation with that power is man's greatest need. - Education, pg. 29

What is synergy? Synergy is the situation in which the whole of something is greater than the sum of all its parts. For example: Clydesdale horses are very strong. One horse alone can pull a weight of two tons! But, when two Clydesdale horses are hitched together, the team can pull a weight of up to twenty-four tons! This is twelve times the weight that one horse can pull by itself!

Much more can be accomplished when there is teamwork than when each individual works alone. But can you imagine what would happen if the horses pulled in opposite directions? It would be chaos, and they wouldn't accomplish anything! Co-operation is necessary to get the job done.

Because of our sinful nature, we cannot carry the burdens and trials of this world on our own. However, when we yoke up with Christ, He pulls the load, and with His help, the burden seems so much lighter! Jesus says, "Take My yoke upon you, and learn of Me...for My yoke is easy, and My burden is light" (Matthew 11: 29, 30 KJV). He promises His burden will be light if we co-operate with Him, and He will never give up on us! "...He which hath begun a good work in you will perform it until the day of Jesus Christ" (Philippians 1:6 KJV). Through the process of synergy, our feeble efforts, yoked together with God's omnipotent power, will be "...able to do immeasurably more than all we ask or imagine, according to his power that is at work within us" (Ephesians 3:20 NIV).

~ Anna Fink

The Highest Aim

That power is Christ. Co-operation with that power is man's greatest need. In all educational effort should not this co-operation be the highest aim? - Education, pg. 29

The young king sat up in bed with a start. He wiped his sweaty brow and whispered, "Lord?" His mind raced back to the dream which had seemed such a reality just moments before.

He had dreamed that a bright light shone down upon him. A voice boomed from above, "Is there something special that you would like Me to do for you, Solomon?"

Solomon answered, "Lord, you have chosen me to be king and to rule Israel in my father's place. But I'm so young, I lack the wisdom to do it. I'm supposed to rule these people, but there are so many of them, it's even hard to count them all. What I would like is wisdom to know how to rule and to decide between what's right and what's wrong. Who can rule such a large number of people, especially your people, and make all the right decisions?" (1 Kings 3:5, 7-10 The Clear Word).

The Lord was pleased with Solomon's request and granted it. James tells us, "If any of you lack wisdom, let him ask of God, that giveth to all men liberally, and upbraideth not; and it shall be given him. But let him ask in faith, nothing wavering. For he that wavereth is like a wave of the sea driven with the wind and tossed" (James 1:5, 6 KJV).

Children sometimes do not understand why parents make the decisions they do. They often forget that their parents have lived for a long time and have acquired wisdom over the years that they as children do not yet have. In the same way, Jesus has been alive for eternity. He knows everything that has been, is, and is to come. Our highest aim should be to connect with Christ, the Center of all wisdom and knowledge. God was pleased when Solomon asked Him for wisdom, and He is just waiting for us to ask for it, too.

~ Victoria West

February 24

The First Time

The true teacher is not satisfied with second-rate work. He is not satisfied with...a standard lower than the highest which it is possible for them [the students] to attain. - Education, pg. 29

A man named Scott owned a cabinet shop in the northern woods of Canada. One day, he hired a young boy named Mark to work for him and learn the art of cabinet-making. In the beginning, Mark didn't have much motivation to do his best the first time, and Scott was compelled to ask Mark to redo several jobs.

One day, Scott asked Mark to make a set of cabinets out of very beautiful and expensive wood. Before Mark started on his project, Scott reminded him to "measure twice; cut once." After a while, Mark came back to him and exclaimed that the cabinets were done! Scott was surprised and inspected the cabinets closely. He discovered that Mark had made a mistake: the cabinets were too large. Being a kind, patient man who was used to dealing with teenagers, Scott didn't get upset, but instead, simply told Mark to remake the cabinets more carefully. Mark started over and made the cabinets a second time. Once again, he made them too big. He made this same mistake several times before he finally completed a correct set of cabinets. The whole time, Scott didn't get impatient or upset. He knew that for Mark to gain the qualities of an excellent worker, he would have to make mistakes and learn from them. But Scott did want Mark to eventually learn to do his best the first time; so he didn't settle for second-best or let Mark get away with less-than-thorough work.

God works in the same way as Scott. He asks you to give Him your heart. But He wants all of it, not just a part. He doesn't want workers who will only give Him second-rate work. He calls for the best there is: people who will go out and do jobs well the first time. Will you completely give yourself to God so that you can work for Him? I challenge you to raise your standards and give God your best!

~ Yannika Stafford

A True Friend

Therefore comfort each other and edify one another, just as you also are doing. - 1 Thessalonians 5:11 NKJV

It was Friday night at the ACTS for Christ Youth Conference, and I was feeling utterly depressed. A friend of mine approached me to see if I was alright, but it was obvious I wasn't. She said something to me that spoke to my heart. "My arms are not as strong as God's, but..." then she hugged me. I was so touched by this that I stayed up late to write about it.

I see you standing here tonight,
In your eyes, a heart full of pain.
Trying so hard to win the fight,
But no ground appears to be gained.

My arms are not as strong as God's,
And I can't win this war for you.
But I will hold you anyway
And be the Father's hands to you.

Sometimes I feel so helpless;
There is so little I can do.
But on my knees and in my mind
I pray and I fight for you.

You cannot see past all the pain
As through this fog you feel and grope.
You must believe me when I say
In the Father, there is hope.

My arms are not as strong as God's,
And I can't win this war for you.
But I will hold you anyway
And be the Father's hands to you.

You don't have to search far to find people who need comfort and love. Why don't you look for such people today? You may not be able to fix their problems, but by hugging them and telling them they're loved, you can be the Father's hands to them.

~ Anneliese Wahlman

True Service

He desires them, above all else, to learn life's great lesson of unselfish service. - Education, pg. 30

"Self-righteous service comes through human effort. True service comes from a relationship with the divine Other deep inside [God].

Self-righteous service is impressed with the 'big deal.' True service finds it almost impossible to distinguish the small from the large service.

Self-righteous service requires external rewards. True service rests contented in hiddenness.

Self-righteous service is highly concerned about results. True service is free of the need to calculate results.

Self-righteous service picks and chooses whom to serve. True service is indiscriminate in its ministry.

Self-righteous service is affected by moods and whims. True service ministers simply and faithfully because there is a need.

Self-righteous service is temporary. True service is a lifestyle.

Self-righteous service is without sensitivity. It insists on meeting the need even when to do so would be destructive. True service can withhold the service as freely as perform it.

Self-righteous service fractures community. True service, on the other hand, builds community." - Richard Foster

I love how Jesus was always willing to serve. He did everything from washing people's feet without complaining, to healing lepers without fretting about contaminating Himself. He had a true servant's attitude.

There are two places in the gospels that say "the Son of Man did not come to be served, but to serve...": Mark 10:45 and Matthew 20:28 (NKJV). Jesus came to earth specifically to serve. Now, understand that when He came to serve, He did not come to serve humanity; He came to serve His Father. But, by serving His Father, He was serving humanity because that was the will of His Father. And He has given us the same job. We are to serve God, and in serving Him, we will be rendering the truest service to mankind.

~ Jessica Hall

I Pledge Allegiance

These principles become a living power to shape the character, through the acquaintance of the soul with Christ, through an acceptance of His wisdom as the guide, His power as the strength, of heart and life. This union formed, the student has found the Source of wisdom. He has within his reach the power to realize in himself his noblest ideals. The opportunities of the highest education for life in this world are his. - Education, pg. 30

One of the most inspiring stories I have ever heard is about a young Navy pilot named Mike Christian who was shot down and held prisoner during the Vietnam War. Mike had grown up near Selma, Alabama. Though his parents had very little money, their family fortune was their character. Mike's parents raised him to be hard-working and loyal. At the age of seventeen, Mike enlisted in the Navy and so impressed his superiors that he was offered a commission.

After being taken prisoner, Mike began working on a secret project. Using a bamboo needle and pieces of red and blue cloth received in rare packages from home, he sewed an American flag on the inside of his blue prisoner's shirt. Every afternoon before Mike and his friends ate their meager prison rations, they would recite the Pledge of Allegiance. No other time of day meant so much to them. But one afternoon, the guards discovered Mike's flag. After confiscating it, they dragged him outside and beat him mercilessly before throwing him back into his prison cell. Later that night, as he lay on his rough sleeping platform, Mike silently picked up his bamboo needle and started to sew a new flag.

Mike's love and loyalty for his country gave him strength even in the harshest of circumstances. The principles that he was taught as a child gave him hope and courage in his darkest hour. If you allow God to educate you with His principles and truths, He will enable you to withstand all of the trials and temptations that Satan throws in your way. Ask God today to give you courage and strength to endure trials and hold high the banner of His love—no matter what.

~ Wesley Donesky

February 28

Leaving the Comfort Zone

He [man] has within his reach the power to realize in himself his noblest ideals. The opportunities of the highest education for life in this world are his. - Education, pg. 30

When Todd was eight years old, he dreamed of joining a little league baseball team, but he was afraid he would not get picked for the lineup; so he didn't try out. Then Todd considered graduating from high school earlier than the rest of his Junior class, but he never got motivated enough to really try. After graduating, he had many ideas for starting up a business, but he didn't want to risk losing the little money he had saved up; so he decided to wait. Later in life, Todd thought about taking biochemistry in college, but since he was afraid that he would change his mind partway through, he decided to stay home. When he was twenty-seven, Todd was going to ask his high school girlfriend to marry him, but he dreaded the thought of rejection so much that he never asked her. Now Todd is forty-nine, and he hasn't done much in life. He has passed up most of his opportunities to grow, explore, travel, and gain useful knowledge.

Life is loaded with daunting experiences: first day of school, first public speech, wedding day, etc. Todd spent the majority of his life avoiding such opportunities, and as a result, he has lived a dull and apathetic existence. His is afraid of moving beyond the familiar position of his pocket-sized comfort zone.

God wants us to live by faith. But often, like Todd, a wall of fear keeps us from leaving our comfort zones and living by faith. Thankfully, there is an answer for this predicament! We can know that God works though our weaknesses to accomplish His will, and that success is only procured by the risk of failure. And 2 Timothy 1:7 says, "For God did not give us a spirit of timidity, but a spirit of power, of love and of self discipline" (NIV).

So why not try living in faith? Step out of the coziness of your comfort zone and know that you have within your reach the power to realize your noblest ideals.

~ Cyrus Guccione

A Leaning Education

In the highest sense the work of education and the work of redemption are one, for in education, as in redemption, "other foundation can no man lay than that is laid, which is Jesus Christ." - Education, pg. 30

The Leaning Tower of Pisa, originally known as just the Tower of Pisa, was designed to be a work of art. Built between 1173 and 1372, its marble floors, columns, and bell tower were supposed to be spectacular. But, the tower was doomed from the very start because of a design flaw. The tower's foundation was dug only three meters deep and was set in unstable soil. Even though the materials were hefty stones, the tower began leaning to one side because of the intense weight bearing down on the weak foundation. Today, the top of the tower is 12 feet 10 inches from where it would stand if the tower were perfectly vertical.

Building a tower on a weak foundation is like gaining an education without having first built a personal lasting relationship with Jesus. He promises, "...Lo, I am with you alway, even unto the end of the world" (Matthew 28:20 KJV). Once we have this never-ending walk, we can focus on the high calling of education.

Too often, more emphasis is placed on the "tower" of book learning than on the "foundation" of Jesus. All wisdom comes from God, the Wellspring of all knowledge. With the proper focus on both aspects of true education, our "tower" will stand straight and strong.

~ Anna Fink

I Need to Save Her

To aid the student...in entering into that relation with Christ...should be the teacher's first effort and his constant aim. The teacher who accepts this aim is in truth a co-worker with Christ, a laborer together with God. - Education, pg. 30

Did you ever meet one of those typical "mean girls" in school? You know, the kind who are snobby, insincere back-stabbers. There was a girl like this at the school I used to attend. Everyone disliked her and avoided her as much as possible; everyone except for my friend Erica. Erica went out of her way to spend time with this girl and be her friend. One day, I asked Erica why in the world she wanted to hang out with such an unkind girl. She simply replied, "Because I need to save her."

The rebuke hit me like a tidal wave. I was supposed to be a Christian, but I sure wasn't acting like one! I should have had the focus that Erica had: saving souls. Erica reminded me of Jesus. During His ministry on earth, He often spent time with the tax collectors and other outcasts of society. He didn't look at their past or their external appearance. In each person, He saw someone who needed a savior and friend. He saw souls whom He loved, and He did everything in His power to introduce them to the love of His Father.

Each day, I ask myself if I can say with Jesus, "He that hath seen Me hath seen the Father..." (John 14:9 KJV). Did I lead others to Him today? Often I fail, as in the case of that girl in my old school. Still, God is willing to forgive and help me to do better. Just think about it! The way I treat others may be the only glimpse of Christ that they will ever see! I need to ask God daily to help me keep that in mind and reach out to others the way Christ did.

~ Rachel Petrello

God's Second Book

But the men who held fast God's principles of life dwelt among the fields and hills. They were tillers of the soil and keepers of flocks and herds, and in this free, independent life, with its opportunities for labor and study and meditation, they learned of God and taught their children of His works and ways. - Education, pp. 33, 34

When God created this world, He spoke everything there is into existence. He created everything in nature to represent His unwavering love for us. I have discovered that the closer I am to nature, the more clearly I can see who God is.

Imagine walking into someone's house and looking around. You would be able to observe what kind of person the owner is by analyzing the contents of his house. This is the way it is with God and nature. When I observe even the smallest blade of grass, I can see who God is by the detail and thought He put into it.

Nature is like a book, with many practical lessons all pointing to God's love for us. Take, for example, the relationship between a mother bird and her hatchlings. She spends much of her life caring for her young, gathering seeds or worms for them to eat and training them for life on their own. Just like the mother bird, God is always taking care of us and providing for our needs. This is just one example of the many lessons nature can teach us about God's unselfish character.

I have also discovered that nature is a great place to meditate on God's word and to contemplate the lessons that it has for me. Nature is also a quiet place where I can escape the rapid pace of this world and its distractions.

So, if you and I want to be drawn closer to our Creator in a special way, we need to go out and spend more time in nature, to ponder His creation and learn the great lessons that it has to offer.

~ Daniel Glassford

March 4

Our Daily Provider

In His dealings with the wanderers in the desert, in all their marchings to and fro, in their exposure to hunger, thirst, and weariness, in their peril from heathen foes, and in the manifestation of His providence for their relief, God was seeking to strengthen their faith by revealing to them the power that was continually working for their good.
- Education, pg. 34

One winter morning in Bangladesh, I came down to breakfast at the orphanage where I lived and found the table empty. Our home-mother, worried by the thought that 106 small children would have to go to school without eating any food, gathered all of us into our leaky tin shack to pray. Some of the babies starting crying and the older children were shivering from the cold. Our home-mother had tears streaming down her face as she informed us that we had run out of food, and it would be a whole week before the sponsors would send us more money. Then she had us get down on our knees, and she prayed to God for strength and food for the children.

After her prayer was finished, she told us that God would provide food for us; He would take care of His children. So, she had us all get ready to go to school. About ten minutes before we left for school, a group of men came to our home-mother and exclaimed with joy that they had miraculously received enough rice, potatoes, and milk to feed over 350 people. They said the nearby villagers had heard that the children in the orphanage were going hungry and had provided the food. That day, we all ate enough food to fill our hungry stomachs.

You know, God really does care about us. Especially when we are put through testing times, we can trust that He will answer our prayers and provide for our needs. Psalms 37:25 says, "I have been young, and now am old; yet have I not seen the righteous forsaken, nor his seed begging bread" (KJV). From my childhood experience, I learned that we may go through hard times, but God is always there with us to be our Comforter and Provider when we need Him.

~ Bristi Waid

A Remedy for Stress

When thou passest through the waters, I will be with thee; and through the rivers, they shall not overflow thee... - Isaiah 43:2 KJV

Have you ever felt as though you can't please anyone? Your life seems to be pulling you in all directions, and you feel as though you're about to snap. Your family wants you to do this; your friends want you to do that, and you just can't get it right. How can we find peace in today's stress-filled environment?

Psalm 103:14 says, "For He knows our frame; He remembers that we are dust" (ESV). God knows how insane this world is, and He wants to help us. He whispers, "Come to me, all who labor and are heavy laden, and I will give you rest" (Matthew 11:28 ESV). Oftentimes though, we try to be strong and hold it all in; but we eventually find ourselves broken and at a dead end. Andy Gullahorn wrote a song to his wife called "Alright Here." I think the words express the way God must feel when He sees us trying to fix everything in our own strength.

Everybody's got their limits
There's only so much you can take
You can dam it up inside you
But one day it's gonna break
When the water overwhelms you
And you've lost the strength to swim
You don't have to be a hero
And keep it all in

You can weep like a baby
You can sink like a stone
You can break and go crazy
Alright here in my arms
You're alright here in my arms

God wants us to come to Him with our stress and worries. His arms are wide, big, and strong enough to hold anything we give Him. Will you let Him hold you?

~ Anneliese Wahlman

March 6

Fight the Battle

And having taught them to trust in His love and power, it was His purpose to set before them, in the precepts of His law, the standard of character to which, through His grace, He desired them to attain. - Education, pg. 34

Last year, I learned a lot—I must have, since I was able to advance to the next grade in school. I learned more about who God really is and what He expects of me. I also was introduced to the word trust. I was encouraged by many friends as I struggled with learning this concept of believing in someone else. But it wasn't just learning to trust people, it was also learning to trust God. This step is most important, as God is the One in control of everything!

While we are advancing in the process of education, we are also involved in an active battle. Satan is working nonstop to keep you from surrendering to Christ and trusting Him, and Satan's greatest ally is your self. Satan works with your innermost thoughts and feelings and attempts to block you from coming to God. Meanwhile, Christ is reaching out His hand, beckoning you to receive eternal life. All of us are caught in the middle of this battle, and we need to make the choice for right. You and I need to guard ourselves against Satan's control.

Only through Jesus' sacrifice and His power can we accomplish this worthy aim. On our own we have no strength or even a full knowledge of true likeness to Christ. God does not expect us to change ourselves into something we cannot fully comprehend, and that is why He has sent the Holy Spirit to guide us and do this work in us. The only roadblock is ourselves. "The warfare against self is the greatest battle that was ever fought. The yielding of self, surrendering all to the will of God, requires a struggle; but the soul must submit to God before it can be renewed in holiness" (*Steps to Christ*, pg. 43).

~ Jo Holdal

Number One Priority

But the people were slow to learn the lesson. Accustomed as they had been in Egypt to material representations of the Deity, and these of the most degrading nature, it was difficult for them to conceive of the existence or the character of the Unseen One. In pity for their weakness, God gave them a symbol of His presence. "Let them make Me a sanctuary," He said; "that I may dwell among them."
- Education, pg. 35

Three years ago, my parents and I decided that I would leave the public school system and, instead, attend a conservative Christian academy in the Philippines. In just a few months, my view of life was transformed. It was something deeper than a change of culture. The biggest struggle I had to face was changing my priorities. All my life, I had been playing the "good" Christian who goes to church regularly, but in reality, I was spending most of my time in secular places without God in my heart. I wanted a relationship with Him, but I did not want Him to take a lot of my time. In the Philippines, I was with Christians 24/7. In this new environment, I started to long for a relationship with God, but I did not know how to approach Him. He understood where I was coming from and patiently took the time to reveal Himself to me. Eventually, He became my priority.

Adolf Hitler once said: "Tell a lie often enough, loud enough, and long enough, and people will believe you." For more than four hundred years, the Israelites were slaves in Egypt. They had to endure daily verbal abuse, working in horrific conditions, and hearing lies every day about their God. In time, many chose to believe these lies. When God released them from captivity, He knew that deep inside, they wanted a relationship with the Divine, but they had been deceived into believing idols were their supreme authority. Through the sanctuary, God let them understand that He wanted to dwell in their hearts. And soon, He became their priority again.

Do you feel that you want to have a relationship with God, but you don't have the desire to make Him first in your life? As you go throughout the day, pray that God will give you the desire to make Him number one. Remember, He is more than willing to patiently work with you to make Himself your top priority.

~ Valdis Cuvaldin

Daddy, Help Me!

So to Israel, whom He desired to make His dwelling place, He revealed His glorious ideal of character... But this ideal they were, in themselves, powerless to attain. - Education, pp. 35, 36

Hannah jumped and lifter her little pudgy hands high toward the ceiling. She just couldn't reach! Dolly had been thrown on top of the bedroom bookshelf earlier that evening. It was now bedtime, and without Dolly, it would be a chore for this little three-year-old to fall asleep. As she jumped, cried, and reached, Daddy heard the ruckus from the living room and decided to investigate. He saw his little girl's predicament and was about to go help her when he decided to watch for a while and see what she would do. She went on in her self-sufficiency for only a moment longer, then cried, "Daddy! Help me! Peeez!" As soon as she cried for him, he was there. As he lifted her up towards her Dolly, she giggled happily.

As I sat in worship, I struggled to remain composed and not start crying. I needed to focus on the message, not on my troubled thoughts. But it was hopeless. God saw me sitting there and wanted to help me, but instead, He waited quietly to see what I would do. Finally, I couldn't take it any longer. I cried in my heart to Jesus, asking Him to help me stay calm, to keep my thoughts focused on Him, and to not give in to my circumstances. I cried, "Daddy! Help me!" Immediately He was there! He lifted me up! My thoughts were of Him, and I wasn't struggling anymore. My all-powerful Father had lifted me onto His shoulders to help me gain what I needed: peace from Him.

Hannah and I both were in situations where we couldn't help ourselves. She couldn't get Dolly off the high shelf; I couldn't get rid of my thoughts and emotions. I am sure you can think of at least one thing that you need help with, help from Someone Else. We all have things we need help with, and we all have a Daddy who can help us. Maybe you can't depend on your earthly father, but you have a Daddy who will always be there. His name is Jesus, and He is there to help you get any "Dolly" that you need off the shelf. If you will only ask, He will come. He is just waiting for you to call, "Daddy! Help me!"

~ Yannika Stafford

God Can Use You

Great was the privilege and honor granted Israel in the preparation of the sanctuary; and great was also the responsibility. A structure of surpassing splendor, demanding for its construction the most costly material and the highest artistic skill, was to be erected in the wilderness, by a people just escaped from slavery. It seemed a stupendous task. But He who had given the plan of the building stood pledged to co-operate with the builders. - Education, pg. 36

A beautiful and extravagant edifice was about to be built. The plans were set. The most costly materials—precious jewels, gold, and textiles—were required. Masters of construction, metal craft, and needlework were in high demand. This building was to be the Sanctuary, where the presence of God would dwell. And who was employed to construct this magnificent work? A band of recently escaped slaves. How ironic!

Do you ever feel like God can't use you? I used to think, Oh, God can't use me! I'm just a high school student, not anyone big or important. Then I worked as a colporteur. I said, "OK God, I'm here to work for you; so if you can use me, go for it!" I was amazed at how God did use me, a girl who was scared to talk to strangers, to get thousands of books about Christ into secular homes!

God often uses little people to do big things. "For ye see your calling, brethren, how that not many wise men after the flesh, not many mighty, not many noble, are called: But God hath chosen the foolish things of the world to confound the wise; and God hath chosen the weak things of the world to confound the things which are mighty..." (1 Corinthians 1:26, 27 KJV). Look at how Joseph progressed from being a slave to becoming the prime minister of Egypt, or how David went from being a shepherd boy to becoming the king of Israel. The Bible is full of stories of how God used insignificant people to do amazing things! God can also use you to accomplish great things for Him!

~ Rachel Petrello

You Are Loved!

Many waters cannot quench love, neither can the floods drown it...for love is strong as death... Song of Solomon 8:6, 7 KJV

The woman looked up at the darkening sky. She had been waiting for this special moment for a long time. The moon shone brightly down upon her as she struggled and wondered when the contractions would end. Finally, the Baby came. He was tiny and perfect, more perfect than she had dreamed. She loved Him with her whole heart. She would remember this night for the rest of her life.

As the years went by, she raised her Son carefully and tenderly. He was to be a great leader someday, and she had the responsibility of raising Him. He grew up to be the Savior of the world. As He traveled and told people about God's love, grace, and forgiveness, the leaders of the country started to hate Him. They mocked Him and tried to sway Him, but He stood strong and refused to waver. When they came to kill Him, He didn't say anything. He just stood there quietly and took it all. They nailed Him to a wooden cross and sunk its base into the ground. They let Him die, just hanging there. He died with love in His heart, love for each and every person who had lived or ever would live on this earth.

I'm sure that, by now, you've guessed Who this story is about. Jesus came down from His heavenly throne and was born in a barn because no one had a respectable room for Him. Why did He do it? Because He loves *you* so much! Even though He had to suffer and die, He would do it again just for you! You matter to God! He created you, and He knows your name. He loves you! And His love is stronger than death.

~ Laelle Teranski

Are You a Happy Foot?

In the preparation of the sanctuary and in its furnishing, all the people were to co-operate. There was labor for brain and hand. A great variety of material was required, and all were invited to contribute... - Education, pg. 37

To build a house, a variety of skilled workers are needed. You need someone to pour the foundation, builders to do all the framing, an electrician to put in the wiring, someone to set up a plumbing system, someone to install heating and air conditioning, painters, a landscaper, and an inspector to make sure safety codes are met. It is not the Master Builder alone who does all the work; many hands are needed.

In the same way, each of us have been given different talents and skills. Some are gifted musically, some thrive in mathematics, others are computer savvy, and some (like me) enjoy hands-on physical labor. Though I know we are all gifted, I often become dissatisfied and envious of the talents others possess. I look at my classmates and wish I could sing like Laura, play guitar like Daniel, cook like Bristi, or explain atomic bombs like Wes. I think less of myself because they have certain skills I wish I had and find myself mentally labeling them as "better."

In reality, I don't have any reason to feel this way. God gave me the talents to fit His plan for my life, and that plan is different from that of my classmates. A lot of skills are needed to accomplish God's work. "Indeed, the body does not consist of one member but of many. If the foot would say, 'Because I am not a hand, I do not belong to the body,' that would not make it any less a part of the body...God arranged the members in the body, each one of them, as He chose. If all were a single member, where would the body be? As it is, there are many members, yet one body" (1 Corinthians 12:14-15, 18-20 NRSV).

Are you a happy foot? Or do you find yourself wishing you were the hand? God gave you talents with a specific purpose in mind. So, don't compare yourself to others! God needs a variety of talented workers in order to build His house!

~ Rachel Petrello

Make Me a Sanctuary

And they were to co-operate also in the preparation of the spiritual building—God's temple in the soul. - Education, pg. 37

God wanted to live with His people, to be in communion with them. On Mount Sinai, He gave Moses the blue prints for a portable sanctuary, a house for Him to live in. The Israelites brought forth the best of their gold to be made into furniture for the sanctuary, and women wove beautiful linen curtains that were as white as snow. The golden furniture, the candle sticks, the altar of incense, the ark of the covenant—all gleamed in the sun as they were being crafted. The vibrant colors of the curtains enclosing the Holy Place rippled in the wind. This beautiful tabernacle was to be God's house, with the very presence of God at its core, the Most Holy Place.

Just as God asked the Israelites to make Him a holy tabernacle to dwell in, God wants to make me a beautiful sanctuary for Him to live in. He desires to create in me the vibrant colors of kindness and courtesy, white purity of character, and the presence of His love at the core of my being. He yearns to fashion His sanctuary in my heart and yours. Paul says in 1 Corinthians 6:19,20, "What? Know ye not that your body is the temple of the Holy Ghost which is in you, which ye have of God, and ye are not your own?...Therefore glorify God in your body, and in your spirit, which are God's" (KJV).

During a week of prayer at my school, the speaker would end his morning and evening worship talks with this song:

Lord, prepare me
To be a sanctuary,
Pure and Holy,
Tried and true.

With thanksgiving,
I'll be a living
Sanctuary
Lord, for you.

~ Anneliese Wahlman

71

True Identity

But ye are a chosen generation...a peculiar people; that ye should shew forth the praises of Him who hath called you out of darkness into His marvellous light. - 1 Peter 2:9 KJV

Have you ever felt like you didn't fit in? I know I have. When I went to school in the 6th grade, I wanted desperately to be accepted. For example, I would come home and cry to my mom that I didn't have enough fashionable jeans or Converse shoes like everybody else. Another way I tried to fit in was with my grades. I have always been taught to do my best in school, but because of my desire to fit in with my classmates, I decided that I would let my grades get lower. I remember one day we had a science test, and I decided not to study. I got to school, and as soon as we began to take the test, I started to mark answers that I knew were incorrect. When I got my score back, I wasn't surprised to learn I had received a low "C." As soon as my friends began to compare scores and mope about their grades, I joined in, complaining, "I can't believe it! A 'C'!" When Mom found out about my grade, she wasn't too pleased. She sat me down and explained that I need to do my best in whatever I do because God has given me talents in order to glorify His name.

Now, what if we stopped attempting to fit in? What if, instead, we tried to stand out for God? Romans 8:14 tells us that those who "are led by the Spirit of God, they are the sons of God" (KJV). This is where we find our identity. Not from how many friends we have, how attractive we are, or how much money we have. We can't even find our self-worth through the good deeds we do or how godly or loving we are, for "all our righteousnesses are as filthy rags..." (Isaiah 64:6 KJV). Furthermore, we are called to do more than just fit in. "Every youth, every child, has a work to do for the honor of God and the uplifting of humanity" (*Education*, pg. 58).

Next time you're tempted to cave in to peer pressure, remember the true identity you have in your heavenly Father. You are called to be "a chosen generation, a royal priesthood, an holy nation, a peculiar people, that ye should shew forth the praises of Him who hath called you out of darkness into His marvelous light" (1 Peter 2:9 KJV).

~ Victoria West

Order

Even before they left Egypt a temporary organization had been effected, and the people were arranged in companies, under appointed leaders. At Sinai the arrangements for organization were completed. The order so strikingly displayed in all the works of God was manifest in the Hebrew economy. - Education, pg. 37

In the army, a soldier must have the appropriate training and development before engaging in battle. Confidence, agility, endurance, and awareness are all characteristics that he needs to be effective. But, along with those abilities, a soldier cannot achieve success without orderliness. Orderliness is one of the most important characteristics that a soldier must obtain. Without orderliness, battles could be lost, unnecessary casualties could occur, and unwanted chaos may take place. Being disorderly can cause many unexpected consequences.

When you live a life of order or disorder, its results are clear and evident in your everyday life. Whatever you do, whether organized or not, affects your thinking and can potentially affect the people around you. If your house is cluttered, your thoughts will be cluttered, and your outlook on life will be less optimistic.

Paul the Apostle wrote in one of his letters to the church of Corinth saying, "Let all things be done decently and in order" (1Corinthians 14:40 KJV). God wants you to be orderly because when your mind is clear and undistracted by the cares of this world, His Holy Spirit will be more apparent in your life, and you will be able to hear Him more distinctly. Will you live a life of confusion and disorder, or commit to be orderly and in harmony with God's standard?

~ Cyrus Guccione

Cleanliness is Next to Godliness

Thoroughgoing sanitary regulations were enforced. These were enjoined on the people, not only as necessary to health, but as the condition of retaining among them the presence of the Holy One. By divine authority Moses declared to them, "The Lord thy God walketh in the midst of thy camp, to deliver thee;... therefore shall thy camp be holy." - Education, pg. 38

About a week ago, I received some money and needed to put it into my wallet. I usually keep my wallet in one of my desk drawers, so that's the first place I looked. I didn't see it in one drawer, so I skimmed the other. Now, I'm not the most organized person you'll ever meet, and I have a tendency to be a bit of a pack-rat. When I looked into my drawers, they were filled to the brim with old school papers, report cards from three years ago, letters, books, and broken pencils. I decided that enough was enough. I yanked out a drawer and began organizing. I threw away paper after paper of old assignments and notes. After it was all organized, I felt a lot better, and that was only one drawer of about seven clogged drawers in my room. I still hadn't found my wallet though, so I moved on to the next drawer. I went through all seven, tossing out unnecessary items and organizing the rest. My wallet ended up not even being in my room, but I felt so much freer knowing that not just the visible parts of my room, but also the hidden places were in order. Later, a friend of mine came into my room and asked me where something was. I pointed to one of my newly organized drawers and proudly said, "It's in there."

In the Israelite camp, God instituted order and cleanliness. This was not only for sanitary reasons, but as a means of keeping God among them. Our God is a God of order. Just look at the universe. Everything has a place, even the stars. Nothing was just randomly strewn about. Look at the human body; it is perfectly organized. We ourselves are an example of order. Ellen White says, in *The Adventist Home*, page 21, that when our homes are orderly, "the ministering angels will have evidence that the truth has wrought a change in the life, purifying the soul..." I don't know about you, but I want to prove that I have changed for Christ by keeping order in my room.

~ Carmen Hartwell

God Wants to Hear You Sing!

As the people journeyed through the wilderness, many precious lessons were fixed in their minds by means of song...Thus their thoughts were uplifted from the trials and difficulties of the way, the restless, turbulent spirit was soothed and calmed, the principles of truth were implanted in the memory, and faith was strengthened. - Education, pg. 39

Recently, I read a book entitled *Princess in Calico*. In the story, a girl named Katura lived on a dreary farm. Her work was monotonous, and everyone around her argued constantly. Katura was very discouraged and wished she could live in a place that was less gloomy and depressing. One day, she received an invitation from her uncle to come visit him for the summer, and she decided to go.

While she was there, Katura was introduced to Tryphosa, a kind old lady who was bed-ridden by illness. Tryphosa was full of God's love and would sing His praises and repeat His words of life whenever she felt sick. This would lift her spirits and give her strength to continue blessing others. Katura, who was not a Christian, was drawn to Tryphosa, soaking up every encouraging word, and was led to give her life to King Jesus, becoming His princess.

At the end of the summer, Katura returned to her dismal farm. But with her new, bright, cheerful spirit, she brought a ray of sunshine to the farm. As she worked, she would sing songs about God's love and grace and repeat to the younger children encouraging words of Scripture.

This story reminds me of my mom when she was a little girl. When she would get sick, like Tryphosa, she knew that God was right there with her. She would sing songs about Jesus, and by thus diverting her mind, she felt better. Even now that she's older, she still sings songs all the time. Sometimes when there are disagreements in our home, my mom will sing or put Scripture music on to soothe our troubled spirits. So, next time you're feeling down and depressed, remember, God is still near, and He wants to hear you sing!

~ Laelle Teranski

Listen for the Lesson

...Many precious lessons were fixed in their minds by means of song. - Education, pg. 39

Do you like music? I love to play the violin, sing, and listen to music. Music can be so relaxing, fun, or interesting. It is powerful and can influence and change the way you think. We can use music to praise God and worship Him and to tell others about Him. God uses music, through His people, to spread the gospel. But have you ever thought that God would use music to speak to you personally?

A couple of weeks ago, I was feeling down and discouraged. Here's what happened: our school was driving home on the bus from filming in the snow, and I was listening to Christian music on my iPod. Something triggered me to start dwelling on a sad subject, and I began to cry. I wanted to simply wallow in sad-sounding songs, and I chose them accordingly. Yet, in every song, it seemed that God was speaking directly to me of His love; every song was reminding me that He was there, and that He could take whatever was causing my sadness and heal me, if I would but let go and surrender my all to Him. From a sad prayer song, to a song about God's love and majesty, to "It is Well With My Soul," God led me to choose specific songs that comforted me and reminded me to trust Him with my struggle. Though it took a few more days for me to finally surrender it all to God, I was very comforted by the amazing experience of God speaking directly to me through music.

Whenever I listen to the songs that God guided me to that night, I am reminded of His love in a special way. I learned more of God's love through the music itself, but also through how He spoke to me in the songs and comforted me in my discouragement. Song has amazing power. When used by God, it can uplift you and teach you lessons of His love. Sing a song today, and listen for God's voice speaking to you.

~ Valerie Jacobson

Let's Sing!

Thus [by song] their thoughts were uplifted from the trials and difficulties of the way, the restless, turbulent spirit was soothed and calmed, the principles of truth were implanted in the memory, and faith was strengthened. - Education, pg. 39

Song has an undeniable power that moves me to the core of my being. When I'm in the audience, beautiful music makes my hair stand on end. And when I play my violin with an orchestra or when my family sings together, I shiver with the thrill of a well-tuned chord or a unique counter-melody. Music can be a great blessing, especially to the musician.

Albert Einstein is known as one of the smartest men who ever lived. As a child however, his parents took him out of school because his teachers said he was too dumb to learn. According to the article "Music and the Brain," by Laurence O'Donnell, "Music was the key that helped Albert Einstein become one of the smartest men who has ever lived. Einstein himself says that the reason he was so smart is because he played the violin...A friend of Einstein, G. J. Withrow, said that the way Einstein figured out his problems and equations was by improvising on the violin."

Ellen White says this about music: "...Rightly employed, it is a precious gift of God, designed to uplift the thoughts to high and noble themes, to inspire and elevate the soul...Let us do everything in our power to make music in our homes, that God may come in" (*Child Guidance*, pp. 523, 524).

By singing and playing uplifting, harmonious music, you can do great good for yourself and those around you. The Bible says, "O come, let us sing unto the Lord..." (Psalm 95:1 KJV). So let's sing, for "a merry heart doeth good like a medicine..." (Proverbs 17:22 KJV).

~ Kevin Corrigan

Don't Talk, Live

Not as a dry theory were these things to be taught. Those who would impart truth must themselves practice its principles. Only by reflecting the character of God in the uprightness, nobility, and unselfishness of their own lives can they impress others. - Education, pg. 41

When I was growing up, there were two families that had a huge influence on me spiritually. One family's influence was good and caused me to take a real interest in spiritual things. Sadly, the other's was bad and caused me to see religion as a pointless list of dos and don'ts. As I introduce you to these families, think about what made their influences different.

I met family # 1 at a homeschooling event. The first thing that impressed me was their conservatism: all the ladies of the family wore skirts! Though I wasn't too keen on the idea of wearing skirts back then, the more I got to know this family, the more I liked them. They were kind, loving, joyful, and showed courtesy to everyone. They had something that made them happy, something that I wanted. They never once said a word to me about their faith, but they lived it. By their example, they planted in me the desire to know God.

Now meet family # 2, who also attended church. They frequently taught Sabbath School, and I admired how they were always on fire for God. In reality however, they just lived for God on Sabbath and the rest of the week were engrossed in the world. Their lifestyle was inconsistent with their professed faith, and their influence caused me to question the Bible's significance. Religion seemed fake, and consequently I fell into a lifestyle similar to theirs.

Think about your own influence; which family do you see yourself as a part of? Do you live your faith? Or is it a once-a-week performance at church? Your influence has the ability to draw others to Christ or push them away from Him. Ellen White says, "Character is power. The silent witness of a true, unselfish, godly life carries an almost irresistible influence" (*Messages to Young People*, pg. 418). So don't just talk; live what you believe!

~ Rachel Petrello

The Blessing of Obscurity

Let your conversation be without covetousness; and be content with such things as ye have... - Hebrews 13:5 KJV

Sometimes I feel small and unimportant. I would like someone to notice something I'm doing, but it doesn't seem like anyone does. Although my desire for appreciation is not necessarily wrong, I find I need a good way to avoid falling into discontent with my daily life. At these times, the following illustration quickly reminds me that I have no reason to complain.

A tall tree stands alone at the peak of a mountain. It is a monument of strength and beautiful symmetry. Naturally, everyone traveling past looks upward and admires this stately evergreen. A small flower lies in the shadow of the same mountain that the tree crowns. No one ever notices it, not individually anyway. When almost every traveler is tucked away in some warm inn, the tree, enshrouded by clouds, battles the fierce tempest. It trembles as the battering wind throws its whole weight against it. It seems to be tested to its limit as the storm rages all through the long hours of the night. But, while the tree battles for its life, the flower, tucked safely out of sight of the raging storm, sleepily nods its head as the gentle breeze rocks it to sleep (adapted from *Patriarchs and Prophets*, pg. 222).

When my father comes home from work and relates one of the difficulties he's trying to master, or when a doctor describes to me his dangerously intricate work, I'm satisfied to be a flower. Someday, God may call me to be a tree. If I'm content in humility, I trust God will give me the grace to also be content in a place of difficulty. For now, I'm thanking God for the blessing of obscurity.

~ Kevin Corrigan

Start with Your Own Plank

Those who would impart truth must themselves practice its principles. Only by reflecting the character of God in the uprightness, nobility, and unselfishness of their own lives can they impress others. - Education, pg. 41

A man goes to his brother and says, "Brother, you have a little speck of dust in your eye. I think you need to take it out."

His brother replies, "Why should I believe you? I don't think I need to worry about anything in my eye. What is a mere speck compared to the wooden plank in your own eye?"

"There's a plank in my eye?"

It is so easy to think that others need to change. I want nations to learn to be at peace with one another and put an end to war. Politicians should stop trying to put down their opponents in a struggle for power. Wealthier people should give aid to those who are sunk in poverty. Criminals should cease their ungoverned acts and simply obey the law. Most importantly, people must realize that they need a personal relationship with God.

So, how do I go about making a difference in this world? How can I show others how to change? The answer is this: it starts in my own life. If I tell others they need to fix issues in their lives, but I struggle with the same problems, they won't see any need to change. Before I can guide others to God, I must have my own personal relationship with Him. I hope that one day someone will be drawn closer to God because they can see Him in me. But first, I must let God change my heart and take the plank from my own eye. Do you want to change the world? It starts with you.

~ Valerie Jacobson

Is It Worth Your Name?

Only by reflecting the character of God in the uprightness, nobility, and unselfishness of their own lives can they impress others. - Education, pg. 41

Late one night, after working as referees for a high school basketball game, Jeff and another referee stopped at a 24-hour convenience store and asked to cash the high school's single paycheck so they could split their earnings. The elderly woman behind the counter agreed to cash the check, but she miss-counted the cash and gave them an extra $20 back. Just outside the store, the two men began to split their money, only to discover that they each had $10 too much. Jeff's junior referee partner thought they should go ahead and keep the extra money as a windfall. But Jeff explained that the money didn't just appear out of thin air; it might even be taken out of the poor clerk's next paycheck, even though it was an innocent mistake. Additionally, he explained that his good name was worth far more than $10; he would never keep something that wasn't his or disrespect himself for any amount. They both went back inside, and Jeff promptly explained to the surprised clerk that she had overpaid them and placed the extra $20 on the counter. The elderly lady quickly glanced down at the money and then back up at Jeff with an amazed look in her eyes. She whispered a grateful "Thank you!" and wiped a tear off her cheek as the men returned to their car.

I don't know how much Jeff impacted both the young referee and the elderly clerk, but I am positive that each of them had a lot to think about that night. Jeff could have very easily kept the money, but he valued his reputation and character far more than a mere ten dollars. I also want to uphold a high standard, so that I can be a living witness and example to those around me. I want to reach souls for Christ, and the best way to do so is by allowing Christ to live and shine through me, so that I may reflect the loveliness of His character. I pray that you will also determine to glorify God in every decision you make, whether big or small, and to make a positive impact upon the lives around you.

~ Megan Metcalf

Frustrations and Fish

True education is not the forcing of instruction on an unready and unreceptive mind. The mental powers must be awakened, the interest aroused. - Education, pg. 41

"Okay, guys, we're going to have a biology lesson!" my dad enthusiastically exclaimed. He then proceeded to inform my brother and me that we would be learning the anatomy of a fish. Since my dad had just returned from a fishing expedition, I put two and two together and realized that we would be dissecting a real fish that used to swim happily in the ocean.

Slowly, a sense of dread crept over me, and I adamantly refused to look at the fish, touch it, or come within a 10-foot radius of it. My dad ignored me and proceeded to gut the fish, explaining each part and how it functioned. Thoroughly grossed out, all I could manage to say was, "Eew! That's disgusting! Can I go now?"

My poor dad—he was probably very frustrated with my unwilling spirit. He was only trying to arouse my interest so that I could learn something useful.

I bet that's how our heavenly Father must feel sometimes. There are so many amazing things He wants to teach us. Yet, because of our unwillingness and unreceptive minds, He can only accomplish a little at a time. Just like my dad couldn't make me like looking at the fish, God can't force us to learn an important lesson. He wants us to be genuinely interested in what He has to teach us, so that He can impart His infinite wisdom to us.

~ Sarah Chang

Full

...A life centered in God is a life of completeness. Every want He has implanted, He provides to satisfy; every faculty imparted, He seeks to develop. - Education, pg. 41

Have you ever felt empty? Not as though you were hungry, but as if something were missing in your life?

So many people today feel that emptiness and try to fill it with material things. Chasing after power, money, fame, relationships, or popularity, they try to find peace and fulfilment. Do they ever find what they are looking for? There are so many unhappy people in the world who are working to fill themselves. But when we put our focus on self, we fail miserably.

I remember going over a new song during an orchestra rehearsal. I played my clarinet part perfectly the first time and felt confident that I could play it well every time. The next time we went over that song, though, I was humbled. I messed up every single note! I had been too sure of myself. It's only when I center my focus on God and His plan that I can truly succeed.

God has placed wants in our lives so that He can show us His infinite love and teach us to be happy. What other Father can care for His children with such tender, affectionate detail? He wants us to recognize that without Him we really are nothing, but with Him we are everything. He has also given us talents, and we are to use them to further honor and glorify Him. But again, all our efforts to accomplish this would be nothing without God as our focus.

I'm not the best clarinetist. But I'm a lot better now than I used to be because God has helped me. Often, I'll be practicing and simply cannot get a part, but when I pray in faith, asking God for help, He shows me how to play it. God wants to do this for all of us. He wants to take care of every want, worry, or trial. So, how can you find peace and happiness? Focus on God, and you'll be filled to over-flowing.

~ Jo Holdal

Holding a Grudge

Be ye angry, and sin not: let not the sun go down upon your wrath...
- Ephesians 4:26 KJV

Whether they are hereditary or acquired traits, we all have defects in our characters. One bad character trait that I struggle with is holding grudges against people. I find that the longer I hold resentment towards someone, the more it just keeps building up, until it wears me down. For instance, I used to have a really close friend. We spent every single moment together. She was the one person that I felt I could just be myself with and not worry that she would think any less of me.

Then one day, she decided she did not want to be my friend anymore. It started out gradually, and I could not see it at first. I thought it was just a phase, but, as time passed, we became very distant. I heard someone say that the reason she did not want to be my friend was because she felt that I gossiped about people, and she wasn't comfortable with that. At that time, I felt very hurt and bitter towards her. The bitterness built into a massive grudge. I would go out of my way to publicly ignore her because every time I saw her with her other friends, I would start feeling bitter. Then one day, I felt impressed that this bitterness that I was holding against her was getting in the way of my relationship with God. If I had talked with her about my feelings at the beginning of the conflict, it would have saved both of us a lot of tears and heartache. But, through this experience, God taught me that I need to watch what I say about people, and I also became more aware of my problem with holding grudges. Negative feedback is never easy to take, but we often have to go through trials to mold us and prepare us for heaven.

Nehemiah 9:17 says that God is "ready to pardon, gracious and merciful, slow to anger, and of great kindness..." (KJV). He is always willing to forgive you and erase your slate of sins. Through prayer, God can help us honestly have forgiving hearts towards others and teach us not to hold grudges against anyone.

~ Bristi Waid

Make Me Whole

...A life centered in God is a life of completeness. Every want He has implanted, He provides to satisfy; every faculty imparted, He seeks to develop. - Education, pg. 41

This quote reminds me of Matthew 7:9-11: "...What man is there among you who, if his son asks for bread, will give him a stone? Or if he asks for a fish, will he give him a serpent? If you then, being evil, know how to give good gifts to your children, how much more will your Father who is in heaven give good things to those who ask Him!" (NKJV).

Before I came to Fountainview, I didn't feel like I had a relationship with God. My prayer life consisted of memorized prayers that really meant nothing. I did not have devotions, except for family worships. I felt empty and longed for something more. At night, I would lie in bed crying, asking God if He could hear me and if He cared. When I came to Fountainview, I started having devotions every morning, but that didn't do much; I still felt like there was a huge abyss between God and me. But, as I began to spend more time with God in His Word, as I took my eyes off myself and looked more to the needs of others, I found myself feeling closer to God. I started to think that maybe He was there listening to me. Now, watching Him answer my prayers every day is the coolest thing on earth! It's like discovering something new each day. I still struggle, but it's a lot easier now because I know that He's waiting for me to talk to Him and share what is on my heart.

If God puts a longing in us for something that is good, then He will satisfy that desire, just like He fulfilled my desire for a relationship with Him. Naturally, we want all our wishes to be granted, but many times our desires aren't good. We need to ask God if a desire is from Him or not. Our lives and desires must be centered around Christ. I know this is hard to do, but I also know that it is possible with God's help. And we can trust that He *will* give us every good thing we ask for.

~ Laelle Teranski

Beautiful

The Author of all beauty, Himself a lover of the beautiful, God provided to gratify in His children the love of beauty. - Education, pg. 41

"No adult can possibly be as wise as a happy child can be. Coming home from church services Sunday night, our family paused in the snow for a moment to study the star-gemmed sky. 'Goodness!' breathed our babe, after an appreciative silence. 'If heaven is that beautiful on the bottom, just think how wonderful the other side must be'" (Burton Hillis, *Better Homes & Gardens*).

Isn't it amazing what our God has done for us? He has put beauty in absolutely everything around us. What's more is that everything in this universe is so practical. Generally, things which are practical are simple and limited, just enough to get the job done. But God, while still being practical, put beauty into everything He created. He creates beyond what is necessary and puts endless possibilities for enjoyment into it.

Our five senses are an example of this. With sight, He gives us beautiful things to look at, such as roses with their amazing shades of color. With hearing, He gives us all kinds of different genres of music to listen to. With taste, He gives us delicious foods of various flavors (salty, sweet, sour). With touch, He gives us textures to feel and warm and cold to experience. With smell, He gives us millions of aromas to tickle the nose. And all just because He enjoys beauty and variety and wants us to be able to do the same. Truly, our God cares about making us happy, even in the smallest details of His creation.

~ Danielle Schafer

Beautiful Thoughts

The Author of all beauty, Himself a lover of the beautiful, God provided to gratify in His children the love of beauty. - Education, pg. 41

In the beginning, God filled our world with wonderful creations that displayed His love for beauty and perfection. "As the earth came forth from the hand of its Maker, it was exceedingly beautiful. Its surface was diversified with mountains, hills, and plains, interspersed with noble rivers and lovely lakes; but the hills and mountains were not abrupt and rugged, abounding in terrific steeps and frightful chasms, as they now do; the sharp, ragged edges of earth's rocky framework were buried beneath the fruitful soil, which everywhere produced a luxuriant growth of verdure. There were no loathsome swamps or barren deserts. Graceful shrubs and delicate flowers greeted the eye at every turn. The heights were crowned with trees more majestic than any that now exist. The air, untainted by foul miasma, was clear and healthful. The entire landscape outvied in beauty the decorated grounds of the proudest palace. The angelic host viewed the scene with delight, and rejoiced at the wonderful works of God" (*Patriarchs and Prophets*, pg. 44).

The earth and the garden of Eden were a reflection of God's character. He created everything perfect, in a way that He knew Adam and Eve would love. He designed them to know what true beauty is and to love and appreciate it. Do you think God meant for us to dwell unnecessarily on unpleasant and depressing issues? Of course not! He wants us to avoid such things and focus on the beauties of His creation. However, I too often find myself thinking about ugly things when I easily could be thinking about something pleasant. God not only created us to love beauty, but He also wants us to think about beautiful things.

"Finally, brethren, whatsoever things are true, whatsoever things are honest, whatsoever things are just, whatsoever things are pure, whatsoever things are lovely, whatsoever things are of good report; if there be any virtue, and if there be any praise, think on these things" (Philippians 4:8 KJV).

~ Sophia Simard

Channels of Blessings

The consecration to God of a tithe of all increase, whether of the orchard and harvest field, the flocks and herds, or the labor of brain or hand, the devotion of a second tithe for the relief of the poor and other benevolent uses, tended to keep fresh before the people the truth of God's ownership of all, and of their opportunity to be channels of His blessings. - Education, pg. 44

Greg owned a small business, with an annual salary of $50,000. He went to a conference where a Dr. Peter Richards inspired his listeners to give a million dollars to the Lord's work. Greg told him it would be impossible for his family to give that much. Dr. Richards asked, "What did you make last year? How much did you give?"

Greg replied, "My salary is $50,000, and we gave $15,000."

"Next year, trust God to help you give $50,000."

"But that's my entire salary!"

Dr. Richards assured Greg, "Trust God, and see how He provides."

With God's help, Greg's business did well, and his family gave $50,000. The following year, God helped them give $100,000. Each year following, they lived on his original $50,000 salary and gave all their extra income to the Lord's work. Within several years, they had given *over* a million dollars.

God set up a system for the Israelites to give Him one tenth of all the income they received, of "all increase, whether of the orchard and harvest field, the flocks and herds, or the labor of brain or hand..." This had a very important purpose in their education.

God's purpose in educating His people was to build their characters. In doing so, He had to be sure that they weren't becoming too proud or selfish. The tithe and offering system was set up to remind the people where their blessings came from. They were also reminded of the way in which they could be channels of blessings through which God can work.

If we allow God to work through us to bless others, we will gain a huge blessing ourselves. We can practice the ways of our Father in heaven, and be loving, unselfish givers.

~ Victoria West

88

If

It was a training adapted to kill out all narrowing selfishness, and to cultivate breadth and nobility of character. - Education, pg. 44

If you can keep your head when all about you
Are losing theirs and blaming it on you;
If you can trust yourself when all men doubt you,
But make allowance for their doubting too...
If you can dream—and not make dreams your master;
If you can think—and not make thoughts your aim;
If you can meet with Triumph and Disaster
And treat those two impostors just the same;
If you can bear to hear the truth you've spoken
Twisted by knaves to make a trap for fools,
Or watch the things you gave your life to broken,
And stoop and build 'em up with worn-out tools:
...If you can force your heart and nerve and sinew
To service your turn long after they are gone,
And so hold on when there is nothing in you
Except the Will which says to them: "Hold On!";
If you can talk with crowds and keep your virtue,
Or walk with Kings—nor lose the common touch;
... If you can fill the unforgiving minute
With sixty seconds' worth of distance run,
Yours is the earth and everything that's in it,
And—which is more—you'll be a man, my son!
– Rudyard Kipling

Would you like to be that kind of man or woman that Kipling is talking about? A man or woman of integrity, trust, wisdom, dexterity, and stamina? Every day, you are to perfect your character into the likeness of God's own character; you are to be gaining victories over temptations, achieving a closer relationship with Jesus, and accomplishing the work He has given you to do. If this is your highest aim, then not only will you overcome the world, but heaven and everlasting life will be yours!

~ Cyrus Guccione

 **Education: Reflecting Your Author**

Wherever in Israel God's plan of education was carried into effect, its results testified of its Author. - Education, pg. 45

A few years ago, I began an accredited study of the violin. It required a lot of practicing hours, and my violin skills grew quickly. I did well on the first music test after a year of intense preparation. As time went on, I began preparing for the next exam. However, I came down with whooping cough, and after that I got almost every virus that came along. This series of illnesses and a few other injuries I had, limited my violin practice for several months. I simply postponed the test for half a year and continued with the program. But, I soon realized that because of my somewhat poor health, it was going to be difficult to spend the amount of time necessary to practice.

My parents and I finally decided that I should drop the program entirely. I could have continued, which I desired to do, but I knew that it would likely be at the expense of my health. Being unhealthy would reduce my ability to think clearly and listen to God's voice, and I knew that nothing would be worth blocking my connection with heaven. Although the change in plans was disappointing, God has blessed me with greater ability, and I know He is still increasing my talent.

The purpose of your education is for you to reflect Christ more clearly. Is it accomplishing this end? Maybe there is something in your training that is overtaxing you, or possibly there's too much going on in your life, and you can barely remember what you're learning long enough to pass the next test. If your education is not healthy, ask God for help; He will either give you strength to go on or peace in choosing a new course. Don't be surprised if God leads you to do something unconventional for your education. For example, God chose for Daniel's secondary studies to be in the court of a heathen king, something Daniel and his parents never would have chosen. Obey God, whether His choice for you is easy or difficult to accept. He promises, "...My yoke is easy, and My burden is light" (Matthew 11:30 KJV).

~ Kevin Corrigan

The Way Less Traveled

Choosing rather to suffer affliction with the people of God, than to enjoy the pleasures of sin for a season; Esteeming the reproach of Christ greater riches than the treasures in Egypt: for he [Moses] had respect unto the recompence of the reward. - Hebrews 11:25, 26 KJV

Robert Frost wrote a poem that really speaks to my heart. In it, he tells a story of man who was walking, when he came to a fork in the road. He stood a long time, unsure of which path to take. He peered down one path as far as he could see; then he looked down the other. He could tell that not too many feet had traveled the second way. Knowing that he must make a decision, for he could not travel both roads, he finally decided to take the second path. He ends the poem with these thoughts:

> I shall be telling this with a sigh
> Somewhere ages and ages hence:
> Two roads diverged in a wood, and I,
> I took the one less traveled by,
> And that has made all the difference.

Because he took the road less traveled, though it may have been the more difficult path, it made all the difference.

Moses was in line to become the next pharaoh of Egypt. Wealth, splendor, and fame were to be his. But he chose a much more difficult road, to follow God's purpose in saving the stubborn nation of Israel. Above the sumptuous calls of Egypt, he chose to follow God's plan for his life. Because Moses had chosen that road, after he died, the Lord resurrected him and took him to heaven. He now has eternity to spend with his God and Creator! Had Moses chosen the temporary pleasures of Egypt, all he would have become was a mummy, slowly decaying in a golden coffin.

Many times we take the easy road in order to gain temporary pleasure and fulfillment. But, while the easy road may bring short-term gratification, Christ's way, though less traveled, brings eternal reward.

~ Anneliese Wahlman

91

We Need Each Other!

Fathers and mothers in Israel became indifferent to their obligation to God, indifferent to their obligation to their children. - Education, pg. 45

Parents, your children need *you*. I appreciate a house and food, but what I really desire is a home where I have my parents' companionship and appreciation. I can see in my peers the same longing for parental involvement in their lives. But youth, your parents need you, too. I have a responsibility to support my parents in such a way that they have the time and energy to give me the friendship, confidence, and support I need.

The only way my family thrives is through working together, but this is not always easy to achieve. We must constantly ask God for power. Without His help, cooperation could not exist in our family, due to our conflicting selfish natures. I find it helps a lot, though, when everyone realizes the benefits of working together.

A number of years ago, my siblings and I were motivated to start helping more with the household chores. We soon found that it was fun to surprise our parents and do an extra job that we had not been asked to do, even if it was small. It was rewarding to see how pleased our parents were when we swept one more room than we were asked to or scrubbed a few extra dishes. But even better is the fact that when we began to help out more, Dad and Mom did all kinds of things with us that they never would have had time to do before. They went exploring with us, built forts, and even played with Legos. The best thing was that through working and playing together, we have become best friends, and rarely do we argue or fight with each other. I now find each day more agreeable and pleasant than the last.

If you choose not to ignore God and the responsibility He has given you in placing you in your family, there will be great rewards here and hereafter.

~ Kevin Corrigan

A Higher Education

These schools were intended to serve as a barrier against the wide-spreading corruption, to provide for the mental and spiritual welfare of the youth, and to promote the prosperity of the nation by furnishing it with men qualified to act in the fear of God as leaders and counselors. - Education, pg. 46

It is not easy being a foreign student in a conservative Christian boarding academy. Take it from someone who has been in one for three years! First of all, you can't just do whatever you want. Second, you have a dress code; and third, you are always accountable to other people. When you add that to waking up early in the morning, having limited free time, and daily manual labor, you might wonder how I survive! Well, let me just tell you about it.

At the beginning of my sophomore year, I felt extremely restrained. I often got frustrated and would whine and question my parents' decision to send me to a Christian school. But, one morning, as I was reading my devotions, I came across a quote that struck me: "With us, as with Israel of old, success in education depends on fidelity in carrying out the Creator's plan. Adherence to the principles of God's word will bring as great blessings to us as it would have brought to the Hebrew people" (*Education*, pg. 50). After reading this, I could clearly see my purpose at this school. Rules were not made to restrict my fun, but to train me how to discern good from evil, to develop my physical and spiritual skills, and ultimately, to prepare me to share the gospel. This quote helped me to view things differently. For example, when I had to give accountability, I appreciated that other people cared about me; or, when I had to work, I was glad that soon I would gather experience in that area of labor. Now I know that being in a Christian academy is the highest education I can get.

Every day, the divine Teacher gives us lessons to prepare us for a higher purpose. The rules that He sets before us are not only to train us to become spiritual leaders and counselors, but also to bring us great blessings. The biggest lesson that a student can take from his training is to become a humble servant in sharing the gospel. This is the true purpose of higher education.

~ Valdis Cuvaldin

God's Cure for Boredom

The pupils of these schools [of the prophets] sustained themselves by their own labor in tilling the soil or in some mechanical employment. In Israel this was not thought strange or degrading; indeed, it was regarded as a sin to allow children to grow up in ignorance of useful labor. - Education, pg. 47

Day 26 of summer # 3 at Fountainview Academy: the digital numbers on the alarm clock read 5:30 am. Its electronic jangling rudely interrupts my peaceful slumber, informing me that the time to rise has come. I groggily roll out of my bed, stumble over to my worst enemy of the moment, and switch it to the 'off' position. An hour later, I find myself in the cafeteria eating breakfast after somehow having mechanically prepared myself for the day. Seven o'clock finds me sitting in the dirt out in the fields, picking weeds from among the green shoots of the baby carrots. Eleven o'clock comes around, and I leave the fields to go inside and clean the school building for an hour. You can't imagine the piles of dirt people track in from those fields!

After lunch, the cafeteria calls my name with all its soiled dishes to scrub and sticky tables to wipe. At 2:00 pm, I'm back in the field until 6:00. It's a typical summer day. When I tell people that I've done this for three summers in a row, the usual response is, "I'm so sorry!" But the truth is, I enjoy it so much! Why go home and be bored when I can stay here and feel productive by working with my hands? Sure it's hard work, and it can get uncomfortable and tedious sometimes. But I've learned so much from staying here during the summer; and I make the best memories with the people around me.

God instituted manual labor back in the Garden of Eden. Adam and Eve were not to just sit around and smell the roses. There may not have been weeds to pick, floors to sweep, or dishes to wash, but they did keep busy. So, next time you feel bored or have nothing to do, find some manual labor; I guarantee that you will find God's cure for your boredom!

~ Carmen Hartwell

April 5

Useful Labor

...It was regarded as a sin to allow children to grow up in ignorance of useful labor. Every youth, whether his parents were rich or poor, was taught some trade. - Education, pg. 47

Working is more pleasant than I often imagine. No, I don't mean a job where I'm getting paid; I'm talking about helping around the house for seemingly nothing. A job accomplished brings me more satisfaction than almost anything else.

One Sunday, my family and I gathered manure from a horse pasture for our garden. It was a lot of work—work that I would generally consider unpleasant. But, as soon as I decided I was going to have a good attitude, I had a lot of fun. It was fantastic exercise, and I could hardly wait to get our vegetables planted! I can't justly describe the feeling that comes with getting a job done cheerfully, but I will say that it's a perfect fit for my nagging desire to do something exciting. I find boredom an impossibility when I choose to be unselfish enough to do something purposeful, even if it's not exactly what I was looking for in the way of entertainment.

Are you feeling down or lazy? Try doing something useful. Put that stack of clothes on your dresser away, empty the trash, or sweep the garage for your dad. Even though doing chores isn't practicing a trade, you're learning the blessing of work which will help make you a success in any job you take on. Though seemingly insignificant, you will be surprised how much satisfaction you receive from even the smallest job well done. "In all labour there is profit..." "...He that gathereth by labour shall increase" (Proverbs 14:23; 13:11 KJV).

~ Kevin Corrigan

Deep Conversation

Not only were the students [of the schools of the prophets] taught the duty of prayer, but they were taught how to pray...
- Education, pg. 47

Paul says to "pray without ceasing" (1 Thessalonians 5:17 KJV). Ellen White writes, "Let every breath be a prayer" (Ministry of Healing, pg. 510). Jesus Himself told His disciples to pray so they wouldn't fall into temptation. It's obvious that we have a duty and a need to pray. But I have found that sometimes, when I kneel down to pray, I just don't know where to start. Have you ever felt that way? I am learning, though, that prayer, even the most simple prayer, should be more than just, "Dear God, please bless my family and friends and help me have a good day." It should be more like a real conversation with God. And no conversation should be one-sided. So then, how do we really pray a heartfelt, unselfish prayer?

Fortunately, the Bible does not leave us in the dark about how to pray. Let's take a look at Jesus' own model prayer, found in Matthew 6:9-13. It begins and ends by praising God. It continues by looking forward to the coming of God's kingdom, which should be our ultimate focus. Jesus reminds us that we should pray that God's will be done, and not our own. Just as we forgive others, we should ask God to forgive our sins too. We don't have to worry about our physical needs, but this doesn't mean we shouldn't ask God to provide for us. Since we don't have the power to withstand temptation, we must ask God to give us His strength to overcome sin.

So, does this mean that we must pray every prayer in this exact order, word for word? No, but it does give us a guide for the type of things we should pray about. Prayer needs to be more in-depth than we usually make it. We should talk to God about greater problems, ask Him for greater strength, and forgiveness for greater sins, but also, we shouldn't forget to ask for the smaller things. You and I need to pray like we're talking to a real Friend who will always listen and can always help. Make your conversations with God a little deeper every day.

~ Valerie Jacobson

My Nation First, Lord

Above every earthly good he [Solomon] asked of God a wise and understanding heart. And the Lord gave him not only that which he sought, but that also for which he had not sought—both riches and honor. - Education, pg. 48

Just before the death of King David, his son Solomon was crowned the new king of Israel. Early on, Solomon realized the enormity of his task and his inability to rule the people in his own wisdom. In contrast to the other greedy kings of Israel, Solomon did not seek to gain riches and honor from his high position. Instead, he knelt reverently before the Lord and prayed, "Now, O Lord my God, You have made Your servant king instead of my father David, but I am a little child; I do not know how to go out or come in...Therefore give to Your servant an understanding heart to judge Your people, that I may discern between good and evil" (1 Kings 3:7, 9 NKJV). In his meek and lowly spirit, Solomon put his nation before himself and unselfishly asked for things that would help him to guide Israel in following after God. Although he asked nothing for himself, God granted him not only a wise and understanding heart, but also riches and honor as a double blessing.

Many times when we are granted the opportunity to exert power, we indulge ourselves with the benefits available to us and seek our own gain. Every one of us is guilty of this tendency, no exceptions. Thinking of others is against my nature, but it is far more rewarding than living for myself. And when I focus on the needs of others, my own cares quickly fade away. A life of selflessness is one of riches and honor in itself; the happiest people on earth are those who live to bless others.

Make yourself rich today; let God teach you to be sensitive to the needs of others and lead you to channel your thoughts away from yourself. Discover a wealth which can only come from heaven above, a wealth which comes from putting others first.

~ Megan Metcalf

A Peculiar People

The discipline and training that God appointed for Israel would cause them, in all their ways of life, to differ from the people of other nations. This peculiarity, which should have been regarded as a special privilege and blessing, was to them unwelcome. - Education, pg. 49

I jumped into the family minivan and crossed my arms. "Why do I have to leave?" I huffed. I had just come from basketball practice on Friday afternoon. Since I had been involved with the basketball program at my school that winter, I practiced five days a week. But, as the days got shorter and sundown got earlier, I could not stay very long at Friday's practice. This was because I had to be home to get ready for Sabbath, and so my parents said. But I didn't understand. Soon we pulled into the driveway. I snatched my gym bag and backpack, slamming the car door and running inside to my room.

As I set my things down, Dad came in and sat on my bed. "I know you probably don't understand why we keep Sabbath the way we do."
"Dad, didn't God make Sabbath for us to enjoy? After all, 'The Sabbath was made for man, and not man for the Sabbath.' So why can't I play basketball on Friday nights? I enjoy it."
"Well, yes, God *does* say that we shouldn't be like the Pharisees and care more about the strict details of what people do on Sabbath than the attitude with which they keep the Sabbath. But, I think you'll find this passage in Isaiah 58 interesting," he said, flipping to Isaiah. "'If thou turn away thy foot from the sabbath, from doing thy pleasure on My holy day; and call the sabbath a delight, the holy of the LORD, honourable; and shalt honour Him, not doing thine own ways, nor finding thine own pleasure, nor speaking thine own words: Then shalt thou delight thyself in the LORD; and I will cause thee to ride upon the high places of the earth,...for the mouth of the LORD hath spoken it'" (Isaiah 58:13-14 KJV).

While we certainly are different from the world, this "set-apartness" should be considered a blessing from God. For instance, the Sabbath really is a blessing to God's people because it allows them to rest from their labors. Yes, we are a peculiar people, but this fact is a great honor.

~ Victoria West

Serving Christ by Loving Others

…Truly, I say to you, as you did it to one of the least of these my brothers, you did it to Me. - Matthew 25:40 ESV

One brisk, wintery day, Charity went to her mailbox and found a strange letter with no return address. It read:

Dear Charity,
I'm going to be in your neighborhood Saturday afternoon, and I'd like to stop by for a visit..
Love always, Jesus

Why does God want to visit me? Charity thought to herself. She looked in her kitchen cabinets and realized that she had nothing to offer Jesus, so she decided to run down to the grocery store to buy some food. With eleven cents left to her name, and her offering tucked under her arm, Charity was making her way back home when a scraggly dressed couple wandered up to her.

"Hey lady, can you help us?" the middle aged man asked. "I ain't got a job, ya know, and my wife and I have been living out here on the street. And well, now it's getting cold, and we're gettin' kinda hungry, and well, if you could help us lady, we'd really appreciate it."

"Sir, I'd like to help you, but I'm a poor woman myself. I'm having an important visitor over tonight; I was planning to serve Him the few things I have," she replied.

"Yeah, well okay, lady; I understand. Thanks anyway." As the couple turned away, Charity felt guilt settle in her stomach.

"Sir, wait!" she called out. The couple stopped. "Look, why don't you take this food. I'll figure something else out."

"Thank you!" The couple smiled.

"You know, I've got another coat at home. Here take this one."

Charity unbuttoned her jacket and slipped it over the woman's shoulders. Now smiling, with no coat and nothing to feed her guest, Charity made her way home. When she got there, she saw another letter in her mailbox.

Dear Charity,
I really enjoyed visiting you today. Thank you for the good food, and I liked the jacket as well!
Love always, Jesus

~ Jessica Hall

Our Royal Heritage

This peculiarity, which should have been regarded as a special privilege and blessing, was to them unwelcome. The simplicity and self-restraint essential to the highest development they sought to exchange for the pomp and self-indulgence of heathen peoples. To be "like all the nations" was their ambition. - Education, pp. 49, 50

Imagine that you are the son or daughter of a great and powerful king. Would you be embarrassed to tell people who you are? Would you be ashamed of your identity? Would you want to just blend in with the common crowd? I don't think so.

Well, I have something to tell you. You are the child of a great King, the greatest King of all, Jesus. You are a part of the royal family, and you have been asked to be a representative of King Jesus, to show His love to the world.

But strangely, many of us, like the children of Israel, reject our royal heritage. We don't want to be different from the rest of the world. We want to fit in, to dress like the world, talk like the world, and act like the world. We are often ashamed to be a peculiar people and try to forget our high calling.

You know, we are but passing through this world. Our heavenly Father has prepared a home for us, and we should work to bring as many souls as possible to this home. We may be thought of as weird or laughed at for a short time, but in the end our reward will be well worth it.

~ Laura Williams

The Devil's Lure

In the rejection of the ways of God for the ways of men, the downfall of Israel began. Thus also it continued, until the Jewish people became a prey to the very nations whose practices they had chosen to follow. - Education, pg. 50

There is a sinister creature who lurks in the watery depths of the ocean. His name is the Angler fish. He makes his home anywhere from the open seas, to the ocean floor, to the continental shelf. The Angler fish has a unique way of obtaining his food. He has a long tentacle protruding from his forehead, between his eyes. He uses this tentacle like a baited fishing line, wiggling it to attract prey, until he can draw them close enough to his jaws to—*CHOMP!* Sometimes, the tentacle emits light to attract the other fish, and sometimes the prey are fooled into thinking the tentacle is food. But, however the victim is lured into the Angler's deadly jaws, he doesn't realize what is happening until it is too late, and there is no escape. The Angler's sharp, lethal teeth are set at an inward incline in his mouth, so food can easily go into his stomach, but not out.

Sometimes, I am just like the Angler's prey. I am attracted to the devil's lure of sin; I'm captivated by it. The devil whispers in my ear that this sin is the only thing that can make me truly happy. What he doesn't tell me is that the very sins I'm pursuing will cause my downfall. The worldly things we cling to in life, things we feel we need in order to be happy, are going to leave us empty and destitute in the end. We need to be surrendering our lives to Christ every day, laying down every sin. It is only His way of life, giving our hearts wholly to Him, and finding our fulfillment in Him that will bring us genuine happiness. The devil is ready and waiting to devour; don't be fooled by his false bait.

~ Anneliese Wahlman

Assimilation

To be "like all the nations" was their ambition. - Education, pg. 50

Have you ever felt like you didn't belong? I'm sure you have, and I know I have at times. Even though I know that where I am and what I'm doing is part of God's will for my life, I sometimes feel the outside pressures to conform and fit in with the expectations of others.

The nation of Israel felt the same way. It's hard to believe that God's own people were feeling that they needed to change who they were in order to get the most out of life. They began to lose their God-given identity and adopt the world's standards. Instead of causing the other nations to look on them with awe, they lost the respect, honor, and riches God had blessed them with.

But, it's not just then in Israel, or now in North America that people lose their identity; it's everywhere and in every age. The world has an irresistible pull on humanity. It offers seemingly innocent, lighthearted attractions and an escape from reality. However, when we look behind the scenes, we realize that it's not all it's advertised to be. Crime, sickness, and homelessness are rampant, often in the very places where frivolity is expressed most freely.

Lately, I've learned a lot about being myself and not letting others decide how I'm going to feel or how I'm going to react to a situation. God is in control of everything we go through, so long as we ask Him to carry us. Christ is there for us through it all, and He will keep us true to His principles. To stay strong in our God-given identity, to prevail no matter the wind, and to resist the strongest temptations, we need to stay focused on God and remain content with His will for our lives.

~ Jo Holdal

It is Well, Part 1

As the tempest that leaves unharmed the flower of the valley uproots the tree upon the mountaintop, so do fierce temptations that leave untouched the lowly in life assail those who stand in the world's high places of success and honor. - Education, pp. 51, 52

When I ponder the lives of great people who have inspired me, one man stands out among the rest: Horatio Spafford, the author of "It is Well with My Soul," one of the most beloved hymns of all time.

Horatio G. Spafford was a prominent lawyer in Chicago during the 1860s. The Spaffords were also close friends and supporters of Dwight L. Moody, the most influential preacher of the day. In 1870, the Spaffords's only son died of scarlet fever when he was four years old. Though the family was devastated, they could not have known that this was only the beginning of tragedies.

Horatio had invested heavily in real estate on the shores of Lake Michigan. In 1871, every one of these holdings was wiped out by the Great Chicago Fire which swept through the city.

In November, 1873, Horatio decided that it would be best for the family to take a holiday. So, he arranged for his family to sail to Europe where their friend, Moody, was holding evangelistic meetings. Just before they were to set sail, a last minute business arrangement forced Horatio to delay the trip. Not wanting to ruin the family holiday, he persuaded his wife and four daughters to go on as planned. He would follow as soon as possible. With this decided, Horatio's family set sail. Only nine days later, Horatio received a telegram from his wife which contained only two words: "Saved alone."

How many of us at this point would feel completely hopeless? Many of us might become angry with God or completely give up in despair. When trials and sorrows come to us, there is but one place we can turn for comfort and help. And that is where Horatio Spafford turned in his time of tragedy.

~ Laura Williams

It is Well, Part 2

The Lord is near to those who have a broken heart, and saves such as have a contrite spirit. - Psalm 34:18 NKJV

On November 22, 1873, the steamship *Ville de Havre,* on which Horatio Spafford's family was traveling, collided with *The Lochearn.* The *Ville de Havre* sank in only twelve minutes, claiming the lives of 226 people, including Horatio's four daughters.

After receiving the heartbreaking telegram from his wife, Horatio boarded the next ship to join her in England. When the ship had reached the approximate location where the *Ville de Havre* had gone down, the ship's steward informed Horatio.

It was here, while looking down into the now peaceful water, during the most trying time of his life, that Horatio penned the words to one of the most loved hymns.

When peace, like a river, attendeth my way,
When sorrows like sea billows roll—
Whatever my lot, Thou hast taught me to say,
It is well, it is well with my soul.

The story of Horatio Spafford has inspired me so much that it gives me encouragement when I face trials or hardships. Even though Horatio experienced horrible pain and loss, he was able to find peace in God. When I experience hard times, I also want to be able to say, "It is well with my soul."

~ Laura Williams

April 15

That Which is Least

The same fidelity was manifest in the palace of the Pharaohs as in the prisoner's cell. - Education, pg. 52

The minutes ticked slowly by as a sixteen-year-old black boy sat on a rough wooden bench, breathlessly awaiting the head teacher's decision concerning his prospective enrollment. In the early post-Civil War years, it was very difficult for African Americans to gain an education due to the heavy racial discrimination that pervaded society.

The boy was on the verge of fulfilling his dream of getting an education. The teacher entered the room, handed him a broom and brusquely commanded him to sweep the floor. The boy looked at the broom, then towards the door and the teacher's rapidly receding form. Jumping up he swept the room not once, not twice, but three times! Then he found a rag and dusted the entire room—windowsills, shelves, baseboards—everything. When the teacher came to inspect the room, not a speck of dirt could be found anywhere. The boy was admitted to the school. His name was Booker T. Washington.

His attention to small details, such as sweeping a room, led him to become a very successful man. He authored fourteen books, founded Tuskegee Institute in 1881, and helped improve relationships between races, which led to the Civil Rights Movement of the 1960s.

By showing fidelity in small as well as big tasks, Booker T. Washington left an example of the way Jesus wants us to be. If He can trust us with small things, He will be able to trust us with big things. "He that is faithful in that which is least is faithful also in much..." (Luke 16:10 KJV).

~ Anna Fink

I Have Prayed for Thee

...Simon, Simon, behold, Satan hath desired to have you, that he may sift you as wheat: but I have prayed for thee, that thy faith fail not: and when thou art converted, strengthen thy brethren. - Luke 22:31, 32 KJV

One evening, two college roommates sat together in their room studying. Both had grown up in the church and were good Christian boys, but this particular evening, one of them felt restless.

"I'm tired of this," he remarked to his friend. "I need some excitement. This Christianity stuff is boring the life out of me. I'm going to go to a party in town and get drunk."

"Why on Earth would you do something like that? You've probably been studying too long. Take a break, and you'll feel better."

"No. I'm going to town. And don't try to stop me, either!"

He grabbed his car keys and dashed out the door. When he got to town, he decided to go to a bar first. Sitting down at the counter, he found his desire to drink was not as strong as he had thought. "Stop being a sissy," he rebuked his conscience. "You're going to drink, and you're going to enjoy it." He ordered a drink, but when it was placed in front of him, he could not bring himself to even sip it. Confused, he left, thinking, "Maybe a party will liven up my spirits." He looked for the rowdiest party he could find and tried to join. Yet, again, he could not bring himself to do any things he had planned on doing. Disgusted with his failed attempt at a worldly night, he drove back to the college.

He dragged himself into his dorm room in the wee hours of the morning. As his eyes adjusted to the dark, he saw his roommate on the floor, kneeling by his bed. Confused, he asked what he was doing.

"After you left, I began to pray for you. I only stopped just now when you walked in the door."

It's the same with us and God. He prays for us when we are talking to Him, and when He's the farthest thing from our minds. What an encouragement to know that, since the beginning, the greatest Intercessor of all time has never ceased to pray for us, that our "faith fail not."

~ Carmen Hartwell

Determination

He remembered the lessons of his childhood, and his soul thrilled with the resolve to prove himself true—ever to act as became a subject of the King of heaven. - Education, pg. 52

If you have determination, you can do almost anything. But this requires a goal in life, a specific point which you are striving to reach. In order for Joseph to prove himself before God and man, in order for him to become a worthy subject of the King of heaven, he had to have determination. He could have turned aside from God, but because he was determined to be true to God, God blessed him, and he prospered.

Ludwig van Beethoven is honored as a musical genius. His accomplishments are even more amazing when we consider the difficulty he had to conquer in order to attain greatness. In his twenties, Beethoven began to lose his hearing. Hearing problems troubled him into the middle years of his life, but he kept it a guarded secret. By the time he reached his fifties, Beethoven was entirely deaf. But he refused to give up. He was once overheard shouting at the top of his voice, "I will take life by the throat!" Many of his biographers believe the only reason Beethoven remained productive for so long was this determination.

Beethoven had a goal in his life, and he was so determined to accomplish his goal that nothing could get in his way. Joseph also determined in his heart not to sin against God, and he was able to accomplish his goal because he experienced a day to day walk with God. When we truly strive for something, God is more than willing to help us achieve our goal as long as it is in line with His will for our lives.

~ Bristi Waid

107

He's Still Working on Me

...He which hath begun a good work in you will perform it until the day of Jesus Christ... - Philippians 1:6 KJV

Are you ever tempted to be discouraged, to think God has given up on you? First of all, you can be sure that only the devil suggests this kind of discouragement. Second, if you feel remorse for the past, it is Jesus pleading with you to surrender to Him. The Spirit does not labor with those who choose not to change anymore. If you know something in your life needs to change, God is waiting to help you. All you need to do is "believe that He is, and that He is a rewarder of them that diligently seek Him" (Hebrews 11:6 KJV). Then go ahead and search for Him.

Likely, if you're reading this devotional, you are seeking God. However, we are all disheartened sometimes by our frequent failures. I think Proverbs 24:16 gives everyone hope to press on: "For a just man falleth seven times, and riseth up again..." (KJV). We know the wicked fall; but the Bible says the righteous man falls, too! In fact, it says that he falls *seven times*—total failure! We may fall as low as is possible, but if we choose to get up, we are counted righteous. When I remember the following stanzas, they give me courage, and I believe they will do the same for you.

There really ought to be a sign upon my heart:
"Don't judge me yet there's an unfinished part."
But I'll be perfect just according to His plan,
Fashioned by the Master's loving hand.

He's still working on me,
To make me what I ought to be.
It took Him just a week to make the moon and stars,
The sun and the earth and Jupiter and Mars.
How loving and patient He must be;
He's still working on me.
- Joel Hemphill

He's still patiently smoothing the rough edges of my character. And He will finish the good work He's begun in you, too!

~ Kevin Corrigan

Champions

In the bitter life of a stranger and a slave, amidst the sights and sounds of vice and the allurements of heathen worship, a worship surrounded with all the attractions of wealth and culture and the pomp of royalty, Joseph was steadfast. He had learned the lesson of obedience to duty. Faithfulness in every station, from the most lowly to the most exalted, trained every power for highest service. - Education, pp. 52, 53

My dog, Lucy, is literally a champion. My mom shows her at American Kennel Club dog shows, and she has earned her championship. But, it takes a lot of work and focus for Lucy to perform well at the dog shows and display her best qualities before the judges. At dog shows, there are lots of distractions. People are all around, and Lucy loves people. The judges also get into the dogs' personal space to examine their mouths and their build. Another diversion is the various refreshments at dog shows. And there are even the other dog trainers' treats that they use to get their dogs to pose. But, my mom uses a squeaker toy or treats of her own to lure Lucy and get her to pay full attention. Also, she has practiced with Lucy to get her to perform well. Even amidst all the distractions of the dog shows, Lucy has been taught to pay attention to my mom through it all, and she therefore gets high points at each show. Consequently, she is now a champion.

God tells us that the world is going to be distracting. In His warning to Cain, He said, "If you do well, will you not be accepted? And if you do not do well, sin is crouching at the door. Its desire is for you, but you must rule over it" (Genesis 4:7 ESV). And the Bible also promises that "God is faithful, and He will not let you be tempted beyond your ability, but with the temptation He will also provide the way of escape, that you may be able to endure it" (1 Corinthians 10:13 ESV). Potiphar's wife tempted Joseph to break God's law in committing adultery with her. But Joseph replied, "My master has not 'kept back any thing from me but thee, because thou art his wife: how then can I do this great wickedness, and sin against God?'" (Genesis 39:9 KJV). Just like Lucy and Joseph, we also need to overcome the allurements and distractions along our walk with Christ. By keeping our eyes focused on Him, we too may become champions.

~ Victoria West

Hold on Tight

Loyalty to God, faith in the Unseen, was Joseph's anchor. - Education, pg. 54

Joseph had many different experiences in his life. In his father's house, he was a favored child; in the house of Potiphar, he was a slave and then a right-hand-man and companion. He was a man of knowledge, having an education from study, observation, and contact with men. Joseph was also in Pharaoh's prison for quite some time. The head jailer was so impressed with Joseph that he put him in charge of all the other prisoners. In the end, Joseph was called to help in an national crisis, which turned into an opportunity for him to be chosen as a leader of Egypt and a preserver of life.

Amidst the ups and downs of life, what do you think enabled Joseph to preserve his integrity? What do you think helped him succeed in everything he did? Faith—that is the answer. Even throughout the hard times, Joseph maintained a close and intimate relationship with Christ. He made it his priority to know Christ better each day, and by doing so, he was able to change a nation.

James 1:6 encourages us to "ask in faith, with no doubting, for the one who doubts is like a wave of the sea that is driven and tossed by the wind" (ESV). Joseph made God his anchor. He asked in faith, and the Lord answered. Joseph's love and passion for God made life bearable when the times seemed impossible.

I know that my life can get hectic and stressful; but I am also learning that holding on to God during those times makes the trails I face more manageable. I love how God wants to help us through those times and wants us to come closer to Him through each experience.

I want to encourage you today to make God your anchor. Hold on tight to Him through good times and bad, and He will keep you in His arms. Let your loyalty to God and faith in the unseen One be your anchor in the voyage of life.

~ Jessica Hall

The Voice of a Father

Loyalty to God, faith in the Unseen... - Education, pg. 54

Sarah was your typical five-year-old girl who loved her mommy and daddy very much and tried to make them happy any way she could. But, little Sarah had never seen her mom or dad because she was born blind.

One night, Sarah sat peacefully on her bedroom floor, quietly humming a playful tune as she combed her doll's hair. Her mom and older sister were downstairs fixing supper, and her dad was picking up some groceries on his way home from work. Suddenly, Sarah began to smell smoke coming from under her closed door. As she began calling for her mom, she heard the sirens of firetrucks racing down the road toward her house. She heard the firemen outside yelling instructions to each other, so she ran to the window to call for help. By this time, flames were creeping under her door, and her room felt hot. Several firemen below saw Sarah in the window and called for her to jump into the net they were holding; the house was about to collapse, and they were unable to enter. Since she didn't know the men below, she couldn't muster enough trust to jump from the window, which was two stories above the net. But then, above the noise of the yelling firemen and the sound of the fire and crashing timbers within the house, she heard a familiar voice that she trusted, that of her daddy calling her name. Realizing the situation, he immediately ran to the net and yelled, "Sarah, jump! The men will catch you!" She knew she could trust her daddy, so without a moment of hesitation, she jumped from the window, landed safely in the net, and was comforted by the embrace of her daddy's arms.

It is tough to trust people you don't know, but when you have a close relationship with them, you know that their word is one you can accept with confidence. When we spend time with God in Bible study and prayer, we will know His voice, and our confidence in Him will grow strong. We will be ready to follow every command because we recognize His still, small voice. Choose today to listen attentively to the voice of our Father in heaven, the voice that brings peace in the midst of the flames.

~ Megan Metcalf

From Surviving to Thriving

Loyalty to God, faith in the Unseen, was Joseph's anchor. In this lay the hiding of his power. - Education, pg. 54

"God, I don't want to do this! I just want to cry!" I prayed. I was sitting in my room attempting to finish my math homework in the few remaining minutes of study hall. But, as I read the problem, I didn't understand how to solve it! I felt God reminding me to trust Him with my problems and give it over to Him, but I was tired. It was the end of the day, and throwing a pity-party for myself sounded much more appealing to me than giving the difficulty to my heavenly Father. For a few seconds, a silent battle raged in my mind as to who I would choose to follow, myself or Christ. I finally decided that I would surrender my will to God and have faith that He would help me. I definitely didn't feel like it, but I knew I wanted to do what was right. I went back to my math problems and suddenly solutions began to form in my mind! God had answered my prayer!

Joseph faced many daunting obstacles in his life. He was sold as a slave by his own brothers and was bought by the Egyptian captain of the guard. After working his way up the ladder of success in his master's house, he was falsely accused of a crime and thrown into prison. I wouldn't blame him if he had decided to sit down and cry. But he made the choice to trust in his father's God. He purposed to do what was right, whether he felt like it or not, and God caused him to not only survive those experiences, but to thrive through them. "But the Lord was with Joseph, and shewed him mercy, and gave him favour in the sight of the keeper of the prison...The keeper of the prison looked not to any thing that was under his hand; because the Lord was with him, and that which he did, the Lord made it to prosper" (Genesis 39:21, 23 KJV).

Faith is a daily choice you and I have to make, a choice to follow Christ whether we feel like it or not. It is the choice to surrender our wills to Him day by day, trusting that He will work in our lives. It is this choice that enables us to have a powerful Christian experience, to not only survive, but thrive.

~ Anneliese Wahlman

I Dare You

Daniel and his companions had been faithfully instructed in the principles of the word of God. They had learned to sacrifice the earthly to the spiritual, to seek the highest good. And they reaped the reward. - Education, pg. 55

> Standing by a purpose true,
> Heeding God's command,
> Honor them, the faithful few!
> All hail to Daniel's band!
> Dare to be a Daniel,
> Dare to stand alone!
> Dare to have a purpose firm!
> Dare to make it known.

How did Daniel live in such a way that his life was worth emulating? Daniel was a man of purpose, principle, prayer, and purity. Daniel purposed in his heart to uphold the law of God. He chose not to eat the king's food, but instead to eat what was pleasing to God. He determined not to compromise concerning what God had revealed to him. Prayer was also a vital part of Daniel's life. He kept communion with God open, making it a point to pray three times a day to demonstrate his reliance upon God. By praying continually, his life was blessed, and he was able to bless others with God's love because he truly had God in his heart. Daniel was very pure in his thinking. He thought about God, and his desire was to please Him. Daniel was faultless when it came to his business dealings, and by being pure in his actions, he was given abundant responsibilities.

I know that it can be easy to conform to the ways and standards of this world. But there are men, even today, who can prove that sticking to God's ways and standards and daring to be a Daniel will lead to success.

Listening to God and following His will may be hard, and you certainly will be held to a higher standard. But I know that if you trust in God and get to know Him better, He will show you what to do. Ask God to help you be a person of purpose, principle, prayer, and purity like Daniel. I dare you!

~ Jessica Hall

Unwavering

Unwavering in allegiance to God, unyielding in the mastery of himself, Daniel's noble dignity and courteous deference won for him in his youth the "favor and tender love" of the heathen officer in whose charge he was. - Education, pp. 55, 56

In a world where values are constantly being compromised, it sometimes feels almost impossible to stay true to Christ. Distractions seem to flood in on me from every direction: media, music, styles, friends, and even school can pull my attention away from Jesus and lead me down the wrong path. How can I stay focused when all around me there are things grappling for my attention? Let's look at the life of Daniel.

Daniel and his friends were taken captive when they were only teens. But early on, they decided to stay loyal to their God. When they arrived at Babylon, they were singled out for the king's special service. In the king's court, they were surrounded by every pleasure imaginable; they were even offered food from the king's own table. Despite the fact that they could have been killed for rejecting the king's gift, they refused to eat the food or defile themselves by drinking wine. Through their loyalty to God, they were blessed immensely, and the kingdom of Babylon prospered under their influence.

How did Daniel and his three friends stay true to God in the midst of all the heathen distractions of the palace? "They placed themselves in connection with the Source of all wisdom..." (*Prophets and Kings*, pg. 486). The only way to withstand the temptations and distractions of this world is to have a relationship with Christ. We cannot hold onto anything that is coming between our Savior and us. Anytime temptations come our way, we can follow the example of the four Hebrews: "In faith they prayed for wisdom, and they lived their prayers" (Ibid.). If we do this, we too can be those "...who will stand for the right though the heavens fall" (*Education*, pg. 57).

~ Wesley Mayes

Trust

…Daniel clung to God with unwavering trust… - Education, pg. 56

Has someone ever failed you? Have people ever broken promises they made or spilled out secrets you asked them not to reveal? Have you ever loved someone, and then had that person turn around and do something that broke your heart? I can think of a handful of times when I have felt hurt in these ways. Often when my trust has been betrayed, I automatically erect a barrier between myself and the people who have hurt me. I don't want to talk to them, be near them, and sometimes I have wished that they were on a completely different planet! I don't trust them anymore, and it takes time to build up a friendship with them again.

In every earthly relationship, there will always be someone who will disappoint or fail you. That's when we are especially blessed to have God in our lives! He is there for us no matter what, no questions asked. Sometimes, I don't really know what He's up to in my life; I don't even know if Jesus is there, and I wonder if I even want Him in my life. But, both you and I need to know that we can trust Him. Even when everything seems to be going wrong, we can trust Him. We need to cling to God! He is the only One who will never move. He will never spill your secrets or break your heart. We can cling to Him when no one else is there for us. When you feel like your world is coming to an end, when you need sympathy or comfort, when you have something exciting to tell and no one will listen, God will be there for you! All we have to do is ask. But you wonder, "Can I trust you, God?" With love, He gently replies, "Trust Me, My child. I will be here. I will be here for you!"

Trust Him when dark doubts assail thee,
Trust Him when thy strength is small,
Trust Him when to simply trust Him
Seems the hardest thing of all.
Trust Him, He is ever faithful,
Trust Him, for His will is best,
Trust Him, for the heart of Jesus
Is the only place of rest.
- Unknown

~ Yannika Stafford

But I Can See You

...Even his enemies were forced to the confession that "they could find none occasion nor fault; forasmuch as he was faithful." While Daniel clung to God with unwavering trust, the spirit of prophetic power came upon him. - Education, pg. 56

"Now faith is the substance of things hoped for, the evidence of things not seen" (Hebrews 11:1 KJV).

During the dreadful days of the Blitz, a British father and son were evacuating a building that had been targeted and pummeled by a German V-2 rocket. Dodging the falling debris, the father kicked down a burning door and ran outside. Finally, escaping the suffocating smoke and scorching fire, the father and son made their way to a large shell hole in the front yard of the building. Desperate for air, the father jumped into the hole, and after regaining his composure, he held up his arms and hollered to his son, "Jump!"

Blinded by the smoke, the boy cried back, "I can't see you!"

The father, scanning the sky, which was tinted black and red by the burning surroundings, yelled to the silhouette of his frightened son, "But I can see you, so jump!" At last, the boy leaped down into the dark smoldering hole, trusting his father's voice. The father caught him and the two took refuge from the chaos.

Just like the father who protected his child in the midst of havoc, Jesus will protect you in the midst of your miseries. But, you must put all your faith and trust in His unfailing love in order to perceive His magnificent works. Faith in Him enables you to face life cheerfully or meet death valiantly. Faith in Him assures you that even if you don't know all the answers, He does. Faith in Him gives you the surety that you are always seen, even when you can't see Him.

~ Cyrus Guccione

True Men

The greatest want of the world is the want of men—men who will not be bought or sold, men who in their inmost souls are true and honest, men who do not fear to call sin by its right name, men whose conscience is as true to duty as the needle to the pole, men who will stand for the right though the heavens fall. - Education, pg. 57

When I was younger, I mowed my neighbors' lawns for cash. I would keep at the job until it was finished because I wanted the reward. However, I didn't do the best job. I wasn't true to my duty. I would leave patches of uncut grass here and there because I was more focused on getting money fast than on doing a good job. This caused me to lose jobs, and it wasn't until I became more mature that I realized the problem was the poor quality of my work.

As a kid, I also had a bad habit of skipping my chores to go and hang out with my friends. When my mom would find out, she would say, "You are who you are in the dark, when no one is watching." Then, after pausing as if to contemplate what she had just said, she would announce, "You are going to have to wash the car, sweep the driveway, and mow the lawn tomorrow, in addition to your other chores."

I would usually pout and whine, "But, Mom, I was only playing a game, and I would have done my chores, but Sammy was going skateboarding and asked me to come and..." I would always end up doing the extra chores the next day.

I think I've grown up a bit since then. I've learned my lesson of integrity. But because I didn't have a close walk with Christ when He first tried to teach me this lesson, I wasn't able to see Him using my experiences as building blocks for my character. My discoveries have led me to make a clearer connection between being an honest, faithful, and successful young man and my walk with Christ. If I want to be honest, true to my duties, and successful in life, I need to have a real connection with God.

~ Daniel Glassford

Unconditional Commitment

The greatest want of the world is the want of men...men whose conscience is as true to duty as the needle to the pole, men who will stand for the right though the heavens fall. - Education, pg. 57

Soon after David Livingstone had begun his work as a missionary to the people of Africa, a missionary society, eager to send men to help, wrote, "Have you found a good road to where you are? If so, we would like to know how to send more men to join you." The dauntless doctor, having hacked his way through the dense jungles of Africa, replied, "If these men of yours will only come if they know there is a good road, I don't want them. *I only want men who will come if there is no road.*"

The world is hungering for men and women who will stick to God's calling no matter what diversions cross their paths. Quite often, God asks me to do things that are out of my comfort zone or that may be embarrassing in front of others. Even though it may be easier to reason these responsibilities away, I want to be committed to make every effort to fulfill God's will. I'll admit, many times I get scared or nervous about doing the things God impresses me to do, such as speaking up front or even talking to someone I don't know. But these experiences strengthen my confidence and trust in God because I am forced to exercise my faith in Him.

What are you willing to do for God? You may not be called to hack your way through an African jungle, but God promises to use your willing heart to achieve extraordinary things. You have only one life to live; what will you do with it?

~ Megan Metcalf

Give Him Your World

A noble character is the result of self-discipline, of the subjection of the lower to the higher nature—the surrender of self for the service of love to God and man. - Education, pg. 57

A man named Bruce Larson worked in New York City counseling people who had to make difficult decisions. Often he would take his clients down to Fifth Avenue and show them a gigantic statue of Atlas. This beautifully proportioned man stood with all his muscles straining to balance the world upon his shoulders. Atlas was supposedly the most powerfully built man in the world, and he could barely stand up under the burden. "Now, that's one way to live," Bruce would point out to his companion, "trying to carry the whole world on your shoulders. But now, come across the street with me." On the other side of Fifth Avenue was Saint Patrick's Cathedral, and inside was a little shrine of the boy Jesus, perhaps eight or nine years old, effortlessly holding the world in one hand. Bruce's point was illustrated clearly. "We have a choice," he would say. "We can try to carry the world on our own shoulders, or we can say, 'I give up, Lord; here's my life. I give you my whole world.'"

Just like Atlas, most of us try to hold our worlds together by ourselves. We strain under the weight and pain, thinking we can handle it all on our own. But we end up hurting ourselves more than we realize when we try to deal with things in our own strength. When we allow ourselves to see things as they truly are, we realize that there is Someone out there bigger and stronger than we are who wants us to hand over our world of worries, suffering, and pain to Him. There is no reason why we need to carry all that on our hearts and bury it there, hiding it like a dark secret. God cares and is eager and willing to listen. He's willing to take our burden on His strong shoulders and carry us though our trials. We no longer need to worry about whether things are going to work out because we already have the assurance that everything is taken care of. Even when it seems like the whole world is against us, we can surrender that burden to Him and know that all is safe in His arms.

~ Laelle Teranski

119

Sinning by Silence

The greatest want of the world is the want of men...Men who do not fear to call sin by its right name... - Education pg. 57

It is better to remain silent and be thought a fool than to open one's mouth and remove all doubt. - Abraham Lincoln

Sometimes silence speaks louder than words. Paul the Apostle urges you to "...make it your ambition and definitely endeavor to live quietly and peacefully" (I Thessalonians 4:11 Amplified Bible). And as President Lincoln stated, not saying anything in certain situations can be beneficial to us; whereas when we speak up, sometimes we embarrass ourselves. Now, obviously this is not the case all the time. So, let's look at another quote from Abraham Lincoln:

To sin by silence when they should protest makes cowards of men.

What does it mean to sin by silence? When the intensity of our fears overpowers and stills the courage of our convictions, especially in a time of injustice, this is sinning by silence. It is being quiet because you don't want to be looked upon as controversial, discordant, or burdensome. It is failing to speak up against teachers and administrators at school, or elders and spiritual leaders in the church, when they undermine the values that they are expected to uphold. It is when we are willfully ignoring the right standards of life and just settling for indifference or neutrality that we commit the sin of silence. Ellen White makes this topic clear in *Testimonies to the Church, Volume 3*: "Indifference and neutrality in a religious crisis is regarded of God as a grievous crime and equal to the very worst type of hostility against God" (pg. 281).

Silence and protesting both have their proper places. But, let's not get them mixed up, or else we will complicate issues more, and worst of all, we'll hurt our Savior.

~ Cyrus Guccione

Those Who Honor Me

A noble character is the result of self-discipline, of the subjection of the lower to the higher nature—the surrender of self for the service of love to God and man. - Education, pg. 57

One of the greatest stories of self-discipline I have ever heard is the story of Eric Liddell, who made history at the 1924 Paris Olympics when he refused to participate in the 100-meter sprint on Sunday, the day he believed was sacred. The world was shocked, and many thought he was giving up his only chance to win an Olympic event. But even under harsh criticism, Liddell stood up for his convictions and ran in the 400-meter sprint instead because it was scheduled to be run on another day. Just before the race began, a bystander gave him a piece of paper with a quotation from 1 Samuel 2:30, which reads, "Those who honor me I will honor..." (NKJV). He ran with that piece of paper in his hand and not only won the gold medal, but set a new world record of 47.7 seconds.

Liddell's victory was not the result of luck or random chance. It was the result of harsh and demanding training. Even from a young age, Liddell trained rigorously for hours on end. But not only did he train his body, he trained his character to stand firm for his beliefs and convictions, no matter what. He trained himself to seek the highest goals by obeying God's laws and trusting his Heavenly Father wherever He led. Even when his racing days were over, he followed God's calling to become a missionary in China, where he died in service for the people of that land.

Every day we have to make decisions to either stand for what we believe in, or back down and follow the crowd. Henry Ward Beecher once said, "Hold yourself responsible for a higher standard than anybody else expects of you. Never excuse yourself. Never pity yourself. Be a hard master to yourself—and be lenient to everybody else." You are held accountable not only to other people, but to God for the choices you make. When you obey God's laws and receive the training He offers you, He will help you succeed in whatever work you are called to do. Ask Him today to help you stand for the right, no matter what.

~ Wesley Donesky

Not Yours

The youth need to be impressed with the truth that their endowments are not their own. - Education, pg. 57

The talents which your Creator has given to you are to be used, not for selfish purposes, but rather for God's purposes. For you see, these gifts are not your own. They belong to God, and only through Him will their true purposes be fulfilled.

When God created you, He put inside of you talents which would enable you to reach your world. These talents may be used to bring people to Christ, or just simply to praise Him. All that you are, everything inside of you, was designed specifically to glorify the God that made you. And by doing this, the people around you will be drawn to glorify Him also. By serving others with your gifts, you are serving God.

We often compare our talents with those of others. But, when you realize the reason why we are given these talents, there is no comparing to be done. We all fit together like a puzzle. Maybe you're a smaller piece with fewer talents, and you feel unimportant. You aren't; regardless of how you see it, the puzzle won't be complete without you.

Figure out the gifts which God has bestowed upon you. Start using them for Him, and not only will the people around you be blessed, but you will be also.

~ Danielle Schafer

Great or Small

The youth need to be impressed with the truth that their endowments are not their own. Strength, time, intellect, are but lent treasures. They belong to God, and it should be the resolve of every youth to put them to the highest use...Every youth, every child, has a work to do for the honor of God and the uplifting of humanity. - Education, pp. 57, 58

There is a problem that currently afflicts a very large number of Christians. It's the mindset of "I'm not good at many things; so I won't even bother trying to do something for God." This is a false mindset. We are all blessed with something we can do for God. From going to foreign countries and preaching and healing, to staying home and being a prayer warrior for those that do go, the Lord has called us all to do something for Him.

I've known children who are fearless in sharing their faith, while, in contrast, I nearly faint at the thought of simply asking a stranger for directions. We all have our spiritual gifts. There are things my neighbor is really good at that I just don't have the ability to accomplish. But, there are things I can do for God that are equally powerful, if I let Him use me and the gifts He's given me.

Adolphe Monod puts it this way: "Between the great things we cannot do and the small things we will not do, the danger is that we shall do nothing." This is so true for us today. We believe that we only need to do "big things" for God, and that the small tasks should be done by someone else who doesn't mind doing that sort of thing. But, great or small, whatever we do in the name of the Lord, for His honor and glory, He will bless. The outcome will not only be a benefit to us, but a contribution towards the uplifting of humanity. This is our Christian duty.

~ Carmen Hartwell

There Is a Work

Every youth, every child, has a work to do for the honor of God and the uplifting of humanity. - Education, pg. 58

Every year, my school goes on a Christmas music tour to California. The tour of my junior year, we were on the road for thirteen days, with at least one concert almost every day. Partway through the tour, I got sick and lost my voice. I don't think I have ever lost my voice that badly before! I sounded like an adolescent male going through puberty! Obviously enough, I had to skip singing in the choir for six or seven concerts.

One of those concerts sticks out in my mind. While I was sitting in the lobby of the church reading a book and the orchestra was opening with "Joy to the World," I felt God impress me to pray for the concert. So, I put down my book and prayed, asking the Lord to pour out a double portion of His Spirit, that the congregation would not just enjoy the carols, but be truly changed by them. I also asked God to visibly grant my request.

After the concert, I didn't think much about my prayer. But the next day, at a different church, our music director told us what we had earned in sales at the concert the night before. From the sale of our CDs and DVDs, we had earned double what we had in any other concert on the entire tour! I felt that this was God's way of showing me that He had granted my request.

There is a work, a talent, that God has given to each one of us. He wants us to use those talents to their fullest potential and glorify Him. Many times though, we compare the gifts we possess with those of our friends or family and become discouraged. Maybe they play an instrument better than we do or have a lovelier voice. But God created each of us with special gifts. He wants us to use and develop those gifts to the fullest and not spend our time wishing we were something or somebody else. During that tour, I couldn't sing, but I could pray, and God blessed my efforts. There is always a work for you to do.

~ Anneliese Wahlman

Small Gems

Children are attracted by a cheerful, sunny demeanor. Show them kindness and courtesy, and they will manifest the same spirit toward you and toward one another. - Education, pg. 240

Guess what today is? Children's Day in South Korea! Children's Day is like Christmas, a time for gifts and fun. On this day, parents spend special time with their children. Since I was born and raised in the United States, my family would celebrate Mother's Day and Father's Day. I felt left out and asked my parents, "We have special days for mothers and fathers, so how come there isn't a day for kids?" Then I found out about Children's Day!

Children are the future, and the little things that we do impress them so much! Bang Jeong-Hwan, the person who helped start Children's Day, wrote an "Open Letter to Adults." One translation of that letter states: "Children are the future of our nation. Let's show respect for children. Children who grow up with ridicule and contempt from others will become people who disrespect others, while children who grow up with respect from others will become people who respect others in turn."

I gained a fuller realization of how much little kids look up to adults and teenagers from one of my friends. She is much younger than I am, but despite her age, she is quite mature. When I first met her, I naturally felt a bond because her name is Sarah too! I simply spent time with her and treated her like a good friend. Later, her mom called and told me that Sarah could not stop talking about me and that she wanted to be "exactly just like me." I never realized the impact that I had on her.

Children need love and attention. If you take time to play with them and read them stories, they will grow and flourish. Instill in them a love for their Creator and share with them gems of His wisdom. They will thank you and always remember you in their hearts!

~ Sarah Chang

No Profit

I made me great works; I builded me houses...I gathered me also silver and gold...Then I looked on all the works that my hands had wrought...and, behold, all was vanity and vexation of spirit, and there was no profit under the sun. - Ecclesiastes 2:4, 8, 11 KJV

An older friend of mine came and preached here at Fountainview a couple of weeks ago. He shared with us a very powerful personal testimony. From a young age, he earned a lot of money by working in the masonry business. He soon bought out his own partner, and, by the age of 18, he was making so much money that buying a brand-new $50,000 truck was a small thing. His business grew and grew, and soon he had crews who were older and much more experienced working on his sites all over the province of British Columbia.

In spite of his success, my friend was not happy. He said that he felt empty inside, that all his money-making and hard work did not give him a lasting sense of satisfaction. Excitement over his material possessions was fleeting. His work prevented him from spending as much time as he should have with his wife and kids. And he was losing his relationship with God. At the highest point in his outward life, he held a pistol in his hands and contemplated ending the continuous cycle of work, gain, and emptiness.

It was then that he realized deep down that he needed God to fill the emptiness inside, and, holding his hand out to God, he pleaded that God would make Himself and the Bible real to him. He came to the decision to give his business over to God and to use it to glorify Him. His business is still thriving, but since then God has given him so many opportunities to witness and change others' lives through his interactions at work. My friend has discovered what God's economy is like: worldly success and material gain is nothing, for in them there is no profit in the scope of eternity; but in living and doing all things for the glory of God, you will find true happiness. Only God can fill the emptiness in your soul. Won't you let Him?

~ Valerie Jacobson

Be That Light

Every youth, every child, has a work to do for the honor of God and the uplifting of humanity. - Education, pg. 58

When my mother, Sharon, was young, she attended a pool party held by a classmate. Everyone was enjoying himself in the refreshing water when suddenly, Sharon felt an excruciating pain grip her calf. Her muscle had cramped while swimming in the deep end of the pool, and she was unable to swim anymore. She began crying, "Help, help!" But those swimming around her thought that, because she was a good swimmer, she was only teasing. She began sinking, screaming for help as she bobbed up and down, but her friends were too busy having fun to realize her desperate need. During her final plea, her friend Carlos, while he stood at the far end of the pool, noticed her and dove in to pull her to safety. Although she was grateful for his help, she was also disappointed that so many close by had not come to her aid.

Many times we, like the friends in the pool, fail to notice the needs and cries of those around us. Quite unlike most of us, Jesus endlessly looked about Him, with eyes keen to discern a sinner in need of God's grace. Whether the sinner's cries were silent or audible, He went to great lengths to rescue them all. We too can do the same by being sensitive to the words, actions, and gestures people use to convey when their souls are in deep despair and silently searching for Christ. Go out of your way to encourage them or perform a deed to brighten their day. As Matthew 5:14 says, "Ye are the light of the world" (KJV). Be that light which imparts life to a careworn world.

~ Megan Metcalf

A Mother

The child's first teacher is the mother. - Education, pg. 275

A mother is a friend
Who's there at every end.
She helps to see the way around
So in her home, joy can abound.

She may not be biological,
But so often she is logical,
There to teach from infancy
All life's lessons with brilliancy.

From childhood to marriage,
She'll love without disparage
Thru the thick and thru the thin
Each time, she'll help you win!

Thank You, God, for my Mother.
She's better than any other.
For each child that is Yours
You give a mom that scores!

On this Mother's Day, thank God for your mom or the mother figure in your life. God has blessed you with the right one to be there for you. Right now, I want to encourage you to read Proverbs 31 and go through that chapter picking out some particular character traits that your mother has.

God has made your mom in a very special way, and today is a wonderful day to celebrate that blessing! "Many women do noble things, but you surpass them all" (Proverbs 31:29 NIV).

~ Jessica Hall

Predestination?

Every youth, every child, has a work to do for the honor of God and the uplifting of humanity. - Education, pg. 58

Do you ever feel like you don't have a purpose in life? As though you're just some random, living mass created to take up space? Your answer should be "No!" Why? Because God has placed you here and now with a specific purpose in mind. You have a job to do that only you can accomplish. Situations and people have been placed in your path to help you grow closer to Christ and to develop His character in you. In this way, you may be better equipped to do the work He has designed you for.

Are you going through a hard time and not understanding the reasons for it? That's okay because God has everything under control, and maybe this trial is exactly what you need right now to show you God's plan for the future. His plan incorporates more than immediate solutions. It also gives us a map to navigate through future obstacles. These trials now seem insurmountable, but your work in handling them is going to help you in the long run by developing your character. Working through these trials will aid you in fulfilling your purpose of glorifying God and helping others.

Recently, I've been facing a difficult situation, and I haven't understood everything. But I've seen God working through it all, and have found my trust in Him growing stronger. I've also been able to talk to others about how my faith has been strengthened and direct them back to God in their difficulties. Through His work in my life, God has been blessing those around me, and He can do that for you, too.

God sends different circumstances to fit us for our lifework. But that doesn't mean that He predestines our futures. You and I choose if we will do the work we are called to do, if we'll proclaim our testimony, and if we'll make the right choices.

~ Jo Holdal

Use Your Talents

By faithfulness in little things, he was prepared for weightier trusts.
- Education, pg. 58

Once upon a time, there was a master who was preparing for a long journey. Before he left, he called his three servants and entrusted different amounts of money to each of them: five talents to Faithful Fellow, two talents to Constant Conscientious, and one talent to Recreant Renegade. Right away, Faithful went out and doubled his money through hard work and investment. Then Constant did the same thing with his two talents. But Recreant dug a hole and buried his master's money, afraid to spoil the one talent he had received.

After his trip, the master came home to settle accounts with his servants. A very excited Faithful ran up to his master and showed him his doubled money. "Well done, Faithful, my servant," smiled the master. "You have been faithful in small things; now I will put you in charge of many things. Come and share in my joy!" Next, an enthusiastic Constant gleefully strode up to his master and showed that he also had doubled his amount. He too received his master's hearty praise.

It was time for Recreant to speak with the master. "I know that your standards are very high. I didn't want to disappoint you. You know how I am when it comes to taking care of things: I always mess up. So I buried the money. Here it is."

The master was furious! "That's a horrible way to live! Why were you so cowardly? The least you could have done was invest it in the bank. I would have at least gained some interest. Give your one talent to Faithful. I know that he will deal wisely with it!" Then the master ordered that Recreant be thrown outside into utter darkness.

God gives every one of us unique abilities. Some of us can play instruments well; others can sing. Some are very technical, and others are good at art. I know that I want to use my talents more wisely; don't you? God has given me talents for a reason: He wants me to be led to use my talents to bring people to Him. Join me in furthering God's work by using the talents He has given us.

~ Jessica Hall

Toiling Labor

...In the humble round of daily toil he [Elisha] gained strength of purpose and nobleness of character, growing in divine grace and knowledge. While co-operating with his father in the home duties, he was learning to co-operate with God. - Education, pg. 58

I once knew a lady who lived in such poverty that she barely had enough food in her house to feed her family. She worked every day in the hot sun, her back aching from bending over for hours, harvesting rice with her bare hands. With two small children to feed and an abusive husband, life was not a happy fairytale. Yet, she kept her sanity through her daily communion with God, which began in the early morning.

Each day, she made time to tell her son Bible stories, and she always encouraged him to make something out of his life by dedicating it to God. Because she could not afford to give her son a good education, when he was old enough to go to school, she sent him to an orphanage. At the orphanage, he was able to attend school. From a young age, he determined in his heart that he was going to make his mother proud of him, because she had sacrificed everything for him. As the years passed, he became a diligent student of science and worked his way through Spicer College in India. All through his life, he held onto the image of his humble, hard-working mother and her devotion to God. Because of her daily toil and nobility of character, he is now a pastor. He is such a blessing to the villagers he serves and now takes care of his aging mother.

Daily toil can wear you down; but if you have Christ in your life, you can get through any circumstance. Since sin entered this world, life has become difficult and unfair, but Jesus has declared, "Come unto me, all ye that labour and are heavy laden, and I will give you rest. Take my yoke upon you, and learn of me; for I am meek and lowly in heart: and ye shall find rest unto your souls. For my yoke is easy, and my burden is light" (Matthew 11:28-30 KJV).

~ Bristi Waid

Real Sacrifice

Elijah, the man of power, had been God's instrument for the overthrow of gigantic evils. - Education, pg.60

When I look at all the stories of great people in the Bible, I am amazed at the ways in which God worked through their lives. Each story inspires me, yet sometimes a little voice in the back of my mind says, "This just isn't fair! Why did all those electrifying experiences happen just to those people. What about me?" I become confused and almost begin to believe that the God we worship today is not the same God whom Moses and Joshua worshiped.

But the more I've studied, the more I've come to realize that the change isn't in God at all; rather, it's in me. The only difference between those great Bible characters and me is that they allowed God to use them. All of them handed their lives over to God in faith and let Him take care of everything. Notice that the quote says Elijah was "God's instrument." He was no super-human. He simply let God rule His life instead of trying to rule it himself.

Giving our selfish lives over to God's control may seem like the hardest thing we will ever do, but it is really the greatest thing. David Livingstone, a missionary to Africa, once said, "People talk of the sacrifice I have made in spending so much of my life in Africa...I never made a sacrifice. We ought not to talk of 'sacrifice' when we remember the great sacrifice which He made who left His Father's throne on high to give Himself for us."

If you want to see God do wonders in your life, first give Him your life. It will seem like a huge sacrifice, until we compare it with what He has done for us. He'll take our lives and make something beautiful out of them, something that on our own we could never achieve.

~ Danielle Schafer

Be Faithful

None can know what may be God's purpose in His discipline; but all may be certain that faithfulness in little things is the evidence of fitness for greater responsibilities. Every act of life is a revelation of character, and he only who in small duties proves himself "a workman that needeth not to be ashamed" will be honored by God with weightier trusts. - Education, pg. 61

I cannot know all of God's purposes. But I do trust that He has a plan and place for me, and if I am faithful in little things, then He can trust me with bigger things.

At school, we have a work/study program in which each student is assigned to a workplace for three and a half hours a day. When I first came to Fountainview, I was appointed to work as a janitor. That was the last place I wanted to work! But, as the months went by, I started to enjoy keeping the school clean. I had a place where I could do something and see the results of my labor. Now, I don't look down on lowly work; rather I take the opportunity to learn new things and make people happy. I have learned that you can change your attitude and mood just by the thoughts you think. If I think about how tired I am and how I just can't wait for the day to finish, then I do become tired, and it takes me longer to do everything. But, if I think about how glad I am to be alive and how good God is, then my spirit is lifted, and I am no longer tired. Even though it may seem that being a janitor is a lowly, unimportant job, it isn't. In some ways, it's just as important as any other job. Just think, if there was no janitor, the school would be a mess! Everything would be very dirty, and no one would enjoy being in the school. But since there is janitor, everything is nice and clean. It may not be perfect, but it's still clean. And I know that, by being faithful in the smaller things (like being a good janitor), I am preparing for the greater work God has for me.

Even if you think you have the most degrading job, or if you think that you have the lowest position in your workplace, remember to always be faithful, because God is preparing you for greater responsibility. Even if we don't receive that greater responsibility until heaven, we can know that God has prepared us well, and that we have followed His plan.

~ Laelle Teranski

133

He Took My Place

For God so loved the world that He gave His one and only Son, that whoever believes in Him shall not perish but have eternal life. - John 3:16 NIV

As my mom looked me in the eyes, I dreaded the punishment I was about to receive. It hurt me to know that I had disappointed my mom. She realized that in order to stop my bad habits, she was going to have to come up with something that hurt a little more than the average spanking. The method she chose was one I've only known her to use once: she wanted me to administer the spanking to her. When I heard this, aching pangs stung my heart; I didn't want to hurt her. Besides, why should she suffer when she warned me so many times, and I still continued my naughty behavior? As she gave me the paddle, I began to cry, "Mama, I can't do it—I can't! I deserve it, not you. Just spank me, please!" My throat tied in a thousand painful knots as I made my plea.

I suppose Mary had similar feelings, but much worse, as she beheld Jesus hanging on the cross. He was physically nailed to a tree, fastened by iron spikes pounded through His hands and feet. Mentally, he was nailed to hell with her sin and the sins of the entire world upon His shoulders. Jesus stayed on that cross as the whole universe watched to see what He would do. They knew He could save Himself if He chose; but instead, He hung there, encompassed by grief and anguish. With every arduous breath, the load became heavier and heavier. Not because Christ's physical state became more agonizing, but because He was bearing the burden of every wrong thought, every cutting remark, every debilitating disease. He felt the pain of the murderer and the murdered, the rapist and the raped, the abortionist and the aborted. When Jesus was hanging on the tree, He took the place of the villain and the victim. He did this for you, a sinner, so that you could inherit eternal life. Didn't He do enough?

~ Sarah-Kate Lingerfelt

The Little Things

None can know what may be God's purpose in His discipline; but all may be certain that faithfulness in little things is the evidence of fitness for greater responsibilities. - Education, pg. 61

Sometimes, I feel that it is hard to see where God is leading in my life. What can I do when I don't know where to turn next? When I feel like this, I find encouragement in David's life. His early years as a humble shepherd boy are a good example to me of faithful commitment to duty.

David was the youngest in his family, and therefore, was given the job nobody else wanted...herding sheep. But even though David had the least desirable job, he did his very best. He even fought off a lion and a bear to protect his flock. He faithfully provided watch-care and loving-kindness to his flock of sheep and praised God through songs that he composed himself. As he worked at his lonely job, God recognized his steadfastness to duty, and when it was time to choose a new king for Israel, David was anointed.

Matthew 25:21 reads: "...Well done, thou good and faithful servant: thou hast been faithful over a few things, I will make thee ruler over many things..." (KJV). As a shepherd boy, no one would have suspected that David would be chosen as king. But God didn't look at his earthly occupation; He looked at his heart.

No matter how I am viewed in the eyes of those around me, God can use me. His plan for my life is infinitely greater than anything I could ever dream of. Even if I have no idea what I am going to do in the future, if I trust in Him, follow His leading, and continue to be faithful in the tasks He sets before me, I know that I can be confident in what He has in store for me.

~ Wesley Mayes

Insignificant

...But all may be certain that faithfulness in little things is the evidence of fitness for greater responsibilities. - Education, pg. 61

Have you ever found yourself dismissing the "little things"? I'm talking about things so seemingly insignificant that you can easily find excuses for evading them without feeling guilty.

It was a sunny Friday morning, and I really wanted to go biking with my best friend. There was only one little drawback: I was home alone, and mom and dad expected me to clean the house. Quickly, rushing through the motions, but not really putting my heart into it, I finished cleaning in no time and was able to go biking. Upon arriving home, however, I found a rather displeased set of parents. In my hurry to get done with the housework, I had simply swept all the dirt under a rug and thought that since it was such a little thing, it wouldn't make much difference. Was I ever wrong!

It wasn't just the fact that I had done a terrible job that was bad; it was also that I had let a harmful habit begin. How could I ever dream of owning a nice home of my own if I couldn't even keep my parents' home clean? This doesn't just apply to home situations; it applies to the workplace and our relationships. The same principle is carried through our entire lives. If you and I can succeed in doing the deeds that are supposedly inconsequential, then we can be assured of success once we get to the "important" tasks.

Do you want to get recognition for your work? Start by doing the humble tasks that seem too lowly and boring to be noticed. You will be noticed, and you'll find that your services are always in high demand.

~ Jo Holdal

136

Unashamed

Every act of life is a revelation of character, and he only who in small duties proves himself "a workman that needeth not to be ashamed" will be honored by God with weightier trusts. - Education, pg. 61

My mom sometimes reads the following poem to the participants of the mission trips she organizes. The poem's authorship is in dispute, but it is often attributed to Dr. Bob Morehead. Regardless of who wrote it, I hope it inspires you as much as it has me.

I am part of the "Fellowship of the Unashamed." The die has been cast. I have stepped over the line. The decision has been made. I am a disciple of Jesus Christ. I won't look back, let up, slow down, back away, or be still. My past is redeemed, my present makes sense, and my future is secure. I am finished and done with low living, sight walking, small planning, smooth knees, colorless dreams, chintzy giving, and dwarfed goals.

I no longer need pre-eminence, prosperity, position, promotions, plaudits, or popularity. I now live by presence, lean by faith, love by patience, lift by prayer, and labor by power. My pace is set, my gait is fast, my goal is Heaven, my road is narrow, my way is rough, my companions few, my Guide reliable, my mission clear. I cannot be bought, compromised, deterred, lured away, turned back, diluted, or delayed.

I will not flinch in the face of sacrifice, hesitate in the presence of adversity, negotiate at the table of the enemy, ponder at the pool of popularity, or meander in the maze of mediocrity.

I am a disciple of Jesus Christ. I must go until Heaven returns, give until I drop, preach until all know, and work until He comes. And when He comes to get His own, He will have no problem recognizing me. My colors will be clear.

Our goal should be to say with Paul, "For I am not ashamed of the gospel of Christ: for it is the power of God unto salvation to every one that believeth..." (Romans 1:16 KJV). Our whole mission in life is to work boldly for Christ. Regardless of your age, career, and personality, your calling is the same: you are to be a member of the "Fellowship of the Unashamed." Is that your goal?

~ Daniel Glassford

137

Be One First

A man that hath friends must show himself friendly... - Proverbs 18:24 KJV

It was 1936, and the Olympic games were in full swing in Berlin. African-American Jesse Owens seemed sure to win the long jump. The previous year, he had jumped 26 feet, 8 1/4 inches—an incredible record that would stand for the next 25 years. However, as he made his way to the long-jump pit, Jesse spotted a tall, blond-haired, blue-eyed German making a few practice jumps. A nervous shiver ran up Jesse's spine. He was sure that Nazi wanted to prove his superiority, especially over a black man. Just then, the tall German sauntered over to Jesse and introduced himself as Luz Long. He smiled and remarked, "You should be able to qualify with your eyes closed," referring to Jesse's outstanding record of the previous year. For the next few minutes the two competitors chatted and got to know each other a little bit. Then Luz made a suggestion. Since the qualifying distance was only 23 feet, 5 1/2 inches, why not make a mark several inches before the takeoff board and jump from there, just to be safe? Jesse tried and qualified easily. In the finals, Jesse set an Olympic record and earned the second of four gold medals. The first person to congratulate him was Luz Long, in full view of Adolf Hitler. Jesse never saw Luz again, but in their brief encounter, the two men formed a friendship that out-valued any gold medal.

Here were two men who were, by common standards, supposed to be enemies. They were on opposite sides of the spectrum. Jesse had every right to be suspicious of the German competitor, and Luz had every opportunity to lord his superiority over Jesse. But, Luz chose to put aside all common preconceptions of what their relationship was supposed to be, and to make a friend rather than an enemy.

Luz Long and Jesse Owens were living out the principle of Proverbs 18:24: "A man that hath friends must show himself friendly" (KJV). In modern terms, the verse is saying that in order to have friends, you need to be one first. Do you feel as though you have no friends? Try reaching out and being a friend to someone else, and you might uncover a friendship of immeasurable worth.

~ Carmen Hartwell

138

Peeling Back the Layers

Not yet was Moses prepared for his lifework. He had yet to learn the lesson of dependence upon divine power. - Education, pg. 62

My home life is something most of the world does not experience. I have parents who love each other and are always there for me. My parents have good jobs that provide for all our needs. We even have enough leisure time to take vacations, go to ballgames, and play golf.

But this year, I decided to leave the comforts of home and go to a boarding academy in British Columbia, Canada. When I told my mom goodbye and watched her drive off, I felt a feeling of confinement. No longer could I jump into the car and take a quick trip to the grocery store, or open the fridge and make myself a meal. Everything was new and strange, and my world felt like it was caving in on me.

Since all the amenities of life seemed to be ripped away from me, I began looking for security in people. Socializing became a god to me, and I began putting my faith in friends. These friends were good people; they made me want to be a better person. But even good people fail, and as my friends failed me, I felt as though I were failing. I hadn't listened to God's message: "Thou shalt have no other gods before Me" (Exodus 20:3 KJV), and my trust in Him was nonexistent. Somehow I knew that in order to find peace in life I needed to trust in the Lord with all my heart and lean not on my own understanding (Proverbs 3:5). However, I was proud and didn't want to acknowledge God. So, He had to take me through a painful, but very rewarding process of peeling away my layers of worldly security blankets.

One afternoon, I sat on my bed and poured my heart out to God. I saw that He had always been there for me, even though I had denied Him so many times and looked for fulfillment in worldly gods. Since that day, it seems like a new layer is pulled off every week, showing me more and more my need for complete dependence upon Christ. And as each layer falls aside, a new beginning starts; I come one step closer to my Savior.

~ Sarah-Kate Lingerfelt

A Better Direction

Apparently cut off forever from his life's mission, he was receiving the discipline essential for its fulfillment. - Education, pg. 62

When you study the story of Moses and his forty years as a shepherd, you will discover that his experience is quite like our own. Before Moses could lead thousands of people through the wilderness, he needed some training. As Israel's leader, he was meant to represent God to the people, and in order to do so, he had to spend a lot of time learning from Him. For this reason, God sent Moses on a journey away from the luxuries of the Egyptian palace, and instead placed him in the countryside as a shepherd.

God knew exactly what he was doing when He put Moses out in the wilderness. Can you imagine what would have happened if Moses hadn't been trained as a shepherd, but instead had gone straight from being a pampered prince to being a mountain man with an immense multitude following him?

Sometimes the situations we are in seem completely pointless, and we are tempted to distrust God's plan for us and wander down our own paths, thinking we know best. But I can assure you that the specific circumstance you are in is training you for the future. We may not understand at the moment why we are in such a situation, but God can see the future, and He knows what will help us in the long run.

Moses went on to become one of history's greatest leaders. And he never would have been able to accomplish this without those forty years of instruction from God. God may ask you to do something which seems completely crazy at the moment, but have faith that He is leading you in a better direction for your life.

~ Danielle Schafer

Ambassadors for Christ

That he [Moses] might become a representative of God, he must learn of Him. - Education, pp. 62, 63

When actors are preparing for a part, they must first learn the characteristics of the person they are enacting. They study their likes and dislikes, accents, ways of walking, facial expressions—everything. In order to properly represent the character, the actor must become intimately acquainted with every aspect of his or her life.

Our relationship with Jesus should be like this. The Apostle Paul put it this way, "Imitate me, just as I also imitate Christ" (1 Corinthians 11:1 NKJV). If we want to show God to the world, we need to spend time with Him and learn what He's all about so that we can become good ambassadors of the faith.

But, how can we get to know Him? First, He reveals to us His character through His written word, the Bible. He tells us, "For I know the thoughts that I think toward you, saith the Lord, thoughts of peace, and not of evil, to give you an expected end" (Jeremiah 29:11 KJV). Here He reveals to us His loving and forgiving nature.

Second, His handiwork, seen in nature, shows us His character. "The sunshine and the rain, that gladden and refresh the earth, the hills and seas and plains, all speak to us of the Creator's love" (*Steps to Christ*, pg. 9). By studying His word and being a student of nature, Christ shows us what He is like. This enables us to represent Him and be a good witness to others.

~ Anna Fink

A Quiet Place

Amidst the solemn majesty of the mountain solitudes Moses was alone with God...Here his self-sufficiency was swept away. In the presence of the Infinite One he realized how weak, how inefficient, how short-sighted, is man. - Education, pg. 63

When I was eleven, I used to get stressed out by schoolwork or friendships that I felt weren't working as they should. At such times, I would take my journal or Bible and go to a secret place in the woods to meditate and pray. This place was a crook in the trunk of a tree, where I could sit about six feet above the ground and listen to the wind rustle through the leaves of the deciduous trees. Sometimes, in the spring and summer, I would also hear the birds singing sweetly. In this quiet place, I would cry out to God, "Father, please help me and give me strength." I would describe all my troubles in detail and pour out my heart to Him. When the wind was strong, it would make the tree I was in sway back and forth. I would feel afraid that I would fall from the tree or that the wind would sweep me away. So, I would pray even more earnestly. In this way, I learned to more fully put my trust in God.

Before Moses led the Israelites out of Egypt, God led him into the wilderness for forty years of training to become a competent leader of His people. Through his training in Egypt, Moses had learned to take things into his own hands and to control by force. This is shown by his killing an Egyptian. God had to take him out of Egypt and put him in contact with the majesty of nature so that his mind could realize the power, simplicity, and awesome grandeur and love of God. He realized how weak and powerless he was and his need of complete dependence upon the Source of all strength.

Are you feeling stressed out or tired from the burdens and cares of life? Are you considering talking with a family member or friend to try to sort things out? Why not take some time, go out in nature, and pour your heart out to God? He understands your every trial and wants to have you draw nigh to Him through His creation. You will leave feeling refreshed and renewed for the day ahead of you.

~ Victoria West

The Empty Chair

...Moses gained that which went with him throughout the years of his toilsome and care-burdened life—a sense of the personal presence of the Divine One. - Education, pg. 63

Pastor John walked up to the house and knocked on the door. The housekeeper answered it, invited him in, and led him to a room where an elderly man lay sick in bed. The pastor noticed an empty chair beside the bed and, assuming it was for him, sat down. Before he had begun to speak, the elderly man called for the housekeeper to bring in another chair, which was positioned next to the pastor. The pastor proceeded to talk with the elderly man and pray with him, for the aged fellow was not expected to live much longer. Afterward, the pastor's curiosity was aroused, and he asked the elderly gentleman the purpose of the empty chair. The old man smiled, and as he explained, the pastor's eyes filled with tears.

A week later, Pastor John got a phone call from the family: the man had passed away. The lady on the phone shared that the elderly gentleman had passed away in a strange position: he had managed to drag himself out of the bed and was resting his head on the seat of the empty chair. With tears, the pastor explained to the family the purpose of the chair. The elderly man had the chair set beside his bed so his Best Friend could sit beside him. He had fallen asleep with his head resting on the lap of Jesus.

Is Jesus real to you like He was to this man? Do you picture Him walking alongside you? Do you talk with Him and hang out with Him like you do with your other friends? I know for me, I often lose the sense that Jesus is actually with me. But the truth is, He is real, and He is physically with us. When I really believe that, my life suddenly becomes filled with peace and joy! With my Creator at my side, all stress and worry disappears, because I know He's in control! Do you have the joy of your Savior being next to you? Do you see Him in your empty chair?

~ Rachel Petrello

Going for Goals

Moses did not merely think of God, he saw Him. God was the constant vision before him. Never did he lose sight of His face. - Education, pg. 63

My parents sat my brother and me down at the kitchen table and began to talk: "We would like to get you guys something fun; so we've decided to get you a trampoline!" After the initial clamor died down, my dad cleared his throat and announced, "However, you children have a part to play. You must be cheerful for thirty days, and *then* you can have your trampoline."

Our faces fell. Thirty days? But, with such a prize before us, who cared about the cost? We made a chart for the allotted time and stuck it on the refrigerator. We used a smiley face magnet to mark our progress: a good day, and Smiley the Magnet moved on to the next square; a bad day, and he moved back. Oh, how we struggled! Sometimes, the magnet moved back several days in a row, but with our eyes fixed on our goal, we plunged forward.

Finally, after about three months, we came to the happy day when we had achieved a full thirty days of cheerfulness! Not only were we given our prize, but we had also learned the lesson of cheerful obedience. With much ceremony, we bore the trampoline home from the store and erected it in the yard. To this day, it provides much enjoyment for me, my siblings, and our many friends. My brother and I never lost sight of our goal, and we won!

Moses wanted to truly know God more than anything. It was his constant thought and aim. Moses was rewarded for his devotion: he saw God. When we desperately want to know God, thoughts of Him will pervade everything we do. If we are focusing on Jesus, He will reward our efforts with a fuller knowledge of Himself.

~ Anna Fink

Waiting

Wait on the LORD;be of good courage, and He shall strengthen your heart; wait, I say, on the LORD! - Psalm 27:14 NKJV

Have you ever been so perplexed about issues in your life that you didn't know what you were supposed to do, and you didn't even really know the reason for your confusion? One day, God showed me many Bible texts that were all about waiting on Him. I didn't think much of them until that night, when perplexities drove me to my knees. It was the best place for me to end up, and I pleaded with God for answers. When I asked Him to clear my mind and speak to me, one of the most distinct messages He whispered was, "Wait." At the time, I didn't know what I was supposed to wait for, but I now believe that God wants me to wait for His direction and for Him to work all things out for the best. This excerpt from the song "While I'm Waiting," by John Waller, has become my prayer:

I'm waiting.
I'm waiting on You, Lord,
And I am hopeful.
I'm waiting on You, Lord,
Though it is painful,
But patiently, I will wait.
I will move ahead, bold and confident,
Taking every step in obedience.
While I'm waiting, I will serve You.
While I'm waiting, I will worship.
While I'm waiting, I will not faint.
I'll be running the race
Even while I wait.
I'm waiting.
I'm waiting on You, Lord,
And I am peaceful.
I'm waiting on You, Lord,
Though it's not easy,
But faithfully, I will wait.
Yes, I will wait.

When life's perplexities crowd in, and you feel so confused it hurts, remember to trust God and serve Him; He will give you strength and peace while you wait on Him.

~ Valerie Jacobson

Do You Have Faith?

To Moses faith was no guesswork...He felt his need of help, asked for it, by faith grasped it, and in the assurance of sustaining strength went forward. - Education, pp. 63, 64

What exactly is faith? Most would say that faith is believing in what you can't see. Although that is true, I'd like to offer a better definition that I learned while colporteuring. My friend J.R. presented this definition during a Bible study: "Faith is simply taking God at His word." At first, I wasn't sure what that meant. But a few weeks later, I learned from a first-hand experience.

One hot day, we were heading towards our territory, a poor Spanish-speaking town called Dos Palos. Because of the town's size and the fact that I'd be canvassing in Spanish all day long, I was sure I wasn't going to sell many books that day. However, our leader encouraged us, and for the next hour, he had us pray aloud in the van. We claimed all the Bible promises we could find, and, in faith, thanked God in advance for helping us get over one hundred books sold. The day went by as usual, selling two to three books an hour, until the last hour of work. All of a sudden, books were being called in over the radio every two seconds! In the last eight minutes alone, twelve books went out! Back in the van we counted up the total and praised the Lord. We had gotten over one hundred books sold!

That day in Dos Palos, I learned the incredible power of faith. It isn't just believing in something unseen; faith is believing God will do what He said He would, and acting on it! It's just like the Bible says: "And all things, whatsoever ye shall ask in prayer, believing, ye shall receive" (Matthew 21:22 KJV). Why don't you give it a try? God will do what He has promised! Have faith and take Him at His word!

~ Rachel Petrello

Holding Hands

Now I beseech you, brethren, by the name of our Lord Jesus Christ, that ye all speak the same thing, and that there be no divisions among you; but that ye be perfectly joined together in the same mind and in the same judgment. - 1 Corinthians 1:10 KJV

Two young brothers frequently walked the railroad tracks to town and back in their bare feet. They always walked on the rails to avoid the sharp stones and rough timber underneath—that is, until they became too tired and lost their balance. Since they never seemed to be able to make it all the way to town without having to walk a stretch on the rail bed, they began to look for a solution. And one day they found it. Walking across from each other on the rails and holding hands made balancing easier, and they were able to walk the whole way above the rocks and splinters.

Side by side, hand in hand is the only way the church can be a powerful witness to the world. We must remember that we are one body. How does it appear if one leg of the body is limping while the rest of the body is overwhelmed with evangelism? How many will listen to church members talk about the love of Christ while their arms are striving in a wrestling match to win a theological battle? The effect on unbelievers is obvious: who is going to believe in the love of God when His church does not love?

Souls outside of the church are not the only ones in danger. The church must pass through a world that is full of deadly detours, and with all our pulling and pushing, some of us are sure to end up on the wrong road. Paul warns us not to argue over unimportant issues: "As for the one who is weak in faith, welcome him, but not to quarrel over opinions" (Romans 14:1 ESV).

Jesus prayed that His disciples might be one so that the world would know that God sent Him, and that God loved them as much as He loved Jesus (John 17:23). To accomplish Jesus' mission for the church, to reach the world with the good news of His salvation for all, we must be united. When others see us choose to be unified even though we may disagree, they will know that the gospel truly has power to change hearts.

~ Kevin Corrigan

147

Use God's Rope

He [Moses] felt his need of help, asked for it, by faith grasped it, and in the assurance of sustaining strength went forward. - Education, pg. 64

I'm climbing a steep rock-face. I have all the right gear, and I know that my Friend is at the top waiting for me. It's a tall cliff, with some parts steeper than others, but I'm confident in my skill and the safety of the ropes. After a while, I feel my grip on the rocks start to slip. As I thrust one hand into my pouch full of chalk, a twang from the rope makes me look up. Oh no! My rope is breaking! "Do you need help?" my Friend, who has been watching, calls down.

I reply, "Uh, no thanks. I'm fine." I wasn't really leaning on the rope before. I reason that I'm strong enough to make it to the top without straining the line further. But soon, both hands slip, and I find myself dangling on only a few fibers of rope.

Embarrassed, but helpless, I realize that I'm in danger and shout, "I need help! Can You please help me?" A strong, new rope sails down from the top, and trusting that my Friend has secured it, I quickly grab hold of it before the last strands of my rope break. Breathing hard, I rest for a while and then carefully attach the new rope to my harness.

"I'll help pull you up, just as I would have if you had leaned on the rope earlier. But you'll still have to climb the rest of the way up," my Friend directs. Reassured that His rope and strength will help me get to the top, I resume my climb with thankfulness and courage.

The world tells us we can climb through life in our own strength, that we don't need a God to help us through. This mindset affects Christians, too, and we often forget how helpless and dependent upon God we really are. It's when we slip and begin to fall that we must remember to look up and see that our Friend and God, who has been holding us all along, is willing and able to help, if we will only ask. Our part, like Moses, is to recognize our sinfulness and our need of God's mercy and ask for help. Believe that God will strengthen you. In faith, let go of your own stubborn will and grasp God's rope instead.

~ Valerie Jacobson

Legacy

In service he [Paul] found his joy; and at the close of his life of toil, looking back on its struggles and triumphs, he could say, "I have fought a good fight." - Education, pg. 68

Have you ever thought about how people will remember you after you die? What will the inscription say that is engraved on your tombstone? Will you be able to say at the end, as could the apostle Paul, that your life was lived for the good of others?

I was about twelve when my great-grandmother died at the age of 97. And though I didn't know her well, the time I had spent with her was precious. Whether it was working in the garden, tending to the children, or fixing meals, my great-grandmother's life was abundant in generous acts of service towards others. Whenever my family came to visit, she was always happily interacting and entertaining my brothers and cousins, creating in us a love for her and what she valued.

Then her health began to dwindle because of heart failure. Her physical activity was reduced to the point of being confined to her bed all day. I remember standing at the head of her bed, along with my family and friends, wondering why this was happening. A week later, as I looked down and dropped a rose six feet below the ground onto her casket, I finally realized how much she meant to me. She left a legacy of selflessness and service to others that I will always remember and cherish.

Observing my great-grandmother's life has led me to conclude that a life of service and giving is the only life worth living. Acts 20:35 says, "...It is more blessed to give than to receive" (KJV). What kind of legacy will you leave? Will people remember you as an egotistical individual with very little kindness, or as a God-fearing, humble person whose character has left a lasting impression and been a beneficial influence? Choose to live a life of giving, and you will leave a legacy of faithful service which will bless those who come behind you.

~ Cyrus Guccione

Love Your Enemies

But I say to you, love your enemies, bless those who curse you, do good to those who hate you, and pray for those who spitefully use you and persecute you... - Matthew 5:44 NKJV

One of the hardest things for me to do is to love every single person around me. It's easy to think, *Oh, I'm a good person; I love people*, but a lot of us have enemies when we don't even realize it. Lately though, God has been showing me just how much He loves each and every person. He even loves those people that I cannot stand to be around. Not only that, He loves them just as much as He loves me. I am no better than anyone else in His eyes. I have also been learning just how powerful prayer truly is. I have put these two things together, and they are totally changing my life. I have started praying for my enemies, each one by name, and asking God to help them in specific areas of their lives. And most of all, I have been asking God to bless them abundantly.

My name, Danielle, means "God is my Judge." Throughout this experience, God has been revealing to me that, not only is He *my* judge, but He is *everyone's* judge. He has shown me that, as a Christian, it is not my place to judge others, but to look for opportunities where I can help people by lifting them up in prayer. Instead of going to them myself and telling them what I think they need to change, I ask the Holy Spirit to speak to them. I ask God what areas of their lives they need me to pray for, and most of all, I ask that God would help me to love them and to see the good in them.

Cursing your "enemies" is one of the easiest sins to get stuck in. But I know you will find that, with God's help, it's possible to get out. The more you pray for these people, the more love you will have for them. By loving others, you are in turn loving your Heavenly Father. He says, "...Inasmuch as ye have done it unto one of the least of these my brethren, ye have done it unto me" (Matthew 25:40 KJV).

~ Danielle Schafer

Outcome

In service he [Paul] found his joy; and at the close of his life of toil, looking back on its struggles and triumphs, he could say, "I have fought a good fight." - Education, pg. 68

Paul, formerly known as Saul of Tarsus, was a politician and a religious leader held in high esteem by many, until he gave it all up to follow Christ. Trials and troubles were certainly his lot, yet through it all he stayed close to God, and at the end he could say, "I have fought a good fight."

Martin Luther was a songwriter, family man, and former monk who headed the Protestant movement and spurred the Reformation on to unimaginable heights. He, too, was persecuted; yet, he always remained at peace with God. He wrote the song "A Mighty Fortress," which has been sung by millions around the world. The hymn expresses faith in God and a calm assurance that all is under His guiding hand. At the end of his life, he could say, "I have fought a good fight."

Jo Holdal is a student, daughter, and Christian. Troubles come and go, but my faith only grows stronger. Daily, I'm drawing closer to God and learning more. Though I haven't made an impact on history, I hope I have impacted the lives of those around me. And when this life is over, I want to be able to say, "I have fought a good fight." I want to hear my Heavenly Father say, "Well done, good and faithful servant; thou hast been faithful over a few things, I will make thee ruler over many things: enter thou into the joy of thy Lord" (Matthew 25:23 KJV). I know that if I am faithful, I will be able to hear those words.

And you can hear those words spoken to you, too! He's just waiting for you to enter His service and fight the good fight. Why not sign up for service and let Him enable you to do honourable deeds today.

~ Jo Holdal

Invest in Heaven

Moses was offered the palace of the Pharaohs and the monarch's throne; but the sinful pleasures that make men forget God were in those lordly courts, and he chose instead the "durable riches and righteousness." - Education, pp. 68, 69

Who won the Oscars ten years ago? How about the Emmy Awards? And the Nobel Peace Prize? What about the gold medal for the Men's Bobsled at the last Winter Olympics? Fame and honor will pass away; these things just don't last. Even if you are famous in your lifetime, how can you be sure you will be remembered? The world calls to us with pleasures and fame. We have only one life to live; we have energy, health, time, and money to devote to whatever we deem worthy. We could spend these talents pursuing that which will bring short-lived pleasure to ourselves. Or, we could invest our many resources into that which will not pass away. "Lay not up for yourselves treasures upon earth, where moth and rust doth corrupt, and where thieves break through and steal: But lay up for yourselves treasures in heaven, where neither moth nor rust doth corrupt, and where thieves do not break through nor steal..." (Matthew 6:19-20 KJV).

God has given us three precious gifts: time, energy, and money. We can choose to invest these gifts in a number of ways. I could choose to be a ballet dancer, violinist, hockey player, screenplay writer, or anything else that tickles my fancy. I could put numerous hours into my personal pleasures, pouring my energy, time, and monetary resources into them. I could become a champion by the world's standards, gaining fame, honor, and prestige. But, would this type of glorification really make a lasting impression? No. My name would probably be forgotten from the earth within five years or less. My life would simply be history to read in a book.

Wouldn't you rather invest your time and energy into something that will last forever—impacting hearts and lives for eternity and having a reward that outshines any other? Jesus wants this lifework to be yours: reaching out to others around you with Christlike selflessness and drawing them to the fountain of Living Water that shall never run dry.

~ Victoria West

Your Influence

Yet there is a future joy to which Paul looked forward as the recompense of his labors—the same joy for the sake of which Christ endured the cross and despised the shame—the joy of seeing the fruition of his work. - Education, pg. 70

Imagine yourself in heaven. Flying around with your new wings and marveling over the beauty and magnificence of everything, you are overwhelmed by all the extravagance and grand colors that you've never seen before. While you happily converse with the ancient monarchs and prophets, you notice an ecstatic young woman searching anxiously for someone. When she finally identifies you, she runs over and warmly thanks you and states that you are the reason why she is in heaven. Unsure what has just happened, you question, "Excuse me, miss, but I'm not exactly sure I know who you are, or what you're talking about!"

Joyfully, the woman goes on to explain that your silent, yet powerful influence had touched her so profoundly that she was inspired to give her life to Christ. Later, when times of religious persecution and oppression arose, she remembered your example, and as a result, she took a stand for Christ and died a martyr's death.

"Great is the responsibility of those who take upon themselves the guidance of a human soul...The work he is doing day by day will exert...an influence that will not cease to extend and strengthen until time shall end. The fruits of his work he must meet in that great day when every word and deed shall be brought in review before God" (*Education*, pp. 280-281).

What you say, how you dress, how you act, even the expressions on your face create an impression on people around you. As a result, they may exert the same influence on others. The far-reaching effects of your influence are unknown. Whether you are aware of it or not, your whole character is always observed by others, most importantly by God. What kind of character are you displaying?

~ Cyrus Guccione

Don't Rebel

Obey them that have the rule over you, and submit yourselves...
- Hebrews 13:17 KJV

Don't rebel. Rebellion has caused pain ever since Satan attempted to overthrow the Ruler of the universe, and it has continued to produce suffering after the fall of man. Think about it: has rebellion ever brought you something worthwhile, something that you could not have obtained in a better way? I believe that the only honest answer you can give is no.

I have often battled against my parents over a decision they made. I would spend a day or two grumbling and complaining, making myself miserable, and then realize that I really agreed with my parents. When I did get what I wanted, it didn't lift my spirits as I expected it to, and many times it became clear that I could have gotten it without sulking. All rebellion has ever given me is an empty feeling of disgust.

The results of the first rebellion were terrible and have brought on the pain of all rebellion since. Think of the God's heartache as He watched His highest angel begin to doubt His love. Contemplate the pain experienced as Jesus and the Father, who had been eternally one, were separated at Calvary. How must it feel to be a fallen angel—to know that you will never again enjoy the complete bliss of heaven? What must the unfallen beings experience looking down with horror on the controversy raging on this planet? As you consider, ask yourself how long you will participate in this terrible curse.

No matter where I look, rebellion causes pain and suffering. Nothing causes more hurt than turning against God. Although it may take many forms—rebellion against your parents, teachers, the government, or other authorities—all rebellion is ultimately against God. "Servants, obey in all things your masters according to the flesh; not with eyeservice, as menpleasers; but in singleness of heart, fearing God..." (Colossians 3:22 KJV). Rebellion is Satan's strategy, and using it makes you partners with the devil and an enemy of God. Jesus loves you more than anyone else could, and He knows exactly what's best for you! Why not choose to trust Him and stop rebelling? Make Jesus your Lord.

~ Kevin Corrigan

God's Will

What is it worth to any life to have been God's instrument in setting in motion such influences of blessing? What will it be worth in eternity to witness the results of such a lifework? - Education, pg. 70

Have you ever stopped and wondered what God's will is for your life? Have you thought about what experiences and tribulations He will set before you in years to come?

God's will for your life is perfectly appointed by Him in order that His works may be shown through your influence. He sets you in the perfect environment on earth for you to trust wholly in Him, so that He can reveal the treasure of a Christ-like life through you. This is God's will for you, me, and all of humanity. In Acts 17:26-27, it states that God "determined" our allotted boundaries, meaning that He already has a designated position for you and me. Why? The answer is found in the next verse, "...so that men would seek him and perhaps reach out for him and find him, though he is not far from each one of us" (NIV).

Isn't that encouraging to know that our Savior and Friend is ever near to each person here on earth? No matter what kind of life God grants you, know that "He will order His angels to protect you wherever you go" (Psalms 91:11 NLT). He may direct you in a path that leads to the life of a physician, a musician, a teacher, or even a martyr—who knows? God does! Will you trust Him?

~ Cyrus Guccione

Not My Will, but Thine

And we know that all things work together for good to them that love God, to them who are the called according to His purpose. - Romans 8:28 KJV

Has it ever seemed like everything was going wrong, and you didn't know why? Have you ever been really opposed to something and then been forced into going against your will?

I experienced this when I was forced to go to Bangladesh on a mission trip in the middle of my sophomore year of high school. My parents made this decision because they thought it was the best thing they could do to help develop my character. Boy, was I ever upset! I wouldn't talk with them for weeks, and then when I did, it was only because it was necessary. While I was there in Bangladesh, I spent most of my time with little orphan children. Through them, God opened my eyes and took me out of my depression and rebellion. By focusing on others, and not myself, I was able to see how truly blessed I am. I had thought this trip was going to mess up my life, but in the end, it did more good than anything else could have. Now, I even have a good relationship with my parents. God used something that was very contrary to my desires to change and mold my character.

Whenever you're faced with difficulties, and you think things just cannot get any worse, remember that even through the difficult times God is right there beside you. He has plans for you. They may not be what you're wanting, but in the long run, if you stick with God's plans, things will always turn around for the better. Jeremiah 29:11 says, "'For I know the plans I have for you,' declares the Lord, 'plans to prosper you and not to harm you, plans to give you hope and a future'" (NIV).

~ Bristi Waid

June 6

No Price Too High

What is it worth to any life to have been God's instrument in setting in motion such influences of blessing? What will it be worth in eternity to witness the results of such a lifework? - Education, pg. 70

Imagine you are walking in the New Earth. The cool green grass tickles your toes. You reach down to pick a blossoming rose and smile as you realize that its scarlet color will never fade and its fragrance will never die!

But the best part is that here in the New Earth, you are with Jesus, all the time! From the very core of your being, you love Him. But, no matter how hard you try, you can't comprehend His love for you! He came to the old sinful world, risking His eternal existence and the peace of the entire universe to die for you. It just doesn't make sense how He could love you that much, even when there was no guarantee that you would love Him in return. But He still loved you. Now there is a never-ending cycle of love flowing between the two of you.

In fact, when sin still reigned, and you first began to experience His love filling your heart, it was so great it spilled over into your relationships with your family and friends. Because they saw an unconditional love in you, you were able to lead them to Jesus. It wasn't always easy to share that love. There were times when you had to sacrifice your time, give up things you wanted to do, and suffer.

However, now that you're here in the New Earth, you know it was completely worth it! Everyone is unselfishly and unconditionally loving and accepting. There are no more insecurities, and no one worries about not measuring up. You don't worry about friends gossiping about you when you're not around. Every girl knows she is a beautiful daughter of God; every boy knows he is an honored man in Christ. The only tears left in your eyes are tears of sheer joy at the peace and happiness of loving and being with the ones you love.

The picture I've just painted for you is the reality of what heaven will be like. If this is picture the end result, is any sacrifice we make in bringing others to Christ too great?

~ Anneliese Wahlman

157

Like Jesus

Of Him all the excellences manifest in the earth's greatest and noblest souls were reflections. The purity and beneficence of Joseph, the faith and meekness and long-suffering of Moses, the steadfastness of Elisha, the noble integrity and firmness of Daniel, the ardor and self-sacrifice of Paul, the mental and spiritual power manifest in all these men, and in all others who had ever dwelt on the earth, were but gleams from the shining of His glory. In Him was found the perfect ideal.
- Education, pg. 73

Writing this set of devotionals has been especially hard for me since English is my second language. Many times, I would get frustrated because I would quickly run out of ideas to write. A person that has helped me through this whole process is one of my closest friends, Jonathan. Enthusiastic and optimistic, he would always encourage me not to give up. One of the things that impressed me most about him was his dedication in editing my papers. Every night he would help me with my homework before doing his own. Prior to reading my composition, he would pray that God would inspire us to make the best out of the draft. You might think that this is one of his greatest qualities. But, if you took time to notice a typical day of his life, you would see, among other things, that he usually sits at meals by the less popular students, he never gets mad, he puts others before himself, and he always prays for his friends. He is dependent upon Christ at all times. For me, he is one of the biggest reflections of Christ that I have ever met.

You will always be amazed by the Bible stories of Daniel and the lions or David and Goliath. You might also be impressed with the obedience of Moses in the midst of trials or the noble character of Joseph. By beholding God, these men became a mirror of His character and an inspiration for a great number of people. Even though the world had these great examples of faith, God chose to ultimately send His Son to earth so we would have a *perfect* example of righteousness to follow. Imagine a character with all the good traits of the great heroes of the Bible, and you will have a glimpse of how Jesus was. I believe that God put deep in our hearts the desire to be like Him. Are you willing, today, to become a reflection of Jesus?

~ Valdis Cuvaldin

158

Perfect Timing

God's greatest gift was bestowed to meet man's greatest need. The Light appeared when the world's darkness was deepest. - Education, pg. 74

As I stepped out into the frosty night, a battle raged in my mind. So far, the semester had been a struggle. Stress from homework, loss of sleep, fighting with my roommate, doubts in my spiritual life, and pressure to return home had built to a point beyond what I could handle. I had decided I would leave Fountainview for good, until a friend offered some encouragement. Now, back and forth the battle raged: should I stay? Or should I go? Softly, it began to snow. I looked up and gasped. Suddenly, I knew the answer.

* * *

The nation of Israel was in trouble. Caught up in the external rules of religion, society had spiraled into spiritual darkness. Humanity was about to reach its lowest point, but just when the darkness was deepest, the Light appeared: the Messiah entered the world. God's timing was perfect.

* * *

Staring up at the falling snow, I began to cry for joy! During a fierce struggle the previous year, I had prayed a specific prayer. I'd been desperate for assurance; so I had asked God for a sign: that, at the time I needed it most, He would make it snow to let me know everything was going to be all right. The snow never came that year, but now as I walked through the magical swirls of white, I realized my prayer had been answered.

God let me know He'd help me make it through—He made it snow—just when I needed it most! God's timing was perfect. If it hadn't been, I wouldn't be here to write this story!

~ Rachel Petrello

Just a Form

Semblance took the place of reality. - Education, pg. 74

Imagine that this last week my neighbor asked me to make some cement stepping stones leading up to her porch. After we had agreed on the price she would pay to have the walkway made, I went right to work building frames to pour the cement into. I had the frames all ready after a great deal of measuring, remeasuring, sawing, and hammering. They were good and strong. Then I had a thought: my neighbor probably would be willing to pay the same amount for the frames as she was willing to pay for the stepping stones. The project had already taken a lot of work; pouring cement would take even more. I was sure she would never know the difference anyway. The next morning I ran over to my neighbor's house and set the forms where the cement stepping stones were supposed to go. Anticipating the money I'd get for half the normal amount of work, I knocked on the door, calling my neighbor out to see the "finished" job. With an incredulous look, she exclaimed, "Where is the cement?"

I answered in surprise, "The frames are there. Why would you need cement?"

This story is obviously ridiculous. But so many Christians, including myself, often make just as silly a mistake. I faithfully follow the rules set out in the Bible, but soon they becomes *just* rules—only a form. God's rules are like the walls of a fortress protecting our relationship with Jesus. But without the relationship inside, the walls are purposeless; they protect nothing of value. We set up barriers to be sure we will not lose Jesus, but we don't actually take any time to be sure He's inside our hearts. We simply miss the point. In this same way, we end up with families without love, friends without friendship, and work without accomplishment—forms with nothing inside.

When Jesus came to this earth, the religious leaders of His time had lost their relationship with Him; they only had a set of rules they rigidly tried to stick to. Jesus pleads with us just as He pleaded with the scribes and Pharisees: "Don't try to get along with just a 'form' as your religion. Be sure to have the blessing of a friendship with Me in your heart."

~ Kevin Corrigan

Thy Law, My Delight

So far from making arbitrary requirements, God's law is given to men as a hedge, a shield. Whoever accepts its principles is preserved from evil. Fidelity to God involves fidelity to man. Thus the law guards the rights, the individuality, of every human being. - Education, pp. 76, 77

You know that feeling you get when you have disobeyed your parents, and you can't look straight into their eyes? It's not a good feeling. When you have done something you know they don't approve of, you can't act normal around them. In contrast, there is such a sweetness in life when you follow your parents' wishes, when you adhere to their commands. You can look them straight in the face and spend time together with no feelings of guilt or shame; you have nothing to hide.

It is the same way with God. We can stand unashamedly before Him, spend time with Him, and look Him straight in the eye when we keep His law. His law also protects those who are weak and humbles those who are strong. It makes society a better place to live. Those who keep it, show love in doing so. All of us want to be loved and appreciated, and God's law makes us feel loved, cared for, and protected. It also preserves "the individuality, of every human being" (*Education*, pg. 77).

We were created to be loving, innocent, and carefree. God's law helps us preserve this identity as sons and daughters of God. We can feel secure in the fact that He loves us and wants what is best for us. Won't you exclaim with David, "...O Lord...Thy law is my delight" (Psalm 119:174 KJV)?

~ Victoria West

Trust and Obey

*...God's law is given to men as a hedge, a shield. - Education,
pp. 76, 77*

I sat on the edge of my bed one balmy August evening, carving a stick with my dad's new pocketknife. Cicadas serenaded me with melodies carried on the gentle summer breeze. As I diligently carved my stick, trying to finish it before my dad came in to put me to bed, I became very impatient with one tiny crevice in the wood. Now, my dad has always told me never to carve toward myself. I was completely aware of his warning, but in my frustration I went against his word and immediately gouged a wound on the side of my thumb. The first time I carved toward myself was also the last time. But to this very day, I still have a scar on my thumb that reminds me of the danger in disregarding instruction.

Just as parents have rules to protect their children, God has rules to protect His children, you and me. God's set of rules has been given to each one of us and can be found in Exodus 20. They are called the Ten Commandments. Just as I ignored my dad's word, many children of God are ignoring His rules, especially the fourth one. This commandment instructs us to "Remember the sabbath day, to keep it holy. Six days shalt thou labour, and do all thy work: but the seventh day is the sabbath of the Lord thy God: in it thou shalt not do any work..." (Exodus 20:8-10 KJV). Jesus kept the Sabbath, but many of His professed followers today are ignoring this commandment and living by what they find most comfortable and socially acceptable.

Christ doesn't want us to miss out on the blessing of the Sabbath. He says, "...The sabbath was made for man..." (Mark 2:27 KJV). You and I have an appointment each week with our loving Creator. We must remember that He has our best interests in mind. He knows that we need a full day of down time and devotion. He doesn't want us to get stressed-out, overworked, and overwhelmed with the pressures of life. He wants to protect us from hurting ourselves. So, He has commanded us to take a day of rest once a week. It is our duty as Christians to trust and obey His law for our own good.

~ Sarah-Kate Lingerfelt

June 12

A Safeguard

...God's law is given to men as a hedge, a shield...To the obedient it is the pledge of eternal life, for it expresses the principles that endure forever. - Education, pp. 76, 77

When I was three years old, my dad was giving my little sister, Morgan, and me a bath. He finished washing Morgan and took her out to dry her off. As he lifted her out, he turned to me and instructed, "Megan, stay in the bathtub while I dry Morgan off, and then I'll get you out when I'm done." I sat in the water for a matter of a few seconds, but when I noticed that my daddy's attention was focused on my little sister, I resolved to exercise my dare-devil skills and get out of the bathtub all by myself; I was a big girl after all. Silently, yet quickly, I stood and lifted myself up onto the wall of the tub. With a speedy last glance in my daddy's direction, I leaped into the air and was sure that after my exciting flight I'd land safely on the soft rug and make my daddy proud that I could get out all by myself. However, my launch didn't turn out as planned: my little, wet foot slipped on the slick edge of the tub and caused me to fall sideways to the floor. My right arm was flung backwards, and it broke when it hit the outer edge of the tub. Oh, how it hurt! As I look back, I can obviously see that following my dad's instruction would have prevented my pain.

God sought to demonstrate His love when He established His Ten Commandments for heaven and earth. Each and every commandment is for our own benefit, so that we may enjoy a wonderful life. Jesus said, "If ye keep my commandments, ye shall abide in my love; even as I have kept my Father's commandments, and abide in His love. These things have I spoken unto you, that my joy might remain in you, and that your joy might be full" (John 15:10, 11 KJV). If the commandments were important for Christ, how much more important are they for us? Just as my dad, out of love, asked me to do something, God, in His love, invites us to observe His commandments.

~ Megan Metcalf

Live with a "Yes" Face

...He [Jesus] went forth to His mission, in every moment of His contact with men exerting upon them an influence to bless...such as the world had never witnessed. - Education, pg. 78

During the days of his presidency, Thomas Jefferson was traveling across the countryside on horseback with a battalion of soldiers. After some time, they came upon a raging river that had flooded because of recent heavy rainfall. The swollen river had risen so high that it had washed away the previously existing bridge, leaving the company in a predicament. Jefferson and his men, unable to find an alternative route, had to ford the river on horseback and fight against the swift current. A traveler, heading in the same direction, stepped aside to watch this fierce battle. After watching many soldiers plunge in and struggle to make it safely to the other side, the traveler asked one of the men if he would be willing to help him cross the river. Without hesitation, the man agreed, and the two soon made it safely across.

As the traveler slid off the horse and thanked the willing warrior for his assistance, one of the lieutenants in the battalion asked him, "Tell me, why did you select the President of the country to ask this favor of?"

The traveler, shocked and embarrassed, admitted that he had had no idea that the President had assisted him. "All I know," said the traveler, "is that on some of your faces was written the answer 'No' to my question, and on others was the answer 'Yes.' His was a 'Yes' face."

Albert Einstein once said, "Only a life lived for others is a life worthwhile." Compassion, humility, and helpfulness should be the essence of our lifework. And just as President Jefferson stood out from among his soldiers, the life of him who seeks the well-being of others will stand out from the crowd. Just as the traveler saw something different in President Jefferson, others should see something different in us. What will the world see in you: a self-seeking character, or a life of compassion for those in need?

~ Cyrus Guccione

June 14

The Touch of the Master's Hand

Here Christ stands revealed as the master teacher...He alone has
perfect understanding of the human soul. - Education, pg. 78

'Twas battered and scarred, and the auctioneer
Thought it was scarcely worth his while
To waste much time on the old violin,
But held it up with a smile.
"What am I bidden, good folks," he cried,
"Who'll start the bidding for me?"
"A dollar, a dollar," then, "Two! Only two?"
"Two dollars, and who'll make it three?"
"Three dollars, once, three dollars, twice;
Going for three..." But no,
From the room, far back, a grey-haired man
Came forward and picked up the bow;
Then, wiping the dust from the old violin,
And tightening the loose strings,
He played a melody pure and sweet
As a caroling angel sings.

The music ceased, and the auctioneer,
With a voice that was quiet and low,
Said, "What am I bid for the old violin?"
And he held it up with the bow.
"A thousand dollars, and who'll make it two?"
"Two thousand! And who'll make it three?"
"Three thousand, once, three thousand, twice;
And going and gone," said he.
The people cheered, but some of them cried,
"We do not quite understand
What changes its worth?" Swift came the reply:
"The touch of the master's hand."
- Myra B. Welch

The master violinist saw the violin's worth when no one else did.
Jesus also sees the worth in a lost soul and perfectly understands the
heart of the sinner. Won't you allow the Master's hand to touch your
life?

~ Anna Fink

165

Association

Christ alone had experience in all the sorrows and temptations that befall human beings. - Education, pg. 78

Have you ever gone through some temptation or trial and felt you were completely alone? Like no one understands you or what you're dealing with?

I have good news: Jesus, the Son of God, has been through it all. He didn't only carry His own troubles though: He carried yours, mine, and every other person's as well. However, He hasn't only carried our troubles; He has shown us a better way to live so we don't have to experience so many of those tough times. He has also given us our friends, family, and others with whom we interact on a daily basis to support us, encourage us, and give us a loving "You can do it!" when we need it. God has placed these people in our lives for a special purpose.

You see, He knows that no man is an island. What if each of us were an island unto ourselves—independent, isolated, and cut off from the needs of others? I shudder to think of what our world would be like if that were true! God wants us to show His character to those around us—to be that shoulder to cry on, that cheerleader, therapist, sounding board, solace, or counselor which reveals His compassion most clearly.

So often I don't realize that I am meant to be like God. I may say I'm a Christian, but that doesn't mean much unless I am actually being Christlike. I am supposed to be there for my brothers and sisters in Christ, to be a light for others to look at and hold up. Then maybe, just maybe, they will see Christ in me.

~ Jo Holdal

I Understand

Christ alone had experience in all the sorrows and temptations that befall human beings...A sharer in all the experiences of humanity, He could feel not only for, but with, every burdened and tempted and struggling one. - Education, pg. 78

There once was a little boy who wanted a puppy very badly. One day, he passed by a house that had a sign posted, reading, "Puppies for sale." He immediately hurried home to scrounge up his money. Returning to the house, he knocked and asked about the pups.

"I hear you've got some puppies for sale, Mister."
"That's right, I do. But they're $25 each."
The boy's face fell, but only for a moment. "Well, I've only got $2.25, but I'd like to see them anyway, please."

The man led him to the backyard where there were five puppies. They were all very excited and were tumbling around with great energy. All except one, that is. In the back corner, a small puppy sat, staring longingly at the boy.

"What's wrong with that one?" the boy asked.
"Oh, that one? Well, she's got a lame leg. I don't expect to sell her anytime soon."
"That's the one I want, Mister. I don't have all the money right now, but can I pay you back a little at a time?"
The man raised his eyebrows. "Now, why do you want that one, son? She'll never be able to run or jump, or do any of the things an active boy like you would want in a puppy."
The little boy smiled and pulled up one pant leg, revealing a leg brace. "That's OK, Mister. I can't do any of those things very well either. We'll understand each other."

When He came down to our earth, Jesus took on our sinful humanity, so that He could more fully understand our weaknesses and faults. He is the only one in heaven who can fully comprehend the nature of man. He was tempted as we are, yet without sin. So the next time you are going through a trial, remember that Jesus knows what you're going through.

~ Carmen Hartwell

167

Trial or Blessing?

Never another of woman born was so fiercely beset by temptation; never another bore so heavy a burden of the world's sin and pain. Never was there another whose sympathies were so broad or so tender. A sharer in all the experiences of humanity, He [Christ] could feel not only for, but with, every burdened and tempted and struggling one. - Education, pg. 78

Thomas Edison invented the microphone, the phonograph, the incandescent light bulb, the storage battery, talking movies, and over 1,000 other inventions. On one evening in December of 1914, after Edison had been straining his finances for years to work on the storage battery, spontaneous combustion broke out in his film room. Within minutes, all the packing compounds, celluloid for records and films, and other flammable goods were ablaze. The heat was so intense and the water pressure so low that the attempts made to douse the flames were useless. Everything was lost, and the damage exceeded two million dollars.

Edison's 24-year-old son, Charles, found his father calmly watching the fire. "My heart ached for him," Charles later said. "He was 67—no longer a young man—and everything was going up in flames. When he saw me, he shouted, 'Charles, where's your mother?' When I told him I didn't know, he said, 'Find her. Bring her here. She will never see anything like this as long as she lives.'"

The next morning, Edison looked over what was left and said, "There is great value in disaster. All our mistakes are burned up. Thank God we can start anew." Several weeks after the fire, Edison delivered the first phonograph.

Like Thomas Edison, we too can look at trials as a blessing if we choose. It may be hard at times, but the Bible says, "...All things work together for good to those who love God..." (Romans 8:28 NKJV). We can remember that, because Jesus suffered, He knows our pain. He knows our sorrows, and He is there for us to help us through our trials.

~ Laura Williams

When I Cry

A sharer in all the experiences of humanity, He could feel not only for, but with, every burdened and tempted and struggling one. - Education, pg. 78

"Jesus will help you."
"God is with you through this."
"The Lord will be with you."

These phrases are often heard when someone is going through a hard time. They are the expected responses, words that easily slip off the tongue to comfort a hurting soul. But to me these words sound cliche, just something we say out of habit.

I used to think of God as a strong, but impersonal Being who was just there while you went through trials. I pictured Him helping and encouraging, but not really being emotionally involved. I was stunned when I learned the truth.

The Bible tells us that Jesus went through everything that we have gone through...and more. He has been "in all points tempted like as we are..." (Hebrews 4:15 KJV). Because He knows our pain, He feels it with us. This excerpt of the song "When I Cry," by the Gaither Vocal Band, sums it up best:

>When I cry, You cry.
>When I hurt, You hurt.
>When I've lost someone,
>It takes a piece of You too.
>And when I fall on my face,
>You fill me with grace.
>'Cause nothing breaks Your heart,
>Or tears You apart
>Like when I cry.

God has already felt all our pain for us, and whenever we are hurting, He cries right along with us. This was a revolutionary thought to me and changed my world. Whenever I am being tempted or going through a hard time, I remember that Jesus not only knows about it, but feels my pain along with me.

~ Anna Fink

Positive Example

What He taught, He lived. "I have given you an example," He said to His disciples;"that ye should do as I have done." "I have kept My Father's commandments." Thus in His life, Christ's words had perfect illustration and support. And more than this; what He taught, He was. His words were the expression, not only of His own life experience, but of His own character. Not only did He teach the truth, but He was the truth. It was this that gave His teaching, power. - Education, pp. 78, 79

Never in my life have I met a boy so dedicated to the Lord as my friend Jonathan. Jonathan grew up as a pastor's kid. He went to church every Sabbath, joined pathfinders, led out in youth services, and played music in church. His whole family is blessed with musical talent, and he seems to be extraordinarily blessed. I'm not sure how many instruments he can play, but I recall at least five.

Yet, somehow, he remains so humble. In class, he is always observing his classmates to find those who might need some help. Instead of focusing on his own problems and stresses, he helps others who are struggling. Many people who are especially gifted put others down to make themselves appear even better, but Jonathan always does the opposite: he always tries to lift others up. At almost every meal, he looks around the cafeteria for someone who is lonely or having a down day and sits with them. He meets them where they are and encourages them. He never condemns anyone; he is a friend. He puts his whole heart into his classes and work. It's difficult to understand how he can be so unselfish. Without even preaching to me, he has convinced me that Jesus is his Best Friend.

It doesn't matter how good we look in church, or that we profess to be Christians. What matters is how we live our daily lives, how we interact with other people around us. "But be ye doers of the word, and not hearers only, deceiving your own selves" (James 1:22 KJV). By following Christ's perfect example and having a relationship with Him, we can have the right motives for our actions. Our actions speak louder than words. Do what you know Christ would have you do, and your actions will show that you are a true Christian.

~ Bristi Waid

Prisms

*Thus in His life, Christ's words had perfect illustration and support.
And more than this; what He taught, He was. His words were the
expression, not only of His own life experience, but of His own
character. Not only did He teach the truth, but He was the truth. It was
this that gave His teaching, power. - Education, pg. 78, 79*

On the mountainside, the crowds gathered to hear an unusual Man
speak. He was new to the small town, and many were curious as to
what He had to say. Some people came not really knowing why, but
within themselves they felt a need to go and listen to this unique
Individual. It was as if something inside was prompting them to go.

When He started to speak, the people were immediately absorbed
in His message. The peasants, the elderly, the children—all were
enthralled by His stories and parables. They were inspired by His
simple wisdom and practical life lessons. He had the ability to
captivate the audience, influence their perceptions, then motivate their
actions. By imparting simple life lessons from nature and revelation,
He instilled in His listeners an inspiration to investigate more about the
so-called "gospel truth." He personified a prismatic ray of light from His
loving Father to the people.

Jesus' life was spent receiving strength from His father in heaven
and then giving that knowledge to His disciples and followers. His
purpose was to give an example of a perfect life for us to follow. His
speech, actions, and everything else were in accordance with the will
of His Father in heaven. He was ever ready to stand up against the
forces of evil and do away with the schemes of the devil.

May it be our prayer to do what Jesus has so lovingly
demonstrated for us to do. May we choose to accept His gift of life and
share it with the world. May we act as prisms of light to our brothers
and sisters, so that God's contagious love and joy can be shared.

~ Cyrus Guccione

Mirror, Mirror, on the Wall
Part 1

To all things untrue and base His very presence was a rebuke. In the light of His purity, men saw themselves unclean, their life's aims mean and false. Yet He drew them. - Education, pg. 79

One night, a girl named Clara had a dream. In her dream, she found herself standing before a great mirror, quoting a line from her favorite fairy-tale. "Mirror, mirror, on the wall, who is the fairest of them all? Wait...what is that?" While gazing at her reflection, she noticed a black spot on her face. As she leaned in for a closer look, the spot grew until her entire face was black with grime! "I must clean this off! I cannot be seen like this!" Desperately, she tried to wash it off, scrubbing and scrubbing, but to no avail. Realizing her face was stained permanently, she began to cry, "Oh, I cannot bear this sight. How dreadfully filthy I am! If only I could be clean again!" Suddenly, she felt a hand rest on her shoulder, and she turned to see who it was.

While Jesus lived on the earth, He showcased God's law and gave a perfect example of following it. When the people looked at Jesus, it was like looking into a mirror. Just like Clara, the closer they came to the mirror, the more clearly they saw how dirty they actually were.

"The closer you come to Jesus, the more faulty you will appear in your own eyes; for your vision will be clearer, and your imperfections will be seen in broad and distinct contrast to His perfect nature. This is evidence that Satan's delusions have lost their power; that the vivifying influence of the Spirit of God is arousing you" (*Steps to Christ*, pp. 64, 65).

~ Rachel Petrello

Mirror, Mirror, on the Wall
Part 2

But whoso looketh into the perfect law of liberty, and continueth therein, he being not a forgetful hearer, but a doer of the work, this man shall be blessed in his deed. - James 1:25 KJV

When we left Clara, she had lifted her blackened, tear-streaked face to see who had touched her. An elderly man stood above her, smiling.

"Little girl, what is troubling you?" he asked. Clara told him the story of her encounter with the great mirror, her bewildering discovery of her dirty face, and how desperately she wanted to be clean. The old fellow smiled, "You are a remarkable little girl! Many people pass by this mirror every day, but they do not take the time to examine what they see. Hence, they do not desire to be clean. You see, the secret of this great mirror is that it reflects not only the exterior, but also the interior. It shows you all your faults, weaknesses, imperfections, and mistakes. Most aren't willing to clean up, so they brush past the mirror quickly, muttering excuses. Even if they try to wash up, they cannot do so by their own efforts. If they would just ask me, the owner of this great mirror, I would happily make them clean."

"Oh, please! Can you make me clean?" Clara asked. In response, the elderly man removed a bar of soap and a handkerchief from his pocket, and began to gently wash her face.

When we come close to Jesus, we see how sinful we really are; but we cannot stop there. As our sins are revealed to us, we need to ask God to make us clean. We cannot be like the man mentioned in James 1:24 who "beholdeth himself [in a mirror], and goeth his way, and straightway forgetteth what manner of man he was" (KJV).

"We shall often have to bow down and weep at the feet of Jesus because of our shortcomings and mistakes, but we are not to be discouraged...He desires to restore you to Himself, to see His own purity and holiness reflected in you. And if you will but yield yourself to Him, He that hath begun a good work in you will carry it forward to the day of Jesus Christ" (*Steps to Christ*, pg. 64).

~ Rachel Petrello

173

Focus

In every human being, however fallen, He beheld a son of God, one who might be restored to the privilege of his divine relationship.
- Education, pg. 79

As I go about my daily life, I sometimes wonder if my focus is in the right place. It seems to me that the best way to grow is to try to build my own relationship with Christ. Now, I realize that my personal walk with Christ is extremely important, but I find myself in danger of becoming too focused on me. Why do I keep failing? Why don't I have the faith that I feel I should? Should I be sensing Christ's presence? Where does the problem lie?

Jesus is our Great Example; He lived a perfect life and gave us the gift of salvation. But if we look at the way He lived, we find something very interesting. Christ was never focused on Himself; His focus was on His Father and on uplifting others. He never condemned those around Him; in each person, He saw potential for something exceptional. Mark 2:15 reads: "And it came to pass, that, as Jesus sat at meat in his house, many publicans and sinners sat also together with Jesus and His disciples: for there were many, and they followed Him" (KJV). Jesus took time for the "rejects" of society, those who were looked down upon and scorned by the priests and leaders. Jesus' words to the woman caught in adultery were, "...Neither do I condemn thee: go, and sin no more" (John 8:11 KJV). Through these words He pointed to the grace and love of His Father. "For God sent not His Son into the world to condemn the world; but that the world through Him might be saved" (John 3:17 KJV).

Although God wants me to spend time with Him, it is impossible to build my faith without sharing Him with others. If I focus too much on the problems that I have, instead of on helping to relieve the problems of others, it will be very easy to become discouraged. God wants to see us reaching out to those in need and living in a way that exemplifies a Christlike character, so that we can win souls for His kingdom. "Let your light so shine before men, that they may see your good works, and glorify your Father which is in heaven" (Matthew 5:16 KJV).

~ Wesley Mayes

Microwave Relationship

Being confident of this very thing, that He which hath begun a good work in you will perform it until the day of Jesus Christ. - Philippians 1:6 KJV

Imagine you are sitting on your couch, just chilling out after work. You're flipping through the TV channels, trying to find something worth watching. Suddenly, an advertisement catches your eye:

"Are you tired of trying to get your relationship with God on track? Are you tired of feeling like you'll never reach that perfect Christian experience? Well, the answer to all your problems is the new spiritual energy drink, Almighty! With Almighty you can drink your way to a personal relationship with Christ. It's instant, easy, and cheap! Simply mix two tablespoons of the powder with water or your favorite fruit juice. It's perfect for the car, the office, or school! Dial the number on your screen right now to order a quart of Almighty for only $19.99! And if you call within the next ten minutes, we'll throw in another half gallon of Almighty and our spiritual happy-mug, all for FREE! Take Almighty today, and you'll have spiritual vibes coming your way!"

To you and me this sounds utterly ridiculous! But in reality, it's not that far from the truth. We live in a microwave generation. We have instant noodles, instant messaging, texting, and e-mail. When we desire something, rather than waiting patiently, we want immediate results. I believe the devil uses this mindset as a trap. He trains us to expect our relationship with God to be formed as quickly as our instant rice, but it doesn't work that way. I think of how many times I have made a commitment to Christ at a conference or week of prayer and expected my spiritual walk to be perfect from then on. But when the spiritual high passes, I seem to lose interest. What you and I need to realize is that forming a relationship with God is the work of a lifetime, just like any other relationship. You don't become best friends with someone by spending time with them only sporadically, but by consistently investing meaningful time together. It's the same way with Christ. It takes unfailing daily devotion to build a strong relationship with God. Rather than depending on the latest quick fix to perfect your spiritual walk, go to THE ALMIGHTY. He has promised to complete the work He has begun in you.

~ Anneliese Wahlman

Heavy Laden

Turning from the ambitious, self-satisfied favorites of this world, He declared that those were blessed who, however great their need, would receive His light and love. To the poor in spirit, the sorrowing, the persecuted, He stretched out His arms, saying, "Come unto Me,...and I will give you rest." - Education, pp. 79, 80

"Diamonds can be found anywhere!" the young man exclaimed. "You just have to grab a shovel and start digging!"

"Hogwash!" His friend retorted, "It isn't possible."

"Oh yes, just look at the headlines of today's newspaper! It reads, 'MAN STRIKES IT RICH IN ACCIDENTAL DIAMOND FIND!' And I'm going to do the same; except it won't be accidental because I intend to spend my life looking for diamonds."

And that is exactly what he did. He sold his house, left his wife and kids, and set off with only the clothes on his back and a pocket full of money. His search took him to many strange and exotic places: the Orient, Europe, Africa, and even Antarctica; but to no avail, for he couldn't find even one diamond. "Maybe I'm just looking in the wrong places..." he mused. So he set off on another wild goose chase to Australia. Finally, after years of searching, when all of his money was used up, he had nothing to call his own besides his clothes and a feeling of abject failure. With nothing to live for, he decided to end his life by jumping off a bridge.

Proverbs 14:12 reads: "There is a way which seemeth right unto a man, but the end thereof are the ways of death" (KJV). This man is a good example of how many of us live our lives. We all have a longing inside of us, a longing for something that maybe we can't identify. We try to find something in this world that will satisfy that longing. It could be money, fame, relationships, or in this explorer's case, diamonds. Whatever it may be, we will never be completely satisfied until we ask God into our lives. His promise in Matthew 11:28 still stands: "Come unto me, all ye that labour and are heavy laden, and I will give you rest" (KJV).

~ Wesley Mayes

Ten Percent

Bring ye all the tithes into the storehouse, that there may be meat in Mine house, and prove Me now herewith, saith the Lord of hosts, if I will not open you the windows of heaven, and pour you out a blessing, that there shall not be room enough to receive it. - Malachi 3:10 KJV

When I was a young girl, my mother taught me the importance of paying tithe. She taught me to give God ten percent of my earnings and how to calculate it. As I contemplated this, I thought to myself, "Tithing is great for when I'm out of school and actually making an income, but for now, that doesn't really apply to me." But the truth is, it does. Maybe I don't have a steady income right now, but didn't God ask for ten percent of everything I have?

What about time? Of the hours I'm not sleeping, is having twenty minutes of devotional time and praying at meals really giving God ten percent of my day? Do I spend my time just doing what I need to do, or helping others? What about talents? Do I play my violin to gain personal praise, or do I play to draw others to God? What about thoughts? Are my sweetest and most frequent thoughts about Christ, or do I spend hours daydreaming?

Looking at it from this perspective, I haven't paid an honest tithe. I really owe God one hundred percent, but I don't even give Him the measly ten percent He's asked for! I need to make some changes in my life, so that I am paying an honest tithe, and maybe you do too. It may seem like a huge sacrifice, especially with our limited time, but God promises to open heaven's windows and pour overflowing blessings upon us! I'm going to give God His ten percent. Are you?

~ Rachel Petrello

Facing Temptation

To the secret place of the Most High, under the shadow of the Almighty, men now and then repair; they abide for a season, and the result is manifest in noble deeds; then their faith fails, the communion is interrupted, and the lifework marred. But the life of Jesus was a life of constant trust, sustained by continual communion; and His service for heaven and earth was without failure or faltering. - Education, pg. 80

Have you ever felt that, no matter how hard you try, you can't stop failing? I know I have. Temptations come my way, and I cave in under the pressure. Sometimes I even get discouraged and feel like giving up. What can I do to stop this pattern of failures? Where can I find the answers?

In my life, I have found that the more time I spend with Christ, the easier it is to resist temptation. Think about it: it's like a young boy and a cookie jar. Say, for instance, that the boy's father tells him he cannot eat a cookie between meals. He tries to resist the temptation, but those cookies look really tasty, and he figures that nobody will notice. So he still gives in and eats one. Now, what if the boy and his father started spending more time together, and grew in their relationship with each other. Would the boy still take a cookie? No; his love for his father would outweigh his desire for a cookie. The cookie would lose its appeal.

It's the same way with Christ. The more time we spend with Him, the closer we will grow and the less we will fall. We have to realize our total dependence upon God's grace and the strength we acquire from experiencing His love for us. Although it may be discouraging at times, always remember that no matter how many times you feel like giving up, Christ will never give up on you.

~ Wesley Mayes

Strong Enough

...The life of Jesus was a life of constant trust, sustained by continual communion... - Education, pg. 80

"Be still, and know that I am God..." (Psalm 46:10 KJV).

But it's too hard, God. There's too much to handle, too much on my mind, too much to worry about. I feel as if I'm drowning in it all.

"Be still..."

But God, I—

"Be still, and know that I AM God."

Okay God...I'm trying. But I need help, Lord.

"Do not be anxious about anything, but in everything, by prayer and petition, with thanksgiving, present your requests..."

How can I not be anxious? Too much to handle, too much–

"...And My peace...will guard your heart and your mind in Christ Jesus" (Philippians 4:6-7 personal paraphrase).

Wow God, I—I can't comprehend it all. I need to trust you, I know. All the time, continually, I need to rely on Your strength. Can you give me that, Lord? I'll give it all to You; just please, give me Your peace! I realize I need You—constantly—because every breath I breathe is Yours.

> For Your love never ceases to amaze
> The one for whom Your only Son You gave.
> I have nothing else to give You back,
> Except all myself, but it seems I lack
> The faith to truly trust in You.
> Just please, Lord, help me through.

Do you ever have so many worries and problems crashing down on you that you feel like you can't stand under the stress? I wrote the above verse a while ago, and God did help me through as I trusted and surrendered myself to Him. Only a constant trust in God can sustain you and me through the trials and difficulties we face every day. And in order to constantly trust God, we must continually commune with Him as our Best Friend who will always listen, our Father who will always understand, our God who is all-powerful—the only One who can make us strong enough to get through.

~ Valerie Jacobson

Jesus Will Help

He did not deal in abstract theories, but in that which is essential to the development of character; that which will enlarge man's capacity for knowing God, and increase his power to do good. - Education, pg. 81

Jesus "did not deal in abstract theories." Instead, He spoke of things which are real to us, things we are able to understand. Because He had no desire to confuse us, He used simple illustrations which are comprehensible to everyone. Jesus' words are perfectly applicable to each one of us right where we are.

When Jesus came as the most humble of all people, born into poverty and obscurity, He didn't intimidate anyone. God did not give Jesus any of the things we think of as making a person valuable, such as a good family name, wealth, education in an exclusive school, an important career, fame, or anything else we see as important. He did this so that none of us would feel as if we needed such things to come to God.

When Jesus spoke, His words had depth. They could keep the most brilliant person studying, growing, and learning; yet even the simplest and youngest child could understand His words. One of the most wonderful things about God is that He wants us to be His friends. He really wants to know us and be known by us—to have a tangible, concrete relationship with us. If you ever need help understanding Him or His Word, just ask Him; He is more than willing to help. In fact, He is eager for you to learn and comprehend more about Him. Don't ever doubt God's desire for you to grow and learn.

~ Danielle Schafer

Counterfeit

...What worse than folly is it to seek an education apart from Him—to seek to be wise apart from Wisdom; to be true while rejecting Truth; to seek illumination apart from the Light, and existence without the Life; to turn from the Fountain of living waters, and hew out broken cisterns, that can hold no water. - Education, pg. 83

This world is full of fakes: fake noses, fake tans, fake leather, fake love, fake everything! And it seems people are discovering more and more to falsify. Hardly anything is genuine; it's hard to find the real deal. But instead of crying for change, we turn a blind eye on these fraudulent practices and make excuses for our neglect. "It's not my problem," we reason, and leave it for someone else to deal with. But who will?

We are trying to get our education from the world, and it isn't teaching us right. You and I have been duped into believing other men's opinions, instead of searching things out and learning for ourselves. We are trying to be wise without God, and our plan isn't working too well. We even have a fake god, called Me, Myself, and I. We have been conned into believing that there is no "higher power" and that we all are our own "god." I have a question: can you or I create someone that will live? Medical technology is advanced, but not that far. We can't do anything without God, in our own strength, not even breathe.

God hasn't made His gifts hard to obtain. Wisdom, truth, light, life, and living water are His joy to bestow upon those who will ask. He has promised, "Ask, and it shall be given you..." (Matthew 7:7 KJV); it's as simple as that. Just ask Him and believe that He can and will do it, and it's yours. I'm so glad He made it that easy, because I know that I don't want to be foolish and fall for all those counterfeits.

~ Jo Holdal

Spiritual Sleepyheads

Whenever He [Jesus] spoke to the multitude, the disciples formed the inner circle. They pressed close beside Him, that they might lose nothing of His instruction. They were attentive listeners, eager to understand the truths they were to teach in all lands and to all ages.
- Education, pg. 85

"Wake up!" my Mom whispered. I groaned and opened my eyes. Instantly, I was awake—my Pastor was looking in my direction. My face turned red as I looked sheepishly at him. I glanced at my watch; it was almost 11:30. I'd been sleeping for over an hour! For the rest of the sermon, I tried to look like I had been wide-awake the whole time.

Church ended a lot sooner than normal that day, and when we got home my Dad commented, "Wasn't that a good sermon today?"

I gulped, "Uh, yeah. It—it was great." I tried to remember the sermon, but it was next to impossible since I had slept for over half of it. I had missed my spiritual food that week, and it left me with nothing to grow on.

Since I've been at Fountainview, my attention span has increased, and it's not just because the sermons are more directed towards my age group. I believe that it is because my growing relationship with Christ has directly affected my ability to pay attention in church. This growing in Christ is vital to each of our lives because we all need to have a better relationship with Him and be more in tune with His will for our lives.

I have discovered through my experiences that if I sleep and do not listen to God's instruction, I will not know where He is trying to lead me. I've realized that I need to be like the disciples, always eager to hear what God has to say about anything, even if it goes against my self-centered heart.

~ Daniel Glassford

July 2

One Tuning Fork

In order successfully to carry forward the work to which they had been called, these disciples, differing so widely in natural characteristics, in training, and in habits of life, needed to come into unity of feeling, thought, and action. This unity it was Christ's object to secure. - Education, pg. 86

In Social Studies class, the most common argument heard, by far, was one between Americans and Canadians. Each group claimed to be better than the other, determining not to be out-done by the other side. The discussions became quite heated sometimes. This is a prime example of disunity. When you decide that your country is better than another person's, this causes division.

Imagine tuning one hundred pianos to the same tuning fork. They are unified by being tuned, not to each other, but to one pitch—one standard, one guiding instrument that is used for all. So with one hundred people, each one looking to Christ, they become "tuned" to the same objective, the same thought. They become more closely connected to each other by looking to Christ than if they took their eyes off Christ and tried to focus on becoming unified by their own efforts.

The snowflake is one of nature's most fragile things; but when billions of them stick together, they can form almost impregnable barriers. A coal from a fire can stay warm for hours if it is placed in a pile with other hot coals; but, when isolated, it cools much more quickly. One Clydesdale horse can pull up to two tons by itself; two Clydesdales together can pull up to 24 tons. Let's see what God can do through us when we are united and in tune to Him.

~ Carmen Hartwell

The Key to Heaven

Peter, James, and John sought every opportunity of coming into close contact with their Master...Of all the Twelve their relationship to Him was closest. John could be satisfied only with a still nearer intimacy, and this he obtained. - Education, pg. 87

The moment that you wake up in the morning, all the inevitable hopes and issues of the new day surge towards you like a typhoon on a raging sea. And these overwhelming feelings can potentially create stress and unnecessary mental pressure throughout your day. But, instead of giving in to the innumerable anxieties ahead, our most prominent calling at the beginning of every day is to muffle these confusing perplexities and expose ourselves to the ever-present "still small voice" (1 Kings 19:12 KJV) through prayer and heavenly contemplation.

Prayer is our key to heaven. Without prayer and continual communion with God, our purpose in life would be unknown and an assurance of peace unattainable. I know that in my life, whenever I take the time to kneel down, speak to God, and surrender my life to him for that specific day, I am filled with a sense of security in God that is absent when I don't spend that quality time with Him. That time spent with God can result in a day of increased victory over temptation, of greater success instead of defeat.

The devil makes use of those who do not make use of prayer. When we disregard the power of prayer, we become careless and oblivious to the fact that we are straying from the right path. "The darkness of the evil one encloses those who neglect to pray. The whispered temptations of the enemy entice them to sin; and it is all because they do not make use of the privileges that God has given them in the divine appointment of prayer" (*Steps to Christ*, pg. 94).

In your life, make it a goal to have an allotted time cut out of your busy schedule to speak with God. Your daily relationship with God should thrive and deepen to a point of perfection, but that all depends on your spending time with Him.

~ Cyrus Guccione

Longing for Love

John's was a nature that longed for love, for sympathy and companionship. He pressed close to Jesus, sat by His side, leaned upon His breast...He [drank] in the divine light and life. In adoration and love he beheld the Saviour, until likeness to Christ and fellowship with Him became his one desire, and in his character was reflected the character of his Master. - Education, pg. 87

I am a very sensitive person. I like to be hugged, loved, and cared for. When I am sad, I want someone to be there to feel for and comfort me. I have longed so many times for someone to take the time to see my need and help me, to "read my thoughts" as it were and to "just know" when to come sympathize and comfort me. John, when he was feeling this way, went to Jesus. He pressed close to Him, finding healing for his soul. And little by little, as John the Beloved looked to, admired, and spent time with his Friend, Jesus, he longed to become more and more like Him. This became John's one desire, and he did begin to reflect ever more closely the character of his Jesus.

When the Bible calls John "the Beloved," the original meaning of the root word is "love that persists and never fails." Jesus didn't just love John, He loved him despite and through all his problems. John, though proud, presuming, and ambitious, was still loved by Christ. Jesus rebuked his selfishness, "disappointed his ambitions, tested his faith" (*Education*, pg. 87). But through it all, Jesus loved John and revealed to him what his heart was searching for—"the beauty of holiness, His own transforming love" (Ibid.).

In my heart, I'm beginning to see that this transforming love of Christ is what I am truly wanting in my life too. I want to have the beauty of Jesus' character shining from my heart. I want to be happy and content, resting in His unfailing love for me. I can have this rest by trusting in Jesus to help and heal me. I need to lean on Him for all my needs and go to Him when I have problems instead of going to my friends who often fail me. I need to go to Jesus, who will always be there to comfort and provide. If I just surrender myself to His love and let Him work in my life, then I will have peace and know that my soul is truly getting what it has longed for.

~ Yannika Stafford

The Way to Victory

So they [the disciples] went on, the crisis drawing nearer; they, boastful, contentious, in anticipation apportioning regal honors, and dreaming not of the cross. - Education, pg. 88

The disciples had been Jesus' companions for about three years. Out of His numerous followers, these twelve men were His closest friends—His family. They ate, slept, talked, traveled, and did everything together. But the entire time that these men were learning at the feet of their Master, their eyes were blinded to a truth of paramount importance. The disciples believed that the Messiah had come to earth to conquer the Romans and make Israel the superpower of the entire world. Now that the Savior was finally here, they spent much time dreaming of the day when He would establish an earthly kingdom. Visions of power, fame, and honor swirled in their minds. However, Christ had come not to establish an earthly empire. He came to prepare men to receive a heavenly empire. His mission was to bring men back to a state of perfect harmony with their Creator, to save them from sin's clutches, by sacrificing His own life on a cross.

When Christ died on the cross, He displayed the greatest, deepest, most infinite love the universe has ever seen. The darkest powers of selfishness and the truest powers of love were in hand-to-hand combat, but love came out the victor! Sadly though, Christ's hand-picked family of disciples didn't see the joy in this victory. Because the disciples had based their experience with Christ on the belief that He would reign as an earthly King, they were crushed when He died; all their hopes and dreams were gone. It seemed their Messiah had failed!

In the same way, if we don't base our Christian experience on the message of the cross we will fail in the end, and all hope will truly be gone. If our focus is only to look good in church, wear modest clothing, and eat the right food in order to appear holy and righteous, then all we have succeeded in doing is turning ourselves into an assembly of modern-day Pharisees. Diet, dress, and church attendance are very important, but if we don't have the cross of Christ in our hearts, all our efforts will be futile. The cross is the only foundation that will stand through this world to eternity.

~ Anneliese Wahlman

Become His Instrument

For them all, Peter's experience had a lesson...But as His hand had been outstretched to save when the waves were about to sweep over Peter, so did His love reach out for his rescue when the deep waters swept over his soul. - Education, pp. 88, 89

It was a foggy winter day in southern England. In a dark, cold alleyway, hunched beside a brick apartment building was an old blind man clutching a cheap violin. He was playing beneath the windows in the hope of getting someone to take pity on him and throw him a few coins. As he was playing, two well-dressed gentlemen came along, and one of them greeted him.

"This is a bad day, friend."

"It is a stormy day," the musician replied, "and the people just will not come out of doors, nor will they open their windows."

"Why don't you make them open them? Play so they will have to listen."

"I wish I could play well," the old fellow replied. Tenderly patting the musician on the shoulder, one of the gentlemen grasped the violin.

"Let me play it," he said.

As the gentleman started moving the bow across the cheap strings, music that seemed almost heavenly floated from the violin. People started to peek out from their frost-covered windows to see where the beautiful sounds were coming from. Excited children rushed out their doors to get a better view of this master. Soon coins were dropping down all over the cobblestone alley.

"Who is playing my violin?" the old man asked. "He must be a master."

"A master he is indeed," the other gentleman responded. "He is Paganini."

Under the influence of the Master, Jesus, Peter was changed into a lovely instrument for God. At first Peter did not want to be conducted by Christ, but his only hope was in Jesus.

You and I are just ordinary people. We don't look amazing on the outside and nobody may want to listen to us. But we have so much potential for making life-changing, inspiring "music." If we give ourselves to the Master, He can and will write amazing orchestrations for our lives. Won't you become His instrument?

~ Jessica Hall

The Angels' Song

His is a love that fails not nor forsakes. - Education, pg. 90

Could we with ink the ocean fill,
And were the skies of parchment made,
Were every stalk on earth a quill,
And every man a scribe by trade;
To write the love of God above
Would drain the ocean dry;
Nor could the scroll contain the whole,
Though stretched from sky to sky.

Oh, love of God, how rich and pure!
How measureless and strong!
It shall forevermore endure—
The saints' and angels' song.
- Frederick M. Lehman

I've had many friends throughout my life. Even though they have tried to be the best friends they can be, they still mess up, and I have gone through times when it seemed as if not one of them really desired to have a relationship with me.

I've never experienced that with God. I've never once wondered whether or not He truly loves me; I've always known that He does. Of course, I have felt as if He couldn't hear me or wasn't answering my questions. But, somehow I have always known that it was me getting between the two of us, never Him. I know I can trust His love, and you can too. No matter what the circumstances, never doubt His love, because that's just what He is—love.

I have never found such perfect words to describe God's love as the words of the old hymn above. God's love is beyond anything we can ever comprehend. It is so rich and pure and completely genuine. The last two lines of this hymn say that God's love is and always will be "the saints' and angels' song." That right there amazes me. God's love is so endless that we can sing about it for all eternity and still have more to say!

~ Danielle Schafer

188

Guiding the Tempted

Human beings, themselves given to evil, are prone to deal untenderly with the tempted and erring. They cannot read the heart, they know not its struggle and pain. Of the rebuke that is love, of the blow that wounds to heal, of the warning that speaks hope, they have need to learn. - Education, pg. 90

"Get off those stones!" the woman screamed, her arms flailing wildly at her 5-year-old daughter, who had been balancing on the bricks that edged the flower bed. I cringed as the mother hit her daughter upside the head and began to scold her. I lived across the street from this family in the suburbs of Anacortes, Washington. It didn't take me long to realize that I didn't like playing in the front yard, where I could often hear parents yelling at their children.

Now maybe that little girl had disobeyed her mother by standing on the bricks bordering the flower bed. But, was yelling the correct way to handle such a situation? Was it the proper way to discipline a child?

"Bold, aggressive, and self-confident, quick to perceive and forward to act, prompt in retaliation yet generous in forgiving, Peter often erred, and often received reproof" (*Education*, pg. 88). But Christ was patient and loving towards Peter and sought "to teach him humility, obedience, and trust" (Ibid.). Jesus dealt tenderly with this easily tempted soul and sought to fortify him in truth.

Do we deal likewise with our brethren, children, and others who are easily tempted or gone astray? Instead of belittling them in our own minds, we should remember that they are sons and daughters of God whom He loves as much as He loves us. They may simply need a loving reproof to guide them back into the way of truth.

The Bible tells us that "speaking the truth in love" is the only way to go about it (Ephesians 4:15 KJV). The key word here is love. You should not focus on finding the "speck in your neighbor's eye," and "not notice the log in your own eye" (Matthew 7:3 NRSV). Being aware of our own imperfections and Christ's compassion toward us equips us to guide our brethren in love.

~ Victoria West

189

Overhaul

A miracle of divine tenderness was Peter's transformation. It is a life lesson to all who seek to follow in the steps of the Master Teacher.
- Education, pg. 91

Peter, a fisherman with a temper and a disciple of Jesus, is the one apostle I can really relate to. I guess that's mainly because he wasn't perfect; he was far from it, in fact, yet he was accepted by Christ. Peter had some major issues: at one point, he acted like a coward and even denied knowing Jesus. However, he followed his Master and yearned for a transformation to take place in his life.

Today, I am striving to come to the understanding of just how much Christ has done for me. I am starting to realize that I must rely on God and God alone to bring about changes in me. The change from a city-oriented, mean girl with lots of attitude to the person I believe Christ would have me be is important and, in the end, is worth whatever I must give up. I may have to give up certain associations and maybe even popularity. Think about it, though: Peter walked away from his livelihood without a second thought. His work, family, friends, his very identity—he was willing to walk away from it all. That makes me wonder, if God came today to take me to Heaven, would I be ready and willing to give up all I have on Earth to follow Him?

I want to be prepared and eagerly awaiting His arrival. It takes more than just wanting though; you and I have to let Christ into our lives to clean us out. We actually have to take that step that will change our way of life forever and commence the journey to perfection in Christ. Do you want to travel that road? I know I do.

~ Jo Holdal

Accepted

Many waters cannot quench love, neither can the floods drown it...For love is strong as death. - Song of Solomon 8:6, 7 KJV

Lord, I walk down the road,
And what do I see?
So many people who are so much better than me!
They're all so talented; how can I ever compare?

God, why did you create me?
You gave life, so I could live.
I wonder why!
I'm a useless, broken sinner.
Your love is too amazing to be real.

I'm lost and worthless,
Broken beyond repair.
Perfect is what I strive to be!
But I've never experienced so many insecurities.

You sent your Son to die
For a wretch like me.
It's confusing—how could love set a person free?
Yet your voice is calling,
And I wonder if I too can be saved.

God! I really want to know why
You gave life, so I could live.
I'm lost and running farther;
Could your love ever reach out to me?

It's hard to believe, but I know it to be true.
I'm so glad that I have chosen You!
I asked, "Could your love reach out to me?"
You answered "Yes!"
And because of that I'm free.

~ Sarah Chang

Investing in God

Commit they way unto the lord; trust also in Him; and He shall bring it to pass. - Psalm 37:5 KJV

My grandparents, whom I call Mom Mom and Poppie, live in Florida, where everyone has countless problems with bugs. Worms crawl up the outside of the house, and there are termites and cockroaches galore. Poppie gave the "bug problem" to the Lord. Instead of paying a company to spray chemicals to get rid of the bugs, he prayed for the Lord's protection and placed the money that would have gone to the exterminators into the Investment Fund at church.

One day, while standing outside his door, Poppie looked up into the sky and saw a large swarm of termites flying directly toward his house. However, just before they reached his house, they turned 90 degrees and landed in the neighbor's yard.

Several years ago, my grandparents also put their van into God's hands by giving to Him the money that would have gone into fixing it. The van had several problems, but after giving money to the Investment Fund, the problems disappeared, and the van still works today. Each and every trouble that comes their way is surrendered to God, so that His will can be done.

My grandparents never seek to look years younger, receive a new car, or gain earthly riches. They simply put their concerns into God's hands and trust in His divine care. I want to have that same trust, that unwavering faith in God's power to take care of every trouble I'll ever have.

~ Megan Metcalf

Blessed Are Those at the Bottom

Blessed are the poor in spirit: for theirs is the kingdom of heaven.
- Matthew 5:3 KJV

> One night, on Guadalcanal, while leading a reconnaissance patrol, we were pinned down by sniper fire and in the ensuing melee, I was all alone, out in the middle of the jungle, not having the vaguest idea of my location...I have never been so scared, but you know what, I discovered the power of prayer at that moment, a power I never had to call upon before, but a power for which I had occasion to be grateful many times during the war, a power I have relied upon throughout my life since then.
>
> - Phillip L. Cochran

The above was written by a combat marine who was fighting in the Pacific Theater of World War II. After reading the marine's experience, I realized I have had very similar experiences. At times, I have been so distressed because I know that I can't continue pursuing a life led by me. I am reminded of Isaiah 64:6: "...And all our righteous acts are like filthy rags; we all shrivel up like a leaf, and like the wind our sins sweep us away" (NIV). It is at these times that I come before God realizing I can't do it anymore by myself; I need a savior.

What amazes me is that when I am in this state Christ blesses me. He proclaims, "Blessed are the poor in spirit..." (Matthew 5:3 KJV). I am a spiritually impoverished person. Just like the thief on the cross, I have come to realize my spiritual deficiency. And yet, Jesus promises me that the kingdom of heaven is mine because I realize I am a sinner in need of a savior. You, maybe, are like the marine under sniper fire, not knowing where you are; or perhaps you are like the thief nailed to the tree; or, most likely, you are like me, exhausted from trying to do everything your own way. Jesus offers hope, and it is always when we begin to think that hope doesn't even exist anymore that He reaches down His loving hand to pull us out of our despair.

~ Sarah-Kate Lingerfelt

Dear God

They saw their own weakness; they saw something of the greatness of the work committed to them; they felt their need of their Master's guidance at every step. - Education, pg. 94

Dear God,

Today was a rough day. It's just so hard not to let the little things bother me! I was reading the book *Do Hard Things*, and it made me feel really guilty. You see, I really didn't want to be at school today. I didn't want to hand any assignments in; I didn't want to work and be in charge of organizing music lessons, or talk to people on the phone. And I was sick and tired of having to deal with people's attitude problems! I just wanted to go home and go surfing! Well, after reading *Do Hard Things*, I realized that MY attitude was in need of a major adjustment.

In this book, the authors explained that teens aren't meeting their full potential because our world today has such low expectations for them. God, am I meeting YOUR expectations for me here at school?

Lord, forgive me. Forgive me for not greeting my trials with a cheery smile, for not seizing the opportunities that You generously place in my path. Forgive me for not rising to the occasion and surpassing what is expected of me. I realize now that everything has a purpose, and that I must strive to do hard things, even when I don't feel like it. I cannot, must not take the path of self-indulgence and give in to the desire to bum around on the beach, paint pictures all day, or read all the books I want.

Thank You for your gentle rebuke; I know that I have your reassurance that You have placed me here for a reason, and that I have a purpose to fulfill here. Help me to look at all the difficulties You give to me as opportunities, and may I always rely on You to give me the courage to face them. I know that You have great things in store for me, God, and that the little trials You send my way now are helping me to prepare for a bigger future. May I be faithful in the little things, so that I may be worthy of your greater plans for my life.

~ Sarah Chang

If a Sparrow Cannot Fall

They [the disciples] knew that His sympathies were with them still. They knew that they had a representative, an advocate, at the throne of God. - Education, pg. 95

The murmur of conversation rose in the chambers where the Constitutional Convention was being held in the early days of the American colonies. A session was being held to address some of the serious problems of the day. During the discussion, Benjamin Franklin arose and said, "Mr. Chairman, we have been groping about in the darkness for weeks, searching after political truth, and have not found it. The longer I live and the more I know, the more do I believe that God governs in the affairs of men; and if a sparrow cannot fall without His notice, it is probable that an empire cannot rise without His assistance." Benjamin Franklin knew that God was interested in their affairs, and if they asked for His help, He was sure to intervene.

When Jesus ascended from the Mount of Olives, He left the disciples behind with the assurance that He cared about them. They had a representative, someone who understood them, who had gone through the same trials and promised to give whatever they asked. "...Whatsoever ye shall ask the Father in My name, He will give it you" (John 16:23 KJV).

Sometimes it is easy for me to get stressed out over an important decision, a big test, or a hard situation, but the God who sees the sparrow fall certainly sees me as I muddle my way through hard circumstances. Yet He is personally interested in my problems and worries, and nothing ever escapes His notice. "...For He hath said, I will never leave thee, nor forsake thee. So that we may boldly say, The Lord is my helper, and I will not fear what man shall do unto me" (Hebrews 13:5, 6 KJV).

~ Anna Fink

The Holy Spirit

...Under the Spirit's teaching they [the disciples] received their final preparation and went forth to their lifework. - Education, pg. 95

Are you equipped to reach your friends and neighbors with the good news, or do you feel that you are not prepared to tell others about Christ? After three years of living with the world's greatest Teacher and learning how to evangelize, the disciples still needed one thing. They needed the Holy Spirit; and with Him, they reached the world.

The disciples were, as a whole, an uneducated group of common laborers. They were absorbed in competing with each other for the highest position. Their spiritual understanding was dim, and they even struggled to grasp some of the lessons Jesus plainly set before them.

However, everything changed during the days spent in Jerusalem after Christ's ascension. As the disciples confessed their sins and prayed for the Comforter, they became unified, allowing God to pour down the blessing He had promised. "No longer were their hopes set on worldly greatness. They were of 'one accord,' of one mind and one soul. Christ filled their thoughts. The advancement of His kingdom was their aim" (*Education*, pg. 95). Beginning at this time, the Holy Spirit's influence did amazing things through the disciples: "To every nation under heaven was the gospel carried in a single generation" (*Education*, pg. 96).

If we, in our time, are to reach the whole world with the good news of Jesus' soon return, we must have the Holy Spirit. He will bring things to our remembrance, helping us to clearly testify for Jesus (John 14:26). How do we receive Him? "...For the Holy Spirit... we may ask; then we are to believe that we receive, and return thanks to God that we have received...The gift is in the promise..." (*Education*, pg. 258). Ask God today for the blessing of the Spirit He has promised to bestow. And then, believing you have His Spirit, go share Jesus with someone else.

~ Kevin Corrigan

A Different Prayer

Ye are the light of the world. - Matthew 5:14 KJV

I love the moon. Growing up, my family and I would take special walks on the night of a full moon. We'd put on our jackets, slip on our walking shoes, and grab our flashlights, just in case we saw a wild animal like a screech owl, raccoon, or fox. We'd then head out the door for our relaxing walk up the road to the top of the mountain, enjoying the light of the moon and the time together. Crickets chirped in the grass and owls hooted to each other from tree to tree, even answering my dad when he mimicked their call. We'd look up into the sky at the billions of stars, often glimpsing a shooting star or two. I loved looking at the moon, inquiring of my parents what the dark spots were and how it could shine so brightly. They explained that the only way the moon can have light is by reflecting the sun's rays. The moon has no light of its own, yet by the power of the sun, it gives us light in the darkness.

This is also true in the Christian walk. We have absolutely no light within us, but Christ, the Giver of light, will shine through us so that we can give hope to every dark corner of the world. Throughout my life, I often pray to God to make me a witness to someone that I meet each day, whether it's a person I see a lot, or someone I'll never see again. But, God has shown me recently that my prayers are in the wrong direction. Instead of praying to be a witness, I should pray for Christ to fill my life with His love. "If Christ is dwelling in the heart, it is impossible to conceal the light of His presence" (*Thoughts from the Mount of Blessing*, pg. 41). When His vital power is in me, I am automatically a light to the world. I have no need to question whether I'm a witness or not. God's divine love overflowing from my heart will be a glimpse of heaven to the person living in this darkened world.

~ Megan Metcalf

Team Effort

They helped every one his neighbour; and every one said to his brother, Be of good courage. - Isaiah 41:6 KJV

"Over here! I'm open!" Shrieks and shouts fill the air as the soccer game gets under way. I just love soccer, whether I'm playing or watching. One reason I like soccer so much is because it's a group effort, and you have to work with others if you want to have the most fun. You could run around the field and kick a ball by yourself, but that gets old fast. With other friends, a game could go on for hours, or until you're all too tired to keep playing.

You know, our Christian walk is kind of like a soccer game. There are two teams, and those on your team are all for helping you out. We go through struggles; we may even fall sometimes, but our teammates are there with outstretched hands to help us get back up. We work together to make sure we keep safe and have fun.

There are so many events in the Bible that would not have happened if it weren't for teamwork. Take, for example, the building of the Tabernacle, which the people united to accomplish; or the re-building of the wall of Jerusalem, completed by a group of newly released captives who worked together with purpose. These biblical examples illustrate the importance of co-operation.

We need to lift up those around us, not tear them down, and by working together we can do it. If we can realize that we're on the same team and have the same goal in mind, we can accomplish greater things. You and I just need to decide to join the team. And really, it's much better to work together than it is to play the game alone.

~ Jo Holdal

Did You Ever Think?

Then was there such a revelation of the glory of Christ as had never before been witnessed by mortal man. Multitudes who had reviled His name and despised His power confessed themselves disciples of the Crucified. - Education, pg. 95

Did you ever think what this world would be
If Christ hadn't come to save it?
His hands and feet were nailed to the tree,
And His precious life—He gave it.
But countless hearts would break with grief,
At the hopeless life they were given,
If God had not sent the world relief,
If Jesus had stayed in heaven.

Did you ever think what this world would be
With never a life hereafter?
Despair in the faces of all we'd see,
And sobbing instead of laughter.
In vain is beauty, and flowers' bloom,
To remove the heart's dejection,
Since all would drift to a yawning tomb,
With never a resurrection...

...Did you ever think what this world would be
If Christ had stayed in heaven—
No home in bliss, no soul set free,
No life, or sins forgiven?
But He came with a heart of tenderest love,
And now from on high He sees us,
And mercy comes from the throne on high;
Thank God for the gift of Jesus!
- *Choice Readings for the Home Circle*, pg. 279

After our fall in the Garden of Eden, we deserved to die. Our sinful behavior warranted immediate punishment, but God had another plan. His only Son would come and live a life of servitude, showing us that although there is sin in this world, it can be overcome through Christ. He wants to help you overcome your sin. Won't you let Him?

~ Wesley Mayes

What's Lacking?

Then was there such a revelation of the glory of Christ as had never before been witnessed by mortal man. Multitudes who had reviled His name and despised His power confessed themselves disciples of the Crucified. Through the co-operation of the divine Spirit the labors of the humble men whom Christ had chosen stirred the world. To every nation under heaven was the gospel carried in a single generation. The same Spirit that in His stead was sent to be the instructor of His first co-workers, Christ has commissioned to be the instructor of His co-workers today...The presence of the same guide in educational work today will produce the same results as of old. - Education, pp. 95, 96

It seems the passion and determination which the disciples possessed is lacking in the world today. Why is this? The promise of Jesus to send us the Holy Spirit is still valid for us now. We could possess the same power which was given to the disciples. What are we lacking? James 4:2 says, "...Ye have not, because ye ask not" (KJV).

I believe that it is our failure to earnestly and persistently request the outpouring of the Holy Spirit that is lacking. God wants to send this gift to us, but most of us have become so caught up in our busy lives that few are left who continue to truly ask for it.

Twelve men, filled with the Holy Spirit, were able to carry the message of a risen Savior to every nation under heaven. Doesn't it make you excited to think that you could do the same?

Why don't we pray earnestly for the Holy Spirit to pour out His power on us so that we will be able to carry the gospel of a coming Savior to the world. I believe it won't be long until we see our Lord returning in the clouds to take us home.

~ Laura Williams

Simply Ask Him

If any of you lack wisdom, let him ask of God, that giveth to all men liberally, ...and it shall be given him. - James 1:5 KJV

Torn were his clothes,
empty his hands,
Chilled to his toes,
no longer able to withstand;
Walking backwards to and fro,
lost in a blizzard,
His body shuddered in the snow.
"Nobody seems to notice
or care if I fall.
Could they really be that heartless,
consider me so small?"
Towards him came a man
with a smile on his face.
"What you need is wisdom
and a little of God's grace."
He knelt down beside him,
reached for his cold hands.
The sky no longer dim,
the road, a whole new land.
"You simply need to pray;
ask for a blessing;
God will show you the way.
His love is always pressing."
the man's tears were gone.
A smile came over his face
like the breaking of dawn
When the sky is filled with lace.
"He's done it for me,
and He'll do it for you.
He'll make you free;
There's just one thing you've got to do...
ask."

~ Danielle Schafer

Professor Nature

To him who learns thus to interpret its teachings, all nature becomes illuminated; the world is a lesson book, life a school. The unity of man with nature and with God...cannot fail of impressing the mind and molding the character. - Education, pg. 100

Come forth into the light of things, let nature be your teacher.
- William Wordsworth

One bright spring day, I was sitting on the porch, listening in silence for God to speak to me. As I patiently waited for the Holy Spirit to take over my thoughts, I soon realized that God wanted to speak to me through nature, His masterpiece. I scanned the horizon and the fresh landscape surrounding me, looking for practical life lessons that God could use to educate me.

First, I noticed the trees, lush with verdure and budding fruits of the season. They stood straight and tall, with branches reaching out far from the mother trunk. I thought of how God wants me to be like a tree "planted by the rivers of water, that bringeth forth his fruit in his season; his leaf also shall not wither; and whatsoever he doeth shall prosper" (Psalms 1:3 KJV). Then I considered the mountains. They stood higher than anything in view except the gold-bordered clouds. They reminded me of what I had learned in my devotions some morning before—to think not of this world, but of heavenly things, and to set my expectations higher than this world's standards. And then the rolling clouds, moving ever so slowly across the dimming sky revealed to me my need to have a definite aim in life and to move confidently in the direction of God's will. He then pointed out to me the man-made things: the roads and trails that make our journeys more convenient and the buildings that provide us with warmth and shelter. These exemplified the talents and skills given to each one of His children to use for His glory.

God is a God of beauty, and what He has done in nature gives education a whole new meaning. His motive in creating nature was to silently testify of His character; and we will be able to find Him in anything, if we but allow God's gentle Holy Spirit to enter our lives every day.

~ Cyrus Guccione

Nature and You

The unity of man with nature and with God, the universal dominion of law, the results of transgression, cannot fail of impressing the mind and molding the character. - Education, pg. 100

In the fall of 2008, my school planned a backpacking trip up Mt. Askom. Since it was my first chance ever to go backpacking, I decided that I wanted to go. We left on Friday and started our long, steep hike. It took me a while to make it to the top, but I persevered and made it just before sundown.

The next day, I asked if I could start out early, so that I could make it to Lake Askom in time for lunch. One of the staff gave me permission, and I was off down the other side of the mountain in the direction of the lake. However, I couldn't see where camp was. I decided to trudge into the woods, every turn expecting to see the lake; but no lake appeared. I thought it was strange that I could have missed such a large lake. I paused to breathe in the beauty of what I had been walking through for the past hour and quickly became aware of how enormously complex the universe around me was. I observed the detail in just one leaf and the beauty in the crystal-clear creek that was running beside me. When I looked up into the sky, I saw the mountain I had just descended and realized how insignificantly small I was in comparison. This brought me back to a verse that I had read in my devotions a few days earlier: "Be still, and know that I am God...I will be exalted in the earth" (Psalm 46:10 KJV). I felt a connection with my Creator that I had never felt before. A whole new world was brought into view, and I felt a great appreciation and love for my God. Suddenly, I had an inspiration that if I followed the creek upstream, I would discover the lake. As I turned to continue my hike, I saw the lake in the distance and soon reached my destination.

Spending time in nature has helped me to realize how inadequate and deficient I am without God. When I was lost in the wilderness, He gave me the idea to hike upstream after my observation of His creation. If you're ever struggling with something, I encourage you to turn to God, and He will see you through.

~ Daniel Glassford

Lessons from Nature

To him who learns thus to interpret its teachings, all nature becomes illuminated; the world is a lesson book, life a school. - Education, pg. 100

One day in PE class, our teacher decided to lead us in a game of follow-the-leader. Coming to the base of what looked like a mountain (though I'm sure it was no more than a hill), we began to climb. After a while, I began to wonder when we were going to come to the top. Over and over I thought I could see the top, only to find that it just kept going up. After this had happened four or five times, I was beginning to feel slightly discouraged. But each time, I seemed to have just enough strength to make it to the top of the next hill. And when we finally reached the top, and I looked out over the incredible view, I decided that every step had been worth the workout.

While climbing (or sliding) back down the hill, I began to ponder how this climb was a lot like life. Our lives can be filled with trials and troubles, making it appear as if we will never come to the end of them. But when we reach heaven and are looking back over the events of our lives, we will see that each trial built and strengthened our characters, preparing us for our final reward. We will quickly realize that heaven was indeed cheap enough.

What wonderful lessons nature teaches us! God's fingerprints can be found throughout it, from the smallest plant to the tallest mountain, each one pointing out how much He loves us.

~ Laura Williams

Topiary Testimonies

...Nature presents an unfailing source of instruction and delight. The heart not yet hardened by contact with evil is quick to recognize the Presence that pervades all created things. The ear as yet undulled by the world's clamor is attentive to the Voice that speaks through nature's utterances. - Education, pg. 100

Topiary is a type of garden art where shapes are created with shrubs and small trees. Shrubs like the boxwood, yew, privet, and ivy are most commonly used. When the plant is very young, wires, sticks, string, and clippers are used to mold the plant into the desired shape. This creates beautiful garden art. However, the plant must be trained from a young age. If someone tried to make a shape out of a shrub that was already fully grown, the branches would snap.

There is a lesson in this for us. We are like these shrubs. When we are young, our minds are soft and pliable, and we can quickly recognize the presence of God in nature. Our ears are better tuned to listen to God's voice.

On the other hand, does this mean there is no hope for older people who have become set in their ways, the stiff branches of old habits that refuse to bend? No! Jesus says, "...Him that cometh to Me I will in no wise cast out" (John 6:37 KJV). He gives all an open invitation to let our minds be shaped for His glory and honor. This transformation can be best accomplished through contact with nature. Its beauties give us a place to study and relax, but most of all, to learn of Him.

~ Anna Fink

The Painter's Message

Let him behold the glorious scenes painted by the great Master Artist upon the shifting canvas of the heavens, let him become acquainted with the wonders of earth and sea, let him watch the unfolding mysteries of the changing seasons, and, in all His works, learn of the Creator. - Education, pg. 101

Why does a painter paint? Sometimes he paints to tell a story. Sometimes to express his great joy or deep sorrow. Sometimes he wants to show you the world from his point of view, or simply to express the breathtaking beauty of nature. No matter the painting, all painters—from the youngest child to the professional artist—have a specific message they want to get across through their painting.

Did you know that God paints too? Look at the majesty of the snow-capped mountains, the colorful autumn forest, the dew sparkling on the grass, the singing birds and opening blossoms, the beauty of a sunset, the starry night sky, and the loveliness of the flowers. God has a message He wants to get across to you, and upon the canvas of nature, He paints it: I love you!

Have you ever found a heart shaped rock? Do you love the quiet calm of a mountain stream, or the thundering waves of the ocean? What kind of flowers make you stop and smile? He made them just for you! Everywhere in nature, God has painted His love for you! So, the next time you take a walk, look and see if you can find "love notes" that were meant just for you!

~ Rachel Petrello

To Give Is to Live

*All things both in heaven and in earth declare that the great law of life
is a law of service...The birds of the air, the beasts of the field, the
trees of the forest, the leaves, the grass, and the flowers, the sun in the
heavens and the stars of light—all have their ministry. Lake and
ocean, river and water spring—each takes to give. - Education,
pg. 103*

The great violinist Niccolo Paganini willed his marvelous violin to
Genoa, the city of his birth, but only on the condition that the
instrument never be played. This was an unfortunate condition
because it is a peculiarity of wood that as long as it is used and
handled, it shows little wear. As soon as it is neglected, it begins to
decay. The exquisite, mellow-toned violin has become worm-eaten in
it's beautiful case, valueless except as a relic.

Just like this violin, our purpose for living should be to help, bless,
and serve others. But, when we live for ourselves and withdraw from
service to others, our lives lose their meaning and purpose.

Sometimes, I feel that if I go out of my way to help someone with a
serious problem, or spend some time with a friend when she needs to
talk, then I will not have the time *I* need to get everything done that *I*
need to do. However, I have found that whenever I have taken the
time to help someone else, I have ended up coming away from it with
a huge blessing.

Living a life of service to others will never leave you with a feeling
of dissatisfaction. You will make others around you happier, and I can
guarantee that you will be happier too.

~ Laura Williams

Seeds

Of the almost innumerable lessons taught in the varied processes of growth, some of the most precious are conveyed in the Saviour's parable of the growing seed. It has lessons for old and young.
- Education, pg. 104

Seeds are the essence of life and growth. From their humble environments, they portray hope, endurance, and patience in their truest forms. Illustration after illustration uses the example of the lowly seed to clearly present the lessons being taught. Even Jesus, the greatest teacher of all time, used seeds in His parables to reflect the lessons and character traits He was trying so hard to teach to His disciples.

Seeds start out small and are totally dependent upon sunlight, water, and air. In the same way, we are dependent on God's grace, compassion, and love. We cannot truly grow or mature without God's innumerable blessings. Seeds start out as insignificant, seemingly empty shells, and only grow because they do not try to draw their strength from themselves. They develop vast networks of roots and branches to receive their strength from the earth, sun, and atmosphere. Similarly, we cannot grow or mature if we try to draw our strength from ourselves. To truly grow, we must draw our strength from the promises in God's Word. The most beautiful plants are the ones that require the most care. Without proper care, they would soon wither and die. If we are not willing to receive God's blessings, we will become dry, withering Christians with little hope for improvement or life. God is the source of our strength and growth. Without Him we will never be truly alive.

Seeds are the ultimate examples of higher education. When a plant reaches its full potential, it enriches the soil around it, provides oxygen for animals, and shelters younger plants. God wants us to reach our full potential, so we will share His blessings with others around us. A comprehensive education is an education received from Christ. With His help, we can grow from small, empty seeds into empowered, fruitful Christians. He wants to educate, strengthen, and empower you. All you have to do is let Him.

~ Wesley Donesky

The Farmer and His Seed

There is life in the seed, there is power in the soil; but unless infinite power is exercised day and night, the seed will yield no return.
- Education, pg. 104

Every spring thousands of farmers make an investment in seeds so that when harvest time arrives, they will have a bountiful return. Our world is dependent on these farmers and their seeds. Unfortunately, though, many people never see the results of this harvest on their dinner plates. Millions in our world are starving, and food shortages have become a major concern for the leaders of many nations.

Two thousand years ago, a Farmer made an investment in billions of tiny seeds. He knew they had great potential if they chose to grow. That Farmer was Jesus Christ, and you are one of the seeds He has invested in. Jesus knows that you can grow and feed the billions of spiritually starving people in the world.

Christ doesn't want any Christian to dry out into an ugly shell, suppressed by grief and discouragement. Through His strength, we can rise above circumstances and shoot past dirty trials. If we only accept God's calling to acquire the rays of light beaming down from His Son, Jesus Christ, we will burst forth and bear fruit.

"Truly, truly, I say to you, unless a grain of wheat falls into the earth and dies, it remains alone; but if it dies, it bears much fruit" (John 12:24 ESV). Today, our world is experiencing a spiritual famine, and as Christians, we are called to revive humanity. If, like Christ, we are prepared to take up our cross and die, we will, like the buried seed, be able to produce fruit that will last for eternity. If we take the opportunity the Farmer has given us, we will bear fruit and flourish in the grace of the cross.

~ Sarah-Kate Lingerfelt

A Pot of Dirt

For a time the good seed may lie unnoticed in the heart, giving no evidence that it has taken root; but afterward, as the Spirit of God breathes on the soul, the hidden seed springs up, and at last brings forth fruit. - Education, pg. 105

Once there was an old king who needed to appoint an heir to take the throne after his death. Since he had no sons, he summoned all the young men of the land to the palace. When they arrived, the king placed a pot full of dirt in front of each of them, and proceeded to say, "In each of your pots of dirt is a seed. I want you to take that pot back to your house and care for that seed. Water it, give it sunlight, and when the time is right, I will summon all of you back to the palace." With this, he dismissed them to their homes.

One little boy watered his seed and set it in the sunlight. Two weeks went by, and his seed did not sprout. No matter what he did, no green appeared in the dirt. He faithfully obeyed the king's instructions.

After a time, all the young men were called back to the palace. When the little boy entered with his pot of dirt, he hid in the back row because all the other young men had gorgeous flowering plants. The king entered and began examining the plants. Each young man tried to make his plant more noticeable to the king, hoping that he would be chosen as heir to the throne. When the king had finished his examination, he called out, "You, the boy in the back with the empty pot, come here." The boy, puzzled and embarrassed, shuffled to the front with his bare pot. The king's eyes lit up as he looked at the boy and declared, "Behold, your future king!" A confused rumble went through the crowd. The king continued, "You see, I gave you all boiled seeds that would not grow, but you all came back with plants of your own creation. This boy, on the other hand, did just what I told him to do: he faithfully cared for the seed I gave him and did not exchange it for another."

Sometimes you and I might feel like the little boy in the back row with nothing but a bare pot of dirt to present to God. However, He wants us to come to Him just as we are. God will exchange our dead seed for His fruitful seed of life.

~ Daniel Glassford

210

Imperceptible Development

The germination of the seed represents the beginning of spiritual life, and the development of the plant is a figure of the development of character. - Education, pg. 105

The Chinese bamboo tree follows a unique pattern in its growth. In the first year after it is planted, it shoots above the ground to a towering height of two inches. In the second year, it's still two inches tall. The next year, and the next, and the next are the same. Though there appears to be no progress, the farmers keep fertilizing and watering the tree. Finally, in the sixth year, the tree that was once only a couple of inches high shoots into the air to a sky-scraping height of fifty feet! You might be asking, "What was happening to the little bamboo tree during the first five years of its growth?" It was putting down roots—strong, sturdy roots, so that it could stand when it became a tall, towering tree.

Many times in our own Christian experience we become discouraged because we feel that we aren't growing in our character. We feel, like the bamboo, about two inches tall spiritually. But what we don't realize is that many times we are blind to our own growth. Imagine a little child. He comes to his mother one day and asks her to measure his height. The very next day he asks to be measured again, but of course, there is no difference from the day before. Does that mean there is no development, that the child's body has quit functioning? Of course not! Just like that child, we can't always see our growth, but God can.

Today, why don't you ask God to give you glasses to see things the way He does? Trust that, though you may appear to be just like the bamboo tree at present, small and weak, He sees your progress and continues to give you spiritual nourishment to help you develop strong, tough roots that run deep into the soil of His love.

~ Anneliese Wahlman

Seeds of Patience

The work of the sower is a work of faith. The mystery of the germination and growth of the seed he cannon understand; but he has confidence in the agencies by which God causes vegetation to flourish. - Education, pg. 105

Once there was a young girl who loved to plant flowers in a small garden near her home. Day after day, she would carefully nurture and care for her precious plants. Her father, seeing that his daughter enjoyed gardening, bought her some special seeds to plant in her garden. The little girl excitedly planted and began to water the seeds. But after several days, the girl noticed that the seeds had not sprouted as quickly as her other plants had. The little girl was bewildered, but day after day she still faithfully took care of her garden. As more time passed, the girl started to become discouraged. Finally, when the third week had come and gone, she felt ready to give up and start over. Just as she was about to dig up the seeds, she noticed a small green sprout poking its head above the soil. Eagerly, with new anticipation and excitement, she cared for the small plant. Soon more sprouts appeared and grew higher and higher until they were the tallest and most beautiful flowers in the whole garden.

In Luke 8, Jesus tells a parable about a farmer who was planting seeds in his field. Some seeds fell on unsuitable ground, but some fell on good ground which caused them to spring up and produce a hundred times more than what was sown. Just like that farmer, we are also sowing seeds. You choose with every word and action whether the seeds you sow will grow joy and happiness, or pain and misery. When you choose to help or encourage another person, you are sowing a seed that will one day blossom into a tall and beautiful flower. But even if your smiles and words of encouragement don't seem to bring immediate results, be persistent. Don't give up. Just like the girl, you will eventually see changes in your life and in the lives of others if you let God work through you.

~ Wesley Donesky

Perfection is a Promise

At every stage of development our life may be perfect; yet if God's purpose for us is fulfilled, there will be constant advancement.
- Education, pg. 106

In Matthew 5:48 Jesus says, "Therefore you shall be perfect, just as your Father in heaven is perfect" (NKJV). I've asked myself before, how can God expect a sinful human race to become as perfect as He is? He never makes mistakes or sins, yet someone with a sinful nature like mine will be perfected before Jesus' second coming?

God created Adam and Eve in His image, endowed with high mental and spiritual powers, flawless beauty and upright stature, to be the crowning act of the creation of this world. No shadow was found between man and his Creator, no imperfection existed in their relationship. Every day, every moment was teeming with divine instruction imparted in direct communion with God Himself. Adam and Eve were created in a perfect state, but were also constantly growing and maturing in their knowledge of spiritual things and were meant to continue growing throughout eternity.

God promises to make us perfect in His sight if we repent of our sins and claim Christ's free gift of His righteousness as our own. If continue to repent and surrender to Christ as He leads, we can be perfect at each stage of spiritual growth. And we will continue growing throughout eternity. "Moral and spiritual perfection, through the grace and power of Christ, is promised to all" (*Acts of the Apostles*, pg. 478). Complete victory is obtained, not through our own success, but through God's assurance and power.

~ Megan Metcalf

213

The Wind

As the plant receives the sunshine, the dew, and the rain, so are we to receive the Holy Spirit. If our hearts are stayed upon Christ, He will come unto us... - Education, pg. 106

Imagine yourself standing in a field of tall grass. The sun is low on the horizon, making the blades surrounding you glow like pure gold. There is a stillness in the air that makes you feel drowsy and dreamy, and as you slowly gaze about, you feel like closing your eyes and sleeping. To your left a tall, spreading oak tree casts a long shadow away from the sun, and you stare in fascination at the silver-green hue of its leaves. All of a sudden, you see the leaves tremble as if in anticipation of something. The grass begins to sway silently, and a leaf flutters slowly to the ground. Suddenly, a great gust of wind rushes down through the branches like a gale on the sea. The grass is blown into solid green waves, and you take a step back in an effort to keep your balance. The cool blast seems to awaken all of nature, and the contrast startles you. Birds begin to sing, and the sky is painted purple as the sun begins to set in the west. Fireflies start to appear, adding their ethereal light to the ambiance of dusk.

There have been so many times in my life when I have felt spiritually drowsy. I'll forget to have my devotions, or I'll get caught up in school work and become distracted. Without the Holy Spirit in my life, it is impossible to stay focused. But, all I have to do is ask for Him, and He comes rushing in like the wind, blowing out all of the apathetic thoughts and feelings and filling me again with life. He can do that for you too. Why don't you ask Him today?

"And suddenly there came a sound from heaven as of a rushing mighty wind, and it filled all the house where they were sitting...And they were all filled with the Holy Ghost..." (Acts 2:2, 4 KJV).

~ Wesley Mayes

Sweet Childhood

Children should not be forced into a precocious maturity, but as long as possible should retain the freshness and grace of their early years. The more quiet and simple the life of the child—the more free from artificial excitement and the more in harmony with nature—the more favorable it is to physical and mental vigor and to spiritual strength.
- Education, pg. 107

One day while walking in the mall, I saw a group of young girls. They couldn't have been more than 10 or 11 years old. They had linked arms and were texting, giggling, and chatting, sporting flat-ironed hair, made-up faces, skin-tight jeans, and designer purses.

I have seen many young children being rushed into growing up too soon. They are pressured by pop culture and their peers to start wearing makeup, get boyfriends and girlfriends, and just begin teenage life much earlier than necessary. Children should enjoy their childhood and not be forced to grow up too quickly. Unnatural excitement from sources such as television, video games, and cell phones cause children to rush into their adult lives of stress, the stimulated highs of electronics, and the complications of relationships.

Children should be raised in nature and taught to see lessons in their simple, carefree lives. They will be less stressed and more drawn to God in these peaceful circumstances. These children will grow up to be strong, healthy, and balanced, ready to face whatever life throws at them with serenity and trust in God.

I remember when I was younger that I really, really wanted to grow up fast! I saw what fun things the older kids and adults were allowed to do: drive, stay up late, and not have anyone telling them what to do. But children, enjoy these sweet years of your life! Yes, growing up is enjoyable and necessary, too, but nothing can compare to those sweet, innocent childhood years when you can play all day without a care in the world. Be happy at whatever stage you find yourself. "Not that I speak in respect of want: for I have learned, in whatsoever state I am, therewith to be content" (Philippians 4:11 KJV).

~ Victoria West

215

Too Late

...Too often His gifts are perverted to selfish uses and made a curse instead of a blessing. God is seeking to change all this. He desires...that His gifts may be to us the blessing that He intended.
- Education, pg. 108

It was almost one in the morning when the phone rang in the Winters's home. Dr. Leo Winters, the highly acclaimed Chicago surgeon, woke with a start. The call was about a young boy who had been tragically mangled in a late-night accident. Couldn't someone else handle it? Not this time. His hands were possibly the only ones in the city, or maybe even the whole region, that were skilled enough to save this life.

The quickest route happened to be through a rather rough area, but with time being a critical factor, it was worth the risk. Then, at a stop light, his door was jerked open by a man in a gray hat and a dirty flannel shirt. "I've got to have your car!" the man screamed, pulling the doctor from his seat. He tried to explain the gravity of his situation, but the man was not listening and sped away. After the doctor wandered around for over forty-five minutes looking for a phone, he finally found a taxi to take him to the hospital. An hour had already passed. He burst through the doors and into the nurses' station, but the nurse on duty only shook her head—too late. The boy had died about thirty minutes earlier. "His dad got here just before he died," the nurse told him. "He is in the chapel. Go see him. He is awfully confused. He couldn't understand why you never came."

Without explaining, Dr. Winters hurried down the hall and entered the chapel. At the front knelt the huddled form of a weeping father, in a gray hat and dirty flannel shirt. Tragically, he had pushed from his life the only one who could have saved the life of his son!

Jesus died for us, but we can never seem to accept this gift. We rush around trying to work out our own salvation, busy, busy, busy, and fail to realize that we are pushing away the only One who can give us what we are looking for. Jesus wants to give us the free gift of His salvation, and the only thing we have to do is accept it and use it as the blessing that He intended.

~ Anna Fink

Seeing in the Dark

By your words I can see where I am going; they throw a beam of light on my dark path. - Psalm 119:105 The Message

As the early morning sunshine hit my face, I popped out of bed and immediately made a mad dash for the nearest window. I peered out in amazement at the new sights, sounds, and smells. I was on my first mission trip, and I had never seen such an impoverished place before. For me, one view was not enough; I was itching to see more. I quickly put on a pair of jeans and bolted out of my hotel room for the closest veranda. As I scrutinized my surroundings, I noticed something lying on the street. Wondering what it could possibly be, I zoomed in on it with my camera. To my horror, I saw a child sleeping on the sidewalk without a blanket as locals strolled by, not seeming to notice the boy who lay where their bustling feet trod. I wanted so badly to go out and work with the street kids, to feed them and give them clothes.

During the course of the day, I sneaked out of my hotel and onto the street. There the street kids entertained me by making small animals out of little reeds. Finally, my dad called me into the hotel and told me to pack my bags because we were leaving for another hotel in a safer district. As I put my belongings on a truck, a flood of emotions rolled over me; I didn't want to leave. But as we left, our driver told us we had been staying in a very dangerous section of town; shootings were frequent, and the street children whom I had given money to, hoping to fill their hunger, really wanted drugs. Prostitutes also strolled the street until the early morning hours, and homosexuals gathered. The driver's words showed me the danger of where I had been that day. I was shocked to think that I had been so captivated by my new surroundings that I was blind to their true nature.

Sin works the exact same way: it enthralls our minds, evoking feelings of self-confidence, and we become less aware of right and wrong. Unless our lives are founded on the principles of the Bible, sin will lead us farther and farther from the safeguard of right-doing. When we come to the understanding of what is right, we look back at our old ways as repulsive and nauseating to our consciences. It is a frightful thought to think of the many times we have played on the devil's playground.

~ Sarah-Kate Lingerfelt

217

Fair Trade?

For what shall it profit a man, if he shall gain the whole world, and lose his own soul? Or what shall a man give in exchange for his soul? - Mark 8:36, 37 KJV

Esau had been gone on one of his frequent hunting trips, and this one had lasted a bit longer than usual. He hadn't eaten in several days and felt as if he would die of starvation any minute. Finally, he came to the open field that was on the edge of his father's farm. He thought of his birthright. When his father died, he would gain the larger portion of the inheritance because, even though he was a twin, he was the firstborn.

As he straggled through the field, he spotted his brother, Jacob, with a pot over a fire. He suspected that the pot was filled with food because Jacob often liked to cook in his spare time. Esau had always made fun of him for liking "women's work," cooking and such, but at this moment he couldn't be more thrilled at the sight of Jacob with a pot of soup. With renewed vigor, he continued over to where Jacob sat and implored his brother, "Please, I haven't eaten in days; please give me some of your soup! If I don't eat now, I fear I may die before I reach home!"

Jacob peered back down into his own bowl and thought for a moment. When he looked up again, he smiled and replied, "I don't know. It's going to cost you."

"Anything, anything! What use is anything I have to me if I am dead from hunger?"

"I want your birthright blessing," Jacob said decidedly.

"Take it! Just let me eat, or I will drop right here."

Jacob smiled. "Good. You may have some soup."

When you think of it, this was an exceedingly foolhardy transaction. But how many times do we ourselves trade things like our honesty, integrity, or purity for worthless pleasures that last for a few moments and then are gone? Next time you are tempted to trade for something temporal, think of the eternal worth of what you are giving up.

~ Carmen Hartwell

Be That Friend

So widespread may be the influence of a single life, of even a single act. - Education, pg. 109

Do you ever get scared when you have to meet new people? Or, even worse, when you have to talk to them? It can be pretty tough sometimes, right?

My family used to travel a lot when I was a little girl, and I absolutely detested going to a new church where I didn't know anyone. Especially when we were in a foreign country where hardly anyone spoke English. It was not my idea of fun. I would walk into Sabbath school and feel self-conscious as the other kids would stare and whisper. Some churches were nice and friendly, while others just felt, well, awkward. During Sabbath school, I would wish so hard for someone to come and talk to me and introduce me to people, so that I wouldn't feel like a misfit. Visiting foreign countries was particularly frustrating to me because I couldn't communicate.

Well, as soon as we would arrive back home, I would determine that no visitor at our church would ever feel like a misfit. I remembered the extremely awkward, uncomfortable feelings I had experienced and made sure to be that friendly person I had so often wished for. I don't know what kind of impact I had on visitors, but I hope my efforts made them feel a lot more comfortable than I felt when visiting other churches.

You also can do the same thing I did! A genuine, friendly smile can do wonders, and talking to strangers isn't as scary as it may seem. Strike up friendly conversations with people in the park or in line at the grocery store. Whether they be new kids at school, new co-workers, or visitors at church, they will be so thankful that they have found a friend—you.

~ Sarah Chang

One Little Ant

A single grain of wheat, increased by repeated sowings, would cover a whole land with golden sheaves. So widespread may be the influence of a single life, of even a single act. - Education, pg. 109

Recently, I went on a weekend campout to a place called Stryne Cabin. Friday afternoon, I was lying on a boulder way up high and soaking up the sun. Now, I didn't see very many animals over the weekend, but one creature that I did consistently see was the ant. While I was on the boulder many ants crawled all over me and annoyed me. I was lying down and trying to snooze, but just as I would be about to fall asleep, one little ant would crawl on me. It was so annoying! I would have to sit up and swat it off, then lie down again and try to sleep. Pretty soon, it would happen all over again. Needless to say, I didn't get much sleep that afternoon.

One thing that amazed me was that one little, tiny ant, which was but a fraction of the size of my body, could annoy me, a big human, so much. Even though it was so tiny, I noticed it, and it made a difference.

This is just like your influence. As much as you may want to get rid of it, you have an influence that will reach a vast amount of people. Everyone you come in contact with, whether you like it or not, will be reached by your influence either for good or for evil. You might just want to hide your light under a bushel, but instead, God calls you to let your light "so shine before men, that they may see your good works, and glorify your Father which is in heaven" (Matthew 5:16 KJV). Even a little ant has an influence.

~ Victoria West

Give to Gain

By casting it away the sower multiplies his seed. So by imparting we increase our blessings. God's promise assures a sufficiency, that we may continue to give. - Education, pg. 110

Christians have a tendency to obesity—spiritual obesity, that is. We go to church and are spiritually fed, but then what? As it is with the physical, so it is with the spiritual: without exercise, we become fat. A sponge that only takes in water and never is wrung out will soon be unable to hold any more. We hoard our knowledge and our blessings, lest we give and become in need ourselves. But God has promised that as we give, we will receive, so that we can continue imparting His blessings to others. All who drink of the Living Water must become a fountain of life.

There is a children's tale of an ant and a grasshopper. The ant spent the summer gathering food and storing up for the winter, while the grasshopper wasted his days singing and playing his fiddle. When the winter came, the ant and his family were warm and snug and had plenty to eat. It was then that the grasshopper realized he had nothing to eat and was going to starve to death. The story was retold by a six-year-old and was given this ending: "After the grasshopper came to the ant and begged for food, the ant unhesitatingly gave all the food he had. The ant didn't have any food left, so he died. But then the grasshopper felt bad and so sad that the ant had died, that he told everyone what the ant had done to save his life." Of course that's not the real ending, but it sure does make a powerful point about the lifesaving force of unselfish giving.

John 12:24 says, "...Unless a grain of wheat falls into the ground and dies, it remains alone; but if it dies, it produces much grain" (NKJV). Jesus gave us everything; He gave His very life away. And now, we can multiply His gift by sharing it with others. But unlike the ant who ran out of resources when he shared, when we give and empty ourselves, we are just making room for God to fill us with renewed blessings.

~ Carmen Hartwell

Unless It Dies

Only through the sacrifice of Christ, the Seed, could fruit be brought forth for the kingdom of God...Life is the result of His death.
- Education, pg. 110

Elisabeth Elliot went to South America to do translation work in 1952. In the space of one year, she experienced three calamities. The first was the murder of the informant who was giving her information about the language and culture of the Colorados, the tribe of Indians she was working for. The second catastrophe was the loss of all the work Elisabeth had done that year. All her files, tapes, notebooks, and vocabulary compilations were stolen, of which no copies or duplicates existed. The same year, her husband, Jim, had been reconstructing a small jungle mission station among the Quichua Indians. During a sudden flood one night, all of the buildings he had rebuilt, plus three new ones, were swept down the Amazon River.

These three experiences of total earthly loss taught Elisabeth and Jim the deep lesson that Jesus taught His disciples: "Truly, truly, I say to you, unless a grain of wheat falls into the earth and dies, it remains alone; but if it dies, it bears much fruit" (John 12:24 ESV). The practical outcome of that lesson was this, according to Elisabeth: "I had to face up to the fact in those stunning losses that God was indeed sovereign; therefore, He was my Lord, my Master, the One in charge of my life, the One who deserved my worship and my service. The road to eternal gain leads inevitably through earthly loss. True faith is operative in the dark. True faith deals with the inexplicable things of life. If we have explanations...if things are clear and simple...there's not very much need for faith. Through these three experiences of loss we came to know Jesus Christ in a deeper way..."

What about you? Are there bad things happening to you? Things that seem like they have no purpose? It may all be so that you will come to know Christ in a deeper way as your Lord, your Master, and the One in charge of your whole life! Christ, the Seed, was sacrificed so that the fruit of a good and righteous character could be cultivated in you and me. We have to lay down our ambitions and pride, and only once self is dead, will there be room for the new life.

~ Anna Fink

Ye Have Done It unto Me

But the law of self-sacrifice is the law of self-preservation...So the life that will be preserved is the life that is freely given in service to God and man. - Education, pg. 110

For just a brief moment, think about one person in your life whom you greatly dislike. The one who, for some odd reason, always seems to irritate you: that person who constantly behaves irrationally, or that loud know-it-all who is always disturbing the peace, or even (perish the thought) your sibling or some other close relative. Have you identified that aggravating individual? Now, try to imagine yourself loving that person. Is it hard? Impossible? Do you even want to try?

Next, think of Jesus Christ, your Savior and omnipotent Benefactor. Think of how much love and devotion He gives and has given to you, His sinful child. Although Jesus can never be annoying or irritating, wouldn't it be a horrid thing if that person whom you dislike immensely were Jesus?

Isn't that an irrational thought? Doesn't that sound a little far-fetched? Why would Jesus be in the place of the person you dislike the most? Look at this verse in Matthew 25:40 in which Jesus is speaking to the multitude: "...Verily I say unto you, Inasmuch as ye have done it unto one of the least of these My brethren, ye have done it unto Me" (KJV). So, according to Christ, you can only love Him to the extent that you love the person you like the least. Wow! When I first came to this conclusion, it was a slap in the face, and it still is every time I think about it.

The next time you remember that bothersome and provoking individual, think of Jesus being in his or her place. How would you treat someone who died for you personally? How should you treat the person who has given you the gift of eternal life? This is definitely food for thought!

~ Cyrus Guccione

Prepared in Advance

...If a human being is wounded or breaks a bone, nature begins at once to repair the injury. Even before the need exists, the healing agencies are in readiness...So it is in the spiritual realm. Before sin created the need, God had provided the remedy. - Education, pg. 113

God created the human body with miraculous ways of recovering from injuries and adapting to the difficulties it has to face. The entire body is covered by a protective layer of skin that functions as a shell over all the muscles, bones, and organs. When the skin is damaged by a cut or scratch, blood immediately begins to flow, filling the opening with tiny platelets that stick together like glue to cover the opening. This process of clotting forms a hardened scab which protects the area underneath from infection, allowing it to heal. Even before it is cut, the skin possesses properties that are ready and waiting to do their part to heal the damaged skin.

It is the same way with God's plan for our salvation. Before sin ever existed in heaven or on earth, God prepared a plan to redeem us. After Adam and Eve fell to temptation, Jesus "offered to give His life a ransom, to take the sentence of death upon Himself, that through Him man might find pardon; that through the merits of His blood, and obedience to the law of God, they could have the favor of God, and be brought into the beautiful garden, and eat of the fruit of the tree of life" (*Early Writings*, pg. 149).

Jesus' blood is the protecting agent that covers the wounds we have from sin, healing the damage. Before you were born, before you had committed your first sin, God provided the remedy so that you could be saved.

~ Megan Metcalf

Only You, Part 1

Perfection exists in the least as well as in the greatest of the works of God. - Education, pg. 114

Once upon a time, there would have been two things that I would have changed about myself in a heartbeat: my slender eyes and my petite height. I really do have tiny eyes. A little girl, who didn't even know me, curiously asked, "Can you see through your eyes?" I was taken aback and wanted to retort, "I can see just fine. Can you see through yours?" In grade school, other children teased me frequently, which constantly made me wish my eyes were bigger. Sometimes, the attention was enjoyable, but usually I simply wished I could "blend in" and be left alone.

God changed my perspective, though, when I was twelve years old. That year, Peru was my first mission trip destination. I loved helping out with Vacation Bible School and playing with the village kids. At first, they were really shy and wouldn't talk to me, but I would smile, and almost every single kid would point at my eyes and smile too. The village kids (especially the little ones) were extremely fascinated with my eyes; I'm pretty positive that not many Asians are spotted in Pucallpa, Peru. Also, I am completely convinced that I was more "approachable" because I was practically the same size, if not shorter, than the children and preteens who attended VBS. Through that trip, God showed me that what I believed to be "flaws" were actually wonderful tools to reach out to others.

It's almost inevitable that people I meet will tease me about my height or my eyes. But I'm okay with it now because I know that God created ME with a special purpose in mind, and it's up to me to discover it and make the most of His blessings.

I'm sure that there are things you might like to change about yourself too. Maybe it's your hair, voice, or nose. Just remember, God created YOU as an individual, and those features which might seem like "flaws" are actually blessings in disguise.

~ Sarah Chang

Only You, Part 2

Upon all created things is seen the impress of the Deity. - Education, pg. 99

Dearest Friend,

I am writing you a letter to tell you how special you are. Remember that I shared with you about how I had a hard time accepting my small eyes and short stature? And how I pointed out that even though we may think we have "flaws," we can choose to see them as blessings in disguise? I want to share one more thing with you.

I once was able to attend a meeting with David Asscherick, and what I learned was so exciting, I had to share it with you! We all have heard sayings like "God made you special," or "There's no one in the whole world that's like you!" But have you actually stopped to think about that concept? I know that every human being has insecurities. We pick on our bodies, worrying that we're too fat or too skinny. We doubt whether people will like us and are afraid others will think we're stupid. We worry about whether we will succeed in life, instead of placing our trust in the Creator.

Pastor Asscherick stated that God loves people. Take a look at Moses. Did you ever think about the fact that God raised Moses from the dead because He did not want to live without Moses as His companion? The same goes for you, my friend. If He wanted to, God could make a clone of you, one that talks like you, acts like you, sings like you. God could cause your friends and parents to think that clone was you and even make YOU believe that clone was you. But there would be one Being in the entire universe who would know that that clone wasn't you: God. God gave you the choice of accepting Him as your Friend, or rejecting His love. And if you reject Him, there will always be a hole in His heart that no one else, but you, can fill.

God isn't interested in a shadow or a marionette of you. He's interested in YOU. And once we find that we can truly believe and accept His love, then we will never have to worry or have insecurities again.

~ Sarah Chang

A Steadfast Tree

The palm tree, beaten by the scorching sun and the fierce sandstorm, stands green and flourishing and fruitful in the midst of the desert.
- Education, pg. 116

Daniel was only twelve years old when he was taken from his home. He was captured and taken to Babylon, a different empire with a strange culture. He had to study a new language and learn new customs and traditions. Babylonians did not have the same religion as Daniel, and he was expected to worship their gods. Daniel was in a difficult position. Even though he was very young, he remembered what his mother had taught him in his early childhood and remained faithful to the God of his forefathers. He did not participate in Babylonian religious activities and rejected the king's best food that had been offered to idols. Daniel prayed three times a day to the living God with whom he had a personal relationship. He was always faithful and trusted God. As a reward for his faithfulness, God helped him receive a high position in the empire where he was able to be a good influence on the people around him.

Like Daniel, we may find it difficult to be a Christian in our world. However, God wishes us to be like a tree that stands steadfast in an unwelcoming and unpleasant desert. It is beaten by the scorching sun and fierce sandstorms. It is hopeless for the tree to survive in the desert if its roots are not strong. The roots are the anchor in the soil that absorb water and nutrition to keep the tree straight and stable. If its roots aren't strong, the tree will wither and die.

The desert is this world that we live in. In spite of difficult circumstances, the tree can bloom if its roots are strong. Then its large, green leaves can provide shelter for tired or wandering travelers passing by. In the same way, a personal relationship with Jesus is the source of healthy roots for our lives. This relationship must be strong in order for us to survive in this world. We cannot do anything without Him, not even breathe. We need His help and strength. We need a relationship with the Life-giver to be able to give life to others. Have you invited Him to be with you today?

~ Elísa Elíasdóttir

All We Like Sheep

The animals themselves are to be his teachers. The ants teach lessons of patient industry, of perseverance in surmounting obstacles, of providence for the future. And the birds are teachers of the sweet lesson of trust. - Education, pp. 117, 118

In Luke 15:4-7, Jesus tells His disciples a parable about a shepherd, who, after counting his one hundred sheep, found that one of them was missing. Immediately, the shepherd left his other ninety-nine sheep in the open country and looked for his single lost sheep. After much searching, the sheep was found and brought back home. Then, once the lost sheep was safe and secure, the shepherd rejoiced with his friends that the lost sheep was found. Then Jesus said, "I tell you that in the same way there will be more rejoicing in heaven over one sinner who repents than over ninety-nine righteous persons who do not need to repent" (Luke 15:7 NIV).

Jesus gave the example of a lost sheep to demonstrate how even when we have sinned and become lost, God will diligently search for us and bring us home if we are willing to be led by Him. The faithful shepherd had only thoughts of love towards his lost sheep. But what was going through the mind of the sheep? He was probably thinking, "Why should I follow the shepherd? It's no fun to have someone tell me what to do all the time. He is probably just trying to keep me away from what I like. Besides, I'm a big sheep now; I can take care of myself!" He probably thought differently after the sun had set, and he could hear the hungry wolves howling all around him.

We might laugh at the foolish actions of the sheep, but don't we do the same thing? So often we think, "It's no fun to have God tell me what to do all the time," or "God is just trying to keep me away from something I might like." The principles and laws presented in the Bible might not always seem fun. But in reality they provide happiness, joy, and life. "All we like sheep have gone astray; we have turned every one to his own way; and the LORD hath laid on Him [Jesus] the iniquity of us all" (Isaiah 53:6 KJV). We have all wandered away from our Shepherd. But no matter what we have done, no matter how lost we are, God will always find us and bring us back home when we ask Him.

~ Wesley Donesky

Thank God for Furnaces!

...We may be surrounded with difficulties, discouragement, and darkness. - Education, pg. 118

Once upon a time, there was a blacksmith named Fabron. He became a Christian, and began to live a life of spiritual excellence, but he was still not prospering materially. In fact, since his conversion, he seemed to be facing more trials than ever. One day, when Fabron's non-Christian friend stopped at the blacksmith's shop, Fabron told him some of the struggles he had been experiencing.

"It seems strange to me that so much affliction should pass over you just about the time when you have become an earnest Christian. I don't want to weaken your faith in God, but you're trying to do your best to be faithful, praying for God's help and guidance, and yet things seem to be steadily worsening. I can't help wondering why."

Fabron was quiet for a long time. I imagine he had been asking himself the same question. "You see this iron which I have here to make a horseshoe? You know what I do with it? I take a piece and heat it in the fire until it is red with heat. Then I hammer it unmercifully to shape it. Next I plunge it into a pail of cold water to temper it. Then I repeat this process until it is finished. But sometimes I find a piece of iron that won't stand up under this treatment. The heat and the hammering and the cold water are too much for it. I don't know why it fails in the process, but I know it will never make a good horseshoe." He pointed to a heap of scrap iron by the door of the shop. "When I get a piece that cannot take the shape and temper, I throw it out on the scrap heap. It will never be good for anything. I know that God has been holding me in the fires of affliction. I have felt His hammer upon me. But I don't mind, because I know this is how He brings me to what I should be. And so in these hard things, my prayer is simply this: 'Try me however You wish, Lord; only don't throw me on the scrap heap.'"

God is working a miracle in our lives every day. Sometimes it may feel as though life is hard, but God cares so much about you that He is always willing to work with you and mold you for His service. "The Lord allows His chosen ones to be placed in the furnace of affliction to prove what temper they are of and whether they can be fashioned for His work" (*The Ministry of Healing*, pg. 471).

~ Jessica Hall

A Lesson of Trust

...As we observe the things of the natural world, we shall be enabled, under the guiding of the Holy Spirit, more fully to understand the lessons of God's word. It is thus that nature becomes a key to the treasure house of the word. - Education, pg. 120

During my junior year, I had the opportunity to go on a winter campout in four feet of snow. It was beautiful, with gorgeous steep mountain slopes and thick white powder on the evergreens. In the trees were some white-bellied, black-capped birds that seemed to be singing with the wind. I stopped to observe them for a while, then grabbed a corn chip from my bag. I broke it into small pieces and held it out in their direction. I could tell by their constant flying in front of me that they wanted the chip. They continued this for a while, then finally one of the birds swooped down and landed close to my fingers in the snow and tried to snatch the chips without landing on my hand. I could tell that he wanted to trust me, but I also observed that he was not so sure that the chips would be worth the risk. It took me some time to gain his trust. A little while later, he came back. This time, he landed on my fingers, and, with a chip in his beak, fluttered a couple of feet away to eat it.

Later that day, while I was sitting by the campfire, my mind went back to the moment with the birds. I was thinking of how my encounter with that bird could parallel my relationship with God. Sometimes I act like that bird, wanting the gift that God is willing to give me, but feeling that it's not worth the risk. When God speaks to me in His still small voice, saying, "Trust me, Daniel," I sometimes don't realize that my entire life depends upon my surrender to Him. At times like these, I must realize that I cannot go through life on my own, and in order to receive God's gift of eternal life, it is essential that I put my trust and faith in Him.

~ Daniel Glassford

Dig Deeper

But the most valuable teaching of the Bible is not to be gained by occasional or disconnected study. Its great system of truth is not so presented as to be discerned by the hasty or careless reader. Many of its treasures lie far beneath the surface, and can be obtained only by diligent research and continuous effort. - Education, pg. 123

There was once a pirate who had a great treasure. On his many voyages and conquests, he had obtained vast quantities of gold, silver, and precious jewels. In order to keep his wealth safe, he decided he must bury it. So he dug, and he dug, and he dug! At about three hundred feet, he laid the bulk of his treasure. Then he filled in the hole until it was only one hundred feet deep. There he laid a fraction of his treasure and finished filling in the hole. Now, anyone looking for the buried treasure would only find the small amount and, thinking he had uncovered all of it, would stop there.

God designed the Bible in a similar way. He packed it with treasures of truth and power! When we read hastily over the surface of a few verses, we may discover some of the treasures they contain. However, the truth is that the real treasure lies farther beneath the surface meaning, and we must dig deeper to find it.

Do you find reading the Bible boring? Maybe you haven't been digging deep enough! Instead of thinking of the typical lesson found in what you're reading, ask God to show you something new, a deeper meaning that applies specifically to your life. You'll be amazed at how powerful and exciting the Bible becomes as you uncover more and more of its treasures!

~ Rachel Petrello

Equal Opportunity

No one with a spirit to appreciate its teaching can read a single passage from the Bible without gaining from it some helpful thought...With the word of God in his hands, every human being, wherever his lot in life may be cast, may have such companionship as he shall choose. In its pages he may hold converse with the noblest and best of the human race, and may listen to the voice of the Eternal as He speaks with men. - Education, pp. 123, 127

Have you ever felt like you don't even have a chance of becoming friends with God? Maybe you weren't raised in a spiritual atmosphere, or you have never studied the Bible before. Sometimes, looking at my pastor, I feel very inferior spiritually. He went to seminary to learn how to study the Bible, and I am only 17 and have no real training. But I have something encouraging to tell you. Though you may not have studied as much as your pastor or someone else you consider way more spiritual than you, you have the same opportunity and ability to study Scripture. Did you catch that? Other people have no advantage over you; they are not more prone to understanding Scripture than you are. They may be further along in the path of actually studying God's Word, but with a Bible available to you, "the sky's the limit." There is no limit to the heights you can attain with the Bible as your guide. You can reach heavenly heights with God's Word speaking to you.

If you got a letter from a good friend, wouldn't you want to read it? I know I would read it the first chance I got. I might even push other responsibilities out of the way in order to read it because my relationship with the person who sent the letter is important. Or, consider getting a new pen pal. I remember being really excited to get a new pen pal. I sent my contact information to the Clubhouse magazine, and they sent me the name and address of the girl I would be writing to. I excitedly wrote her a letter, telling her about myself and asking lots of questions. When her letter arrived, I eagerly devoured the greeting from my new friend. I wanted to get to know her better.

Don't you want to know God better? He has written you a very special letter to tell you about Himself. In order to have know Him, you need to learn as much as you can about Him. God wants to speak to you. Won't you let Him?

~ Victoria West

232

In the Storm

...The Lord hath His way in the whirlwind and in the storm, and the clouds are the dust of His feet. - Nahum 1:3 KJV

The wind shrieked down on the small boat, whipping the waves into towering whitecaps. As Jesus' twelve disciples struggled at the oars, trying to keep the vessel headed into the wind, a gigantic wave crashed down over the deck, threatening to wash them overboard. A jagged streak of lightning exploded across the sky, and in that brief instant of light, a gust of wind tore the sail from its rigging. As the rain and waves rapidly filled the tiny vessel, the men scrambled to bail the water out, but just as soon as it was emptied, it was filled again. It seemed as if all the elements of nature had focused their anger on that little boat bobbing helplessly on the Sea of Galilee.

In the midst of all this confusion, there was but one glimmer of peace. On the back of the boat lay Jesus in deep slumber, as if there were nothing at all to be worried about. While the rest of the disciples continued their struggle at the oars, one stumbled back to where Jesus lay, grabbed his shoulders, and shook Him: "...Master, carest Thou not that we perish?" (Mark 4:38 KJV).

Jesus awoke, stood to His feet, and in a voice clearly heard above the roar of the wind and waves, He spoke the words: "...Peace, be still" (Mark 4:39 KJV). Suddenly, as if some unseen force had blown back the clouds, the moon came out, illuminating a golden pathway in front of them. The wind chased itself away, and the waves died down. The stars, reflected in the still, dark water, looked like a thousand fireflies.

Do you have a storm in your life? Are the waves of sin threatening to drown you? Jesus is there, just waiting for you to call out to Him, and before you know it, you will have His peace in your life.

~ Wesley Mayes

The Unity of the Bible

When thus searched out and brought together, they will be found to be perfectly fitted to one another. Each Gospel is a supplement to the others, every prophecy an explanation of another, every truth a development of some other truth...Every principle in the word of God has its place, every fact its bearing. - Education, pp. 123, 124

"I do not believe in the Bible. It is not even realistic to think that a book like this can change my life. Consider an important question that rarely gets asked: with more than forty authors living centuries apart, how can the Bible still be united? Were these authors well-equipped with the tools to detect fraud or identify self-deception in the books they wrote?" How many times have you met people who have similar views to the ones above? How can we defend the unity of the Bible in a logical, reasonable way? What does the unity of the Bible have to do with our relationship with God?

Reading the Bible superficially will not give anybody a deep understanding of it. At first glance, the Book may appear as a random combination of a history textbook, children stories, and some sermons. But, if someone is willing to search it with patience, prayer, and an open mind, the hidden truths of the Bible will be revealed. Only then will they discover the amazing unity of the word of God. Isn't it astonishing that more than 44 authors wrote 66 books at different times in history, and still there is a mysterious unity between all of them? In the Old Testament, the future coming of the Messiah is disclosed. In the New Testament, the prophecy is fulfilled. Both testaments have one theme: Christ's plan of redemption for us.

The unity of the Bible shows us that God inspired its words. He gathered and inspired a group of people to write over a period of 1,500 years, so that today, the world would have a book revealing His character. How great is His care and love for us! He is very anxious to connect with us through His Word. Through it we may be "thoroughly equipped for every good work" (2 Timothy 3:17 NKJV). Have you discovered the purpose that Jesus has for your life through reading and connecting with His word?

~ Valdis Cuvaldin

That Which Is Beyond

Man, created for fellowship with God, can only in such fellowship find his real life and development...He who with sincere and teachable spirit studies God's word, seeking to comprehend its truths, will be brought in touch with its Author; and, except by his own choice, there is no limit to the possibilities of his development. - Education, pp. 124, 125

The Bible is like a telescope. If a man looks through his telescope he sees worlds beyond; but if he looks at his telescope, he does not see anything but that. The Bible is a thing to be looked through to see that which is beyond; but most people only look at it and so they see only the dead letter.

- Phillip Brooks

The Bible is indeed a telescope into the mind and thoughts of God. It is a way for Him to speak to us. The Bible is filled with words of comfort and hope to encourage and guide us as we walk the path of life. It is also a textbook, the most important textbook, that teaches us how to live happy and productive lives. And most importantly, it is a map that shows us the way to forgiveness, salvation, and eternal life.

However, this book does us no good if it is left on the shelf to collect dust. It seems that so often we forget that people were willing to suffer persecution and even death in order to have in their possession this book that we so often take for granted. I think the following verse by Lynn DeShazo says it best:

Martyrs' blood stains each page;
They have died for this faith.
Here them cry through the years,
"O heed these words and hold them dear!"

~ Laura Williams

235

Seek No Further

Created to find in God his highest joy, he [man] can find in nothing else that which can quiet the cravings of the heart, can satisfy the hunger and thirst of the soul. - Education, pp. 124, 125

Have you ever had a craving for something and couldn't be satisfied unless you had it? Or maybe you've searched for something special and experienced a great happiness when you found it?

There was a woman who lived in Samaria who had a thirst for something more in her life. This woman searched for love, going from husband to husband, yet she found no true fulfillment. Her heart felt empty and rejected. But a single day would change her life forever; that day was the day she met Jesus as she drew water from the city well. He startled her when He asked her for a drink from her pitcher. She couldn't understand why a Jew would talk to a Samaritan woman, especially asking a favor of her, because the Jews and Samaritans despised each other. Jesus showed this outcast soul how important she was to Him; she was a person of value in the sight of God. Although He appeared to be the one dependent upon her kindness by asking for a drink, it was actually the woman who He was there to reach. He offered her the water of everlasting life, the water that would satisfy the cravings of her heart. Yet, she didn't realize that this Man whom she was speaking to was the Messiah she had looked forward to meeting all her life. The Messiah Himself was beside her, and she knew Him not.

Many souls are searching far and wide for a spring of water that will quench their thirst when Jesus' offer of everlasting life is right next to them. Jesus earnestly wants everyone to accept "the divine grace which He alone can impart...[the] living water, purifying, refreshing, and invigorating the soul" (*Desire of Ages*, pg. 187). Christ is the answer to every longing within my heart. Money, friends, or material possessions cannot satisfy that thirst which only Christ can quench. Are you searching to fill the cravings of your heart? Seek no more. Accept Christ's calling when He bids, "Come unto me, all ye that labor and are heavy laden, and I will give you rest" (Matthew 11:28 KJV).

~ Megan Metcalf

Heaven's Entrance Exam

So we see that they were unable to enter because of unbelief.
- Hebrews 3:19 NRSV

Have you heard? The most exciting educational opportunity still has a vacancy for you! God has offered you eternity to study His entire creation. And best of all, the only omniscient Teacher in the universe will be leading the expedition! There is an entrance exam, but all people can pass it if they want to. The test is made of one question: will you trust God no matter what? The Bible says that the Israelites were not able to enter into Canaan because of their unwillingness to trust in God. We know that Canaan is a representation of Heaven. With this in mind, we can see that unbelief ends in losing our heavenly inheritance. When God asks, "Do you trust Me," what will you say?

On a particularly eventful day a few years ago, I had a chance to watch God test the residents of Seattle. We were driving to Sea-Tac Airport, when suddenly we began bumping up and down vigorously. As we rocked back and forth, we thought we must be having a major car breakdown. That's when we noticed that the car in front of us was having similar troubles. In a few seconds, traffic slowed to a stop, and I watched as wild-eyed people came streaming out of the supermarket beside us. I will not forget that earthquake easily. In God's providence, not a single person was hurt and very little property was damaged. Still, the next day, everywhere you went you could hear scared and distressed people discussing the earthquake. Although we were extremely confused during the earthquake, my family and I were never really afraid.

So, what's the difference between us and the fearful people we overheard? It certainly was not some natural fearlessness we had and they were missing. The difference is simple. We had found a trusting relationship with God, and they had not. The only way to be truly fearless is to have the completely fearless God by your side. He is soon going to allow some big tests to come upon this world, and you don't want to be someone who is scared by a small earthquake. Choose to build a trusting relationship with God starting today. And someday soon, you will find yourself in heaven learning things you had never imagined!

~ Kevin Corrigan

237

Simple Things

Death and life are in the power of the tongue... - Proverbs 18:21 KJV

Do you ever say things and immediately regret saying them? I do this so often I have lost count. I wish someone could invent something that will stop unkind words from ever leaving my mouth!

Actually, we do have something that will stop those words; it's called a mind. See, most of the time when we say something unkind, it's because we have spoken impetuously. Sometimes we purposely say mean things, but then too, we haven't really thought through the total consequences of that action.

I know for me, when I get into an argument, I'm in it to win. I often don't let anything stop me from coming out on top, even if it means bashing someone's reputation or hurting their feelings. And you know, I have hurt so many people that way. Because even if I say mean things as a joke, people don't always take it the same way. And really, should we be joking with people that way?

If we are Christians as we profess to be, then we should be acting like Christ. He never bashed anyone, or hurt their feelings. He brought healing and peace when He spoke. His words were ones of comfort and hope, and if necessary, a gentle rebuke, but always done in a loving and caring way. So, when I'm "dissing" my friends, am I really being like Christ? I don't know what you think, but that doesn't seem possible to me. Many times, though, I find myself excusing my behavior: "Oh, it's just a little thing; they know I don't mean it." But do they really? I've heard it said that in every jest there is a seed of truth; so where does that place us when we're constantly "dissing" those around us?

It's the simple things that add up in the end; it's those little comments made under your breath that end up being vented later on. To go to heaven, I must have a relationship with God that expresses itself in the way I treat others (1 John 4:20,21). I'm not going to let a simple thing like not controlling my tongue keep me from being there. What about you?

~ Jo Holdal

Your Two Wolves

The mind, the soul, is built up by that upon which it feeds; and it rests with us to determine upon what it shall be fed. - Education, pp. 126, 127

Once upon a time in a Cherokee village, there was a young man who desired to become wise. He went to his grandfather, the wisest man in the village, and asked him to teach about life. The grandfather gazed at his grandson, and pondered this question for a moment before answering. Then, very slowly, he began to speak: "A fight is going on inside me, inside you, and inside everyone who lives. It is a terrible fight between two wolves. One is evil—he is anger, envy, sorrow, regret, greed, arrogance, guilt, resentment, lies, and ego."

The young man didn't see how this connected with his life, but his grandfather was wise, and this was what he had asked for, so he continued to listen. The old man continued:

"The other wolf is good—he is joy, peace, love, hope, humility, kindness, benevolence, sympathy, truth, and faith. They are fighting for the control of your soul."

The grandson pondered this analogy for a minute. Finally, he ventured to inquire, "Which wolf will win?"

The grandfather stated plainly, "The one that is fed."

Though this story is a legend, it speaks volumes of truth. Survival of the fittest decrees that that which has strength will triumph. If we think of our minds in terms of a fight between two animals, the same principle applies. Our character is made up of our habitual thoughts and actions. The thoughts we choose to dwell on, the attitudes we assume, the decisions we make feed one wolf or the other. By being fed, one wolf will grow while the other starves. Thus, one will dominate the other. It's up to you to decide the outcome of the fight. Which wolf will you feed?

~ Carmen Hartwell

Unplugging Yourself

It is within the power of everyone to choose the topics that shall occupy the thoughts and shape the character. - Education, pg. 127

God gave us the awesome ability of free choice, which means that we have the power to choose our thoughts. Everything that we think, listen to, and observe has a direct effect on the way we act and feel. It was in the summer of 2007 that my parents finally decided to let me buy an iPod. I couldn't wait to get my used Nano. *Now I can listen to music wherever and whenever I want*, I thought. It wasn't long before I had my earphones in all day long. At first I only listened to great Christian music, but eventually I began to listen to music that, while it wasn't necessarily "bad," wasn't always overtly Christian.

One day I heard that my cousin was going to Fountainview Academy; so I applied and was accepted. When I got there I suddenly found myself without an iPod because only juniors and seniors had the privilege to use such devices. Later that year, I realized that while my music hadn't been "bad," it was creating static between God and me. I had become so accustomed to having my earphones in, that I never had time to reflect on the important things of life, like observing the wonders of nature around me, or making new friends. Now, without this constant distraction, I started making new friends, and life was just plain happier. I felt so much more cheerful and free!

Now that I am a junior and have iPod privileges, I enjoy it so much more. My music is an addition to my life, not an addiction. I have time to chat with my friends, study my Bible, and enjoy time in nature. It really is true that one's thoughts and inputs shape his character. Why not try "unplugging" for a while from the constant informational or entertainment overload. Take time to take a hike out in nature and listen to God's message of love spelled out in every bird's song and sparkling waterfall. Take time to really listen to people. You'll find out that not only does God have things to tell you, but He also needs you to be an example to those around you.

~ Daniel Glassford

Lasting Love

He who through the word of God has lived in fellowship with heaven, will find himself at home in heaven's companionship. - Education, pg. 127

One evening, Lt. John Blanchard, a soldier in Florida during WWII, wandered into the post library and found a book to read. The feminine handwriting in the margins intrigued him; so he turned to the front of the book and found the name of the previous owner, a Miss Hollis Maynell. John did some research and found her address in New York. The following day he was shipped overseas. For 13 months the two corresponded by letter and began to open their hearts to each other. He asked for her picture, but she refused by saying that if he really loved her, it wouldn't matter what she looked like.

Finally, the day came when they were to meet in Grand Central Station. Hollis had instructed, "You'll recognize me by the red rose that I'll be wearing on my lapel." As John stood waiting, a young woman came toward him, eyes blue as flowers. He started toward her forgetting that she was not wearing the rose—and then he saw Hollis Maynell standing behind the pretty girl. Her hair was graying, but she wore a red rose on the rumpled lapel of her brown coat. So deep was John's longing for the woman whose spirit had captured him that he approached her; he didn't hesitate. "I'm Lt. John Blanchard," he introduced himself, "and you must be Miss Maynell. I am so glad to meet you. May I take you to dinner?" The woman's face broadened into a smile. "I don't know what this is about, son," she answered, "but the young lady in the green suit who just went by, asked me to wear this rose. And she said if you asked me out to dinner, I should tell you that she is waiting for you in the large restaurant across the street!"

John had fallen in love with Hollis' spirit and character by reading the written thoughts of her heart. Likewise, we can fall in love with God by reading the Bible, the written thoughts of His heart. We will know Him so well, that when we at last are in heaven, we will finally find ourselves at home with the One who has captured our heart.

~ Anna Fink

The Living Word

With the word of God in his hands, every human being, wherever his lot in life may be cast, may have such companionship as he shall choose. In its pages he may hold converse with the noblest and best of the human race, and may listen to the voice of the Eternal as He speaks with men. - Education, pg. 127

Once there was a woman living as a missionary in a small Chinese village with her husband and two small children. While they were in China, Japan entered World War II. Soon the Japanese army began advancing deep into China. In a short while, they were within miles of the woman's house. A Chinese general informed the village that they would have to evacuate immediately. At that time, the woman's husband was assisting a village that was several days journey away. She knew that her two small children would not be able to survive the long, dangerous journey to the village where her husband was. As she thought about what to do, she noticed a small Bible calender sitting on her kitchen table. On it was written a verse for each day. The verse for that day read: "The angel of the LORD encampeth round about them that fear Him, and delivereth them" (Psalm 34:7 KJV). That night she lay awake listening to the rumble of enemy artillery in the distance. As she remembered the verse on the calender, she prayed and entrusted her life and the lives of her children to God. When she awoke the next morning, she noticed that something was different. There was complete silence everywhere. Nothing was moving except for some farm animals that had been left behind by the fleeing villagers. Later that day the Chinese general returned to the village. When the woman asked him why he had returned he said, "The enemy has changed direction and is now heading east." The woman returned home, praising God for saving her family from certain death.

Throughout history, God has used the Bible as His chosen means of communication with mankind. When you read the Bible, you are not simply reading words that were spoken long ago. You are listening to God speaking to you now. If you listen, you will hear His voice saying, "Fear not: for I am with thee" (Isaiah 43:5 KJV). When you hear the artillery of the devil rumbling in the distance, you can entrust your life to God and say with confidence, "If He is with me, who can be against me?"

~ Wesley Donesky

I Want to Want Thee

He who through the word of God has lived in fellowship with heaven, will find himself at home in heaven's companionship. - Education, pg. 127

If you could go to heaven where there is no pain or death, no natural disasters, with the beauty of nature all around, and a mansion of your own, all the food you ever dreamed of, and all the friends you ever loved, would you be happy if God weren't there? For anyone who is deeply in love with Christ, this couldn't be the case.

Some people have gone through their entire life doing "the Christian thing," even getting baptized, but never truly falling in love with God. They don't sing from their heart or think of Him throughout the day. They have no desire to spend more time than necessary on their knees in prayer. They look forward to heaven for its security, but aren't so sure they want to meet the Man who got them there. They see others around them who love God, but don't see how it is possible for them. They wish to feel the same way about their Creator, but haven't the slightest clue where such a love could possibly come from.

If you are struggling with falling in love with God, tell Him! He has countless methods of wooing you to His heart. Just ask and He will be sure to do everything in His power to bring you into a loving relationship with Him. I want to suggest a prayer that I have prayed time and time again to renew the strength of my relationship with God.

O God, I have tasted Thy goodness, and it has both satisfied me and made me thirsty for more. I am painfully conscious of my need for further grace. I am ashamed of my lack of desire. O God, the triune God, I want to want Thee; I long to be filled with longing; I thirst to be made more thirsty still. Show me Thy glory, I pray Thee, so that I may know Thee indeed. Begin in mercy a new work of love within me. Say to my soul, "Rise up my love, my fair one, and come away." Then give me grace to rise and follow Thee up from this misty lowland where I have wandered so long.

~ Danielle Schafer

I'm Just a Toaster

Every breath, every pulsation of the heart, is an evidence of the care of Him in whom we live and move and have our being. - Education, pg. 131

Have you ever been trying to use a toaster or some other small appliance and been frustrated because it wouldn't work? Let me point out an interesting fact about toasters (I've learned this from experience): toasters only work if they are plugged into the outlet. Profound, I know. You can put your toast in, clean out the crumb tray, and even hold down the lever till your finger falls off, but it still won't work if it's not plugged into the power source.

You know, all our power comes from God. You may be thinking, "Yeah, I know that!"; but do you really? How many times do we display some skill or talented action and take the credit for ourselves, forgetting the One who can perform all skills and arts beyond perfection? All power to do anything and everything comes from God. When your eyelids first flutter open in the morning, that is an act of God. When your lungs are filled to their capacity with oxygen, that is God breathing into them. Most of the time, we don't even realize He's the one enabling us to do even the most seemingly effortless tasks; but He is. Whether you're walking to the grocery store, gazing at a beautiful sunset, feeling salty ocean spray on your face, hearing imposing thunder roll in the clouds, or appreciating the love of a friend, you can only experience these things because you are running on the fuel of the eternal God. If He withdrew His power for a nanosecond, we would cease to exist. I would not exist; therefore, my fingers could not type, and you would not be reading this. God is the one who gives us to power to do everything. We're just powerless toasters. Unless we're plugged into the Power Source, we can do nothing.

So, next time you're complimented on the lovely song you sang in church or the inspiring poem you wrote, give the glory to God. Praise Him for giving you the power to do such things. I know I have a difficult time doing this. I want to take the credit all for myself, but I can't. God is the One who has given us every talent we possess, including the power to simply exist. So, let's try to live and speak in such a way that gives the credit to Whom it belongs.

~ Anneliese Wahlman

244

Never-Ending Money Wallet

He that hath pity upon the poor lendeth unto the Lord; and that which he hath given will He pay him again. - Proverbs 19:17 KJV

When I was little, I used to think it would be really cool to have a never-ending money wallet. Let me explain: this wallet would be full of all sorts of bills—$100s, $50s, $20s, $10s, $5s, and $1s. If you pulled a bill out of its spot in the wallet, another bill of the same amount would "grow" back in its place. This would give me the opportunity to go shopping and buy whatever I wanted, while still having the same amount of money I started with! A never-ending amount!

Now, I can see that there was a selfish motive behind my wanting a never-ending money wallet. But, what if you could have a never-ending money supply to end all your financial troubles, donate generously, and go on lots of mission trips? Wouldn't you love to have one of those never-ending money wallets? I sure would. Well, guess what? God promises us that He will repay abundantly what we give to help the poor. "That which he hath given will He pay him again" (Proverbs 19:17 KJV). God will fill our storehouses richly if we keep our priorities straight and remember that all comes from Him.

However, we need to make sure that we realize this important principle: we are but stewards of God's wealth. We are not to use money to serve our selfish purposes and buy whatever we feel like buying. We are to wisely budget and donate money to charities or offerings at church and freely give to God's purposes. If we keep this line of reasoning, God will bless us many times over and will keep our wallet lined with a never-ending supply of money.

~ Victoria West

Subjects of His Care

Every breath, every pulsation of the heart, is an evidence of the care of Him in whom we live and move and have our being. From the smallest insect to man, every living creature is daily dependent upon His providence. - Education, pg. 131

I was in my room one evening and mindlessly began to sing the hymn, "I Sing the Mighty Power of God" while I tidied up. As I was singing, I began to think about the words. There's a line in the last verse that says, "Creatures that borrow life from Thee are subject to Thy care." I paused a moment to actually think about what I was singing, and I was struck with the awesome significance of it. Just being a creature of God automatically subjects us to His watchful protection. As soon as we're born, He's got our back. And not only that, but the very next line says, "There's not a place where we can flee, but God is present there." For the rest of our lives, there's nowhere we can go and nothing we can do to get away from the care of our Father. What an amazing promise!

It is only by the mercy and care of the life-giving God that all life is sustained on Earth. Seeds grow because God breathes life into them. The earth spins on course because God is directing it. The rain, the clouds, and the sunshine come to be with a word from His mouth. If the sustaining care of God were to be removed but for a moment, every tree, flower, insect, sea creature—everything that has life would perish. Every breath you take, every beat of your heart is a gift of preserving power bestowed from the hand of God Himself. Without Him, you would cease to exist.

God is keeping us alive every single moment of the day. Does that not give us reason to praise Him? Why don't you sing the mighty power of God today?

~ Carmen Hartwell

September 4

A Voice Behind You

He has an intimate knowledge of, and a personal interest in, all the works of His hand. - Education, pg. 132

One cool November night, my church youth group was playing capture-the-flag in the woods behind my friend's house. Being in the mountains of North Carolina, the property had multiple levels, all descending to a creek at the bottom. I began quietly crawling upstream to a trail that would lead me to secretly enter the opposite team's territory. I came to a small drop-off which I planned to slide down to reach the trail, and, holding onto a tree on the edge of the bank, I slowly lowered my legs over the edge. Just as I was about to jump down, I heard a voice behind me saying, "Don't jump! Pull yourself back up and go down another way." That's weird, I thought. There is nobody near me–I am completely alone. I decided to obey the voice and pulled my legs back onto the ledge. I went further down the trail to a place where it leveled off and then made my way back to the spot just below where I was going to jump. I looked up and saw a 12-foot rock cliff that dropped straight down to the ground. I instantly realized what could have been my fate if God had not told me to pull myself back up: I would have hurt myself pretty badly falling 12 feet to the ground. God protected me that night from a danger of which I was unaware.

I know for certain that God is taking care of me and guiding my life, and I also know that He will guide yours. He promises that if you obey His still, small voice, He will protect you. Put your trust in God's word. In Isaiah 30:21, He says, "And thine ears shall hear a word behind thee, saying, This is the way, walk ye in it, when ye turn to the right hand, and when ye turn to the left" (KJV).

~ Megan Metcalf

The Prayer That Never Fails

We need to know of an almighty arm that will hold us up, of an infinite Friend that pities us. We need to clasp a hand that is warm, to trust in a heart full of tenderness. - Education, pp. 132, 133

I'm afraid of the dark—well, not so much of the darkness itself, but rather of what the darkness hides from me. It really is silly, to think that the God of the universe who created everything from sweet peas to the Grand Canyon, who wiped out entire nations with a wave of His hand, who even created me, can't take care of me in the dark. I sometimes get so caught up in worrying, that I forget how important I am to God and how much He desires to do what's best for me.

I'm sure I'm not the only person in the world who struggles with fear. I'm also probably not the only person who has prayed and asked for God's protection. But, I'm often still scared when I've finished praying, even though He has always kept me safe.

Each of us, to some degree, has a hard time trusting someone, whether it be God or just another human being. If you have a hard time trusting God, I want to teach you a short and simple prayer that has changed my life. I have probably heard this prayer a thousand times, and maybe you have too. But it wasn't until I actually tried it that I was able to see how powerful it really is. It's the simple request of a hopeful father, calling out to Jesus: "...Lord, I believe; help my unbelief!" (Mark 9:24 NKJV). Not once has God failed me when I've prayed this prayer. "Cast yourself at His feet with the cry, 'Lord, I believe; help *Thou* mine unbelief.' You can never perish while you do this—never" (*The Desire of Ages*, pg. 429).

~ Danielle Schafer

God? Really?

It was the Maker of all things who ordained the wonderful adaptation of means to end, of supply to need. It was He who in the material world provided that every desire implanted should be met. It was He who created the human soul, with its capacity for knowing and for loving. And He is not in Himself such as to leave the demands of the soul unsatisfied. - Education, pg. 133

Have you ever needed someone in your life who will just be there no matter what? Someone who loves you despite your faults, despite your unkind actions, and despite how wretched you feel? Your friends just don't understand you or what you are going through. You feel lost, alone, and helpless. "Does anyone care?" you ask. "Does anyone love me for who I am? Does anyone love me despite all my cares and the problems I cause?"

Friend, there is Someone who can be a positive answer to those questions. His name is Jesus. But you say, "Jesus doesn't love me. I don't know if I love Him either!" To that, I must reply, no! God can't not love you! That is who He is—*love*! Even if you turn your back on Him, He will never give up on you. John 3:16 says, "For God so loved *you*, that He gave His most special gift to you: His only Son! All you have to do is want His Gift and believe in Him. Then you will not perish! You will have everlasting life!" (my paraphrase).

Don't give up on God. Give Him a chance to work in your life. Think of all the times He has worked in your life in the past. Maybe you have been saved in certain life-threatening situations. Maybe you had someone come and encourage you and make your day better. Do you really believe that those situations could all be due to chance? No! I don't believe it! God has a plan for *you*, and that is why He has kept each and everyone of us alive: so that we can have the chance to get to know Him better and be a living testimony of the miraculous things He can do in our lives. When you feel depressed, stressed, sad, or lonely, look to Jesus for companionship and love! He will give it to You, and the peace that passes all understanding will be yours (Philippians 4:7). Just please believe in Him! He is the only One who will never fail you.

~ Yannika Stafford

249

On the Mountain

We need to know of an almighty arm that will hold us up, of an infinite Friend that pities us. We need to clasp a hand that is warm, to trust in a heart full of tenderness. - Education, pg. 133

In your relationship with God, have you ever fallen and lost sight of Him? When the road gets rough, does it seem that sometimes God has left you to fend for yourself, deserted and alone? Where is He?

Let's say you're on top of a mountain. Snow is falling all around you, covering everything with a beautiful blanket of white. Anything that you might have considered unsightly is blotted out, and the landscape looks fresh and new. But as you descend the mountain, the snow turns to rain. What was once beautiful is now dismal and bleak. Instead of being white, everything is dark and wet. The rain soaks through your clothes and makes you cold, and in your hurry to leave, you slip on a wet rock and land in the mud. Everything seems to be going wrong.

Now, let's compare the mountain to your spiritual walk, and let's say that the snow is like God. When you are at a high point in your spiritual walk (on top of the mountain), everything is great; you can feel God's presence in your life, and anything that might be going wrong is covered by the joy that you have in Christ. But then your faith fails, and it seems as if God is no longer there (down the mountain), and all of the hard circumstances that didn't matter before now threaten to crush you. What has happened to God? Is He still there? Yes, of course He is. Although the situation has changed, He hasn't forsaken you. Rain and snow are just different forms of the same thing, and although God seems harder to see in the rain, He is always there for you. He promises, "...I will never leave thee, nor forsake thee" (Hebrews 13:5 KJV).

~ Wesley Mayes

More Than a Concept, Part 1

No intangible principle, no impersonal essence or mere abstraction, can satisfy the needs and longings of human beings in this life of struggle with sin and sorrow and pain. - Education, pg. 133

You have to know more than just the fact that God exists. It can't just be a concept; it has to be real. You have to see it, smell it, hear it, touch it, taste it, and feel it. It must be more than a theory, or a mere acquaintance. You need a friend. You can't just know about God; you need to actually know Him.

How can you get to know God? One way is through His Word. The Bible is God's letter to us. In each story, God reveals something about His character, as well as a lesson to learn from. As you read the inspired words, God's heart and mind are laid open before you.

Another way is prayer. Prayer is more than asking God to bless your food and forgive your sins. It's talking to Him as you go about your day, asking for help and advice, telling Him a joke, or sharing your heart's secrets with Him. Prayer is opening your heart to God like you would to your best friend.

You can also get to know God through nature. The handiwork of Him who numbers the hairs on your head and notices a sparrow fall showcases His care for even the minutest details of your life.

As you begin to discover who God is through reading the Bible, talking to Him in prayer, and marveling at His works, something amazing will happen: He won't be just a concept, a doctrine, or a mere theory anymore. He will be real. God will be your Friend.

~ Rachel Petrello

251

More Than a Concept, Part 2

We need to know of an almighty arm that will hold us up, of an infinite Friend that pities us. We need to clasp a hand that is warm, to trust in a heart full of tenderness. - Education, pg. 133

Yesterday we saw that in order for God to be more than a concept, we need to get to know Him and not just know about Him. But, is God somebody we really want to know? Sometimes we tend to think of God kind of like a landlord, someone who's just there to make sure we follow all the rules. We don't want to waste time getting to know someone who's bossy.

While God does want to be our Lord, He also wants to be our friend because He knows what we've been through. "The Elder Brother of our race is by the eternal throne...He knows by experience what are the weaknesses of humanity, what are our wants, and where lies the strength of our temptations; for He was in all points temped like as we are..." (*The Desire of Ages*, pg. 329).

Are you suffering anxiety and pain? Jesus fell on His face, sweating drops of blood while He cried in the Garden of Gethsemane. Has a friend walked out on you? Jesus' friends fell asleep when He needed them most, and one of His closest friends denied knowing Him three times. Have you been abused or abandoned? Jesus hung on the cross, bloody, almost naked, stripped of His dignity, and mocked and rejected by the whole world!

You know, a friend is someone who can relate to what you're going through. There's not one thing that's happened to you that Christ didn't experience in some way. Who can relate to you better than that? God is tired of being your landlord. He wants to be your friend because He's been there. He knows your needs and struggles, and He's offering you a shoulder to lean on! He promises He'll never leave you nor forsake you, so what are you waiting for? Ask Him to become more than a concept; ask Him to be your Friend.

~ Rachel Petrello

September 10

Chance or Design?

The deepest students of science are constrained to recognize in nature the working of infinite power. But to man's unaided reason, nature's teaching cannot but be contradictory and disappointing. Only in the light of revelation can it be read aright. "Through faith we understand." - Education, pg. 134

Millions of years ago... We have all heard this phrase many times. It's in our textbooks, nature movies and documentaries, magazines, and we hear it at zoos and national parks. The theory of evolution is a large part of the conservation movement and seems to coat the science world.

This theory that the world is millions of years old is not new. However, it has only become popular in the last few hundred years. Before this, the majority of people believed that this world was created by intelligent design.

Many atheistic scientists have claimed that the theory of creation is a religion, while the theory of evolution is science. Yet, the reality is that it takes faith to believe either one. Which would you rather put your faith in? In the beginning...chemical soup and rocks, or in the beginning...God?

G.K. Chesterton writes: "It is absurd for the evolutionist to complain that it is unthinkable for an admittedly unthinkable God to make everything out of nothing, and then pretend that it is more thinkable that nothing should turn itself into anything."

I don't know about you, but I would rather put my faith in God. Just go outside into nature and observe the beauty, detail, and order. There is no question but that this world was made by an incredible Designer.

~ Laura Williams

Dirty Business

Its [the Bible's] principles of diligence, honesty, thrift, temperance, and purity are the secret of true success...That which lies at the foundation of business integrity and of true success is the recognition of God's ownership. - Education, pp. 135, 137

The CEOs of the "Tower of Babel" project thought it would be the most ambitious business venture yet. They thought that when the plan was completed, they would become rich, be respected, and most importantly, they would not have to depend upon God anymore. So, they quickly made the necessary arrangements and started building the tower. Everyone was working hard; everything was going according to plan. But one day, something went very wrong.

The Bible tells us that God was watching His people from the very beginning of their building project. He was hurt to see that they were trying to get away from Him. As the tower got taller and taller, He decided to stop its construction. In His mercy, He chose to spare their lives, but their consequence has continued to this day: He jumbled their language.

The people who decided to build the Tower of Babel tried to seek independence from God by doing dirty business. They tried to deny Him, so they could live their wicked lifestyle. In modern society, there are many people who get rich by doing corrupt commercial activities. They might appear to have great success, but it won't last for long. Proverbs 14:12 says, "There is a way that seems right to a man, but in the end it leads to death" (NIV). God will, one day, reveal their vicious plans of cheating. A truely successful businessman is aware that everything given to him belongs to God. He will allow Divinity to direct the future of his business. He acknowledges that diligence, thrift, temperance, and purity are essential for the success of the company.

Have you ever found yourself in a situation where you did a little "tricky business"? If you're trying to keep God out of your business, one day you'll end up spiritually, if not physically, bankrupt. Dirty business just isn't worth it. Let us ask God to give us the power to do the right things for the right reasons in every situation we face.

~ Valdis Cuvaldin

Do a Good Job

That which lies at the foundation of business integrity and of true success is the recognition of God's ownership. The Creator of all things, He is the original proprietor. - Education, pg. 137

Job was a very honest, and upright man who loved God with his whole being. He was one of the few men on earth who hated and shunned evil, and was very blessed. He had a wife, seven sons, and three daughters, and owned seven thousand sheep, three thousand camels, five hundred teams of oxen, and five hundred donkeys. Job was the most influential man in all the East!

One day, when the angels were reporting to God, Satan came too. "What have you been up to?" God asked.

"Oh, You know. Going here and there, checking things out," replied Satan.

"Have you noticed My friend Job? The one who is honest and true to his word, totally devoted to Me and hating evil."

"I've noticed him. Who wouldn't? You give him everything, and You take care of him and all his family and possessions. You bless everything he does! But I bet that if You reached down and took everything away from him, he would curse You, and then who would You brag about?"

"Go ahead and take away all that is his. Just don't lay a finger on him" (personal paraphrase of Job 1:6-12).

Over the next little while, Job went through a lot of suffering. Satan put his hand on all that Job possessed: all his children, animals, and almost all his servants were taken away. Eventually, Job himself was afflicted with sore boils from his head to his feet. However, Job was able to keep his faith throughout this time of great loss.

Job understood that all of his possessions were from God. "'The LORD gave and the LORD has taken away; may the name of the LORD be praised'" (Job 1:21 NIV). Job had just been doing his best with what God had given him, and even though he did not understand why it was being taken away, he still blessed his Father's name. He decided that whatever God gave or took away from him, he would still do a good job.

~ Jessica Hall

Lessons from Geese

For all that makes confidence and co-operation possible, the world is indebted to the law of God, as given in His word, and as still traced, in lines often obscure and well-nigh obliterated, in the hearts of men.
- Education, pg. 137

I love to watch geese heading south for the winter. It's a beautiful sight to watch their "V" formation in action as they go by. As you observe them, you might also be interested in what science has discovered about why they fly that way. Scientific study has shown that as each of these big birds flaps its wings, an uplift or updraft is created for the bird immediately following. By flying in a "V" formation, the whole flock adds at least seventy-one percent more distance to their flying range than if each bird flew on its own. It was also discovered that when a goose falls out of formation, it suddenly feels the drag and resistance of trying to go it alone and quickly gets back into formation to take advantage of the lifting power of the bird immediately in front. When the lead goose gets tired, he or she rotates back in the formation and another goose takes the lead. It's a beautiful picture of cooperation and teamwork.

Perhaps you've also noticed that there's a lot of honking going on up there. This is to encourage the leader. It's also a signal to keep up speed. Finally, when a goose gets sick or is wounded by a gunshot and falls out of the formation, two other geese will also fall out and follow the wounded or sick goose to help and protect it. They stay with this hurting one until it is either able to fly again or is dead, and then they launch out on their own or with another formation to catch up with their original group.

The cooperation of these geese shows us a picture of the way God wants us to work together, in our homes, families, with our friends, and in our business dealings. God has laid out principles in the Bible that are still to be the basis of how we deal with each other today. Even though humanity has pushed God aside, the faint tracings of His law are still etched in our hearts, and God uses these pricks to our conscience to bring us back to the cooperative way of life He intended for us to live.

~ Anna Fink

Bad Day?

Though He slay me, yet will I trust in Him...When He hath tried me, I shall come forth as gold. - Job 13:15, 23:10 KJV

Ever had one of those days where everything seems to go wrong? You start the day with uncooperative hair; then it progresses to falling asleep in class. Your friends give you strange looks because of your...unique hair-do, and you have a pop quiz in science that you were not prepared for in the least. This then flows nicely into missing the bus, arguing with a younger sibling, forgetting to feed the cat, having to eat Brussels sprouts for supper again, and to top it off, going to bed late because you were working on a project due the next day that you had conveniently saved for the last minute. Sound familiar?

If anyone knew about bad days, it was Job. Talk about trials—and I don't mean just missing the bus! Think of your worst day; then imagine having it about five hundred times consecutively, and maybe you'll get about one third of Job's experience. But, he remained positive because he knew God had it all under control. There was a grander plan that he couldn't see, and he refused to despair. He understood that something tried in the fire comes out better in the end.

1 Peter 1:7 says, "That the trial of your faith, being much more precious than of gold that perisheth, though it be tried with fire, might be found unto praise and honour and glory at the appearing of Jesus Christ..." (KJV). We have impurities and imperfections that need to be refined, and God sees this. He is the only One who can fully and properly refine us for His purpose, and He knows the best way. As an earthly refiner doesn't waste his time on worthless metal, so the Great Refiner wouldn't spend time on that which has no value to Him, but only on that which He perceives to have potential. So, instead of complaining when you encounter a hardship, trust in the Lord and rejoice that He has found you worthy of His refining fire.

~ Carmen Hartwell

An Omnipresent Voice

He may disregard that voice, he may seek to drown its warning, but in vain. It follows him. It makes itself heard. It destroys his peace.
- Education, pg. 144

Have you ever heard God's voice speak to you? Are you acquainted with His silent promptings throughout your day? I remember distinct moments in my life when I heard God's voice, maybe not audibly, but it was evident to me that He was speaking. In times of temptation, the Holy Spirit would alert me to the point that I would have to stop and think about what I was doing wrong and correct myself.

But after a while, His voice became fainter. It was hard enough to hear in the beginning, but then it became almost inaudible beneath the noise of my frenzied distractions. I was putting so many things higher than God on my "important" list, that I hardly spent any time with Him throughout my day. Some of those things were not necessarily bad: friends, education, work, sports. However, all these things may have their proper place, but it is not in the place of God. It was like they had become my own little gods. After all, I had invested more time in them than I had in the real God. So, after much soul-searching, along with question and answer sessions with God, I finally realized what I had been getting myself into. My priorities had become tangled and distorted, and I hadn't asked Him to help me through my difficulties. It was like climbing up a steep mountain with the intent of reaching the pinnacle, but always falling down and never being able to reach my destination. Now I had to start to climb all the way back up again.

I must recognize that I cannot win these battles against self on my own. But "I can do all things through Christ who strengthens me" (Philippians 4:13 NKJV), and God's voice will always be there to guide me, no matter what the situation. You may think that you can defeat your temptations and overcome your weaknesses on your own, but in the end, discouragement awaits all who take that path. God's way is best because He knows the end from the beginning! His voice speaks to you. It makes itself heard. It follows you, not for the purpose of destroying your peace, but because He knows you can't make it on your own.

~ Cyrus Guccione

258

Just Let Go

"What shall it profit a man, if he shall gain the whole world, and lose his own soul? Or what shall a man give in exchange for his soul?" This is a question that demands consideration by every parent, every teacher, every student—by every human being, young or old.
- Education, pg. 145

An interesting system has been used for capturing monkeys in the jungles of Africa. The goal of this system is to humanely capture monkeys for shipment to zoos in North America. To accomplish this, heavy bottles with narrow necks are partially filled with sweet-smelling nuts and placed deep in the jungle. The next morning, the captors return to find a monkey trapped by each bottle. This is accomplished because the monkey, attracted by the smell and appearance of the fruit and nuts, puts its hand into the bottle to extract the food. Because of the bottle's narrow neck, the monkey cannot remove his hand unless he lets go of the bait. The bottle is too heavy to carry away, and the monkey struggles in vain to escape. His greed and fear of letting go eventually cost him his freedom and his lunch.

Luke 18:18-24 tells a story about a rich young ruler who wanted freedom and eternal life. He knew that his wealth and position could not satisfy the longings of his heart. So he asked Jesus, "Teacher, what must I do to be saved?" Jesus answered, "Sell all that you have and give it to the poor. Then you will have treasure in heaven." That rich young ruler turned around and walked away very sad. His heart was tied so tightly to his possessions that he couldn't let go, not even to free himself and gain eternal life!

Do you have something in your life that you can't seem to let go of? As long as you are holding on to what you have in this world, you will always be a captive of Satan. Yet, even though you can't free yourself, there is still a way to escape. Letting go requires will power, perseverance, and lots of prayer. God has promised to give you what you need, when you need it. All you have to do is trust Him; it's that simple. Stop, pray, and just let go.

~ Wesley Donesky

Phobia of Failure

The beauty and fruitfulness of the land were lost sight of through fear of the difficulties in the way of its occupation. - Education, pg. 149

Everyone has a fear of failure. We worry about what people will think of us if we mess up. Oftentimes this fear is so great that it becomes debilitating. For myself, I sometimes become so afraid of falling short that I don't even try. For instance, one weekend my school drove down to Rosario Beach in Washington for a campout. On Friday afternoon, a group of students were playing soccer, and one of my friends, Rachel, tried to get me to join in. Now, I'm not very good at sports, so I resisted her. Still, Rachel kept at me. I eventually decided to give it a try, but as soon as I saw everyone running around, I changed my mind! On Sunday, Rachel and a couple of other friends asked me to play volleyball. I walked over to the net feeling about as awkward as a duck trying to knit a sweater. When the ball was served in my direction, I watched it sail over the net...and land in front of me in the sand. Someone spoke up, "Uh, I think that was for you." I had such a crippling fear of failure that I didn't budge an inch when I saw the ball coming!

Moses had sent out twelve spies to search out the Promised Land for the purpose of conquering it. When they returned, ten of the spies could only speak of the obstacles they would have to overcome in order to possess the promised land. They talked of the giants and their weapons of war. They looked at the Promised Land, but they only saw looming failure. However, the other two spies, Caleb and Joshua, saw things differently. They saw the obstacles through God's eyes. They knew God had promised them the land, so when they gazed upon it, success was their only option.

So in reality, the only thing that keeps us from doing great things for God today is fear. Fear is what kept the ten spies from possessing Canaan and what kept me from being successful in actually hitting the volleyball. We need to move beyond our anxiety and believe God's Word. This way, when the volleyball is served in your direction, you can hit it hard with the hand of faith. Why not ask God to help you overcome your fear so you can do great things for Him?

~ Anneliese Wahlman

260

Empty?

By his own bitter experience, Solomon learned the emptiness of a life that seeks in earthly things its highest good. - Education, pg. 153

Solomon had it all. As the son of a mighty warrior-king, his every need and want was met. God had especially blessed Solomon with certain capabilities so that he could ably and justly rule his father's kingdom. "Noble in youth, noble in manhood, the beloved of his God, Solomon entered on a reign that gave high promise of prosperity and honor" (*Education*, pp. 153, 154). But it was not to last. Pride separated Solomon from God, and he began to pursue worldly ambitions. It was an unsatisfying quest, which led Solomon to later write: "Then I looked on all the works that my hands had wrought, and on the labour that I had laboured to do: and, behold, all was vanity and vexation of spirit, and there was no profit under the sun" (Ecclesiastes 2:11 KJV).

Sometimes it takes a while to hit home, but I myself have been in that discontented state. I was dissatisfied with my insignificance, so I tried a new job to get noticed, and...I was still unhappy. I thought, "Maybe my talent will make others appreciate me more," which led me to practice piano like a maniac. And sure, I got attention, but...I was still unhappy. I wanted this, I wanted that, and...I was still unhappy. It wasn't until I focused on God that He was able to fill the God-shaped hole in my heart. Then, bit by bit, I felt content; I felt secure. I was truly happy and had complete peace.

In this day and age, it is easy to get caught up in this "make me happy" attitude. From the latest iPod to microwave dinners, or the laundry detergent that is "exactly what you want," there is always some new gizmo that is sure to put a smile on your face and make you think, "All I need is this!" It's a lie. Material things will only bring an empty happiness. It doesn't even have to be material things. You might want a better relationship with your friends, status, recognition for your hard work, or a job promotion. But, in order to be truly satisfied, you must first find God. He will truly make you happy. It's not a gimmick or a fad; it's the truth. I hope that you will be able to experience the happiness that only God can give.

~ Sarah Chang

261

Unshakable Faith

Against this man, Satan brought scornful charge: "Doth Job fear God for nought? Hast Thou not made an hedge about him, and about his house, and about all that he hath on every side?...Put forth Thine hand now, and touch all that he hath;" "touch his bone and his flesh, and he will curse Thee to Thy face." - Education, pg. 155

Job was one of the richest and most righteous men of his time. God had blessed him with a great number of animals, loyal servants, wonderful children, and a faithful wife. What more could Job ask for? At first glance, it might seem that there was an "agreement" between him and God: "I worship You; You bless me." One day, Satan decided to try Job's faith by taking every blessing that God gave Him. In only a few days, most of his animals and servants were lost, all of his children were killed, and his health was terribly afflicted. Even when he found himself in this terrible situation, Job did not get discouraged. Even when his wife urged him to curse God, he replied, "...You are talking like a foolish woman. Shall we accept good from God, and not trouble?" (Job 2:10 NIV).

What a great example of faith we can find in Job! Even when Satan took everything he had, he still chose to remain loyal to God. Job depended upon Him so much that even when he questioned his own sanity, he did not give up on His Creator. As a result of his incredible trust in the Divine, Job was tremendously blessed with sons and daughters and even more riches than he had before.

Would you like to have the unshakable faith of Job that goes beyond any human understanding? Sometimes God may bless us greatly, but sometimes He may put us to the test. If you find yourself in this kind of situation, do not worry. Cast all your cares upon God, trust Him fully, and He will not only bless you again, but He will also fill the emptiness you had before. God allows trials in our lives to mature our faith and to increase our dependency upon Him. My desire is to have the faith of Job one day. As you go through your daily schedule, take time to reflect upon the characters of the great individuals of the Bible and practice a dependency upon God that will stand in the midst of trials.

~ Valdis Cuvaldin

Where I Belong

My soul longs, indeed it faints for the courts of the LORD; my heart and my flesh sing for joy to the living God. - Psalm 84:2 NRSV

Have you ever missed someone so much that you longed to hear their voice? As I have gotten to know God better, He has awakened a love for Him in me, and lately I've realized that I miss God. The whispers I hear in His word and my heart make me more eager to hear His audible voice. This excerpt from a song by Chris Rice expresses the longing in my heart for God:

I heard about the day You went away,
You said You had to go prepare a place
And even though I've never seen Your face,
I'm missin' You.
Cause somewhere behind those stars,
Is Someone who belongs to me
And I know in my deepest heart,
There's a place for You
Until I find the place You made for me,
I'm missin' You.
I dream about Your promise to return,
And I wake up hanging on Your every word
But for now my feet are planted here on earth,
Still I'm missin' You.
And even though they say that I'm a fool,
I know You see me waiting here for You
And I pray that somehow You'll get here soon,
Cause I'm missin' You.

Are you as excited to see our Savior as I am? I just can't wait till I see Him coming with clouds of angels, the sheer brilliance lighting up the dark world around me. I will eagerly stare into the light and search for the face of my dearest Friend, and as His eyes meet mine for the first time, I will hear His voice in my heart: "This is the end to which I have loved you. But truly, it's only the beginning. I've missed you too, but now we'll spend eternity together!" And when He meets me at the gates of New Jerusalem, I will hear with my ears the voice my heart knows, "Well done, good and faithful servant. Welcome home." I will be where I belong at last. Will you join me?

~ Valerie Jacobson

A Simple Prayer

Trust in the Lord with all your heart; do not depend on your own understanding. Seek His will in all you do, and he will show you which path to take. - Proverbs 3:5, 6 NLT

When I was reading Hosea tonight, Lord, I heard You speaking to me. You know I struggle with trusting your voice when it goes against my wants. It amazes me how much the prophet Hosea trusted You. First, You told him to go marry Gomer, a whore. Hosea knew that You saw the end from the beginning; he believed You knew what was best for his life. Lord, I need to confess: my faith is not that strong. If You told me to marry someone who was openly an adulterer, I would come up with lots of little excuses. I wouldn't want to ruin my reputation.

So many times my pride gets in the way. It blinds me to the great potential I would have if I chose to listen to Your voice. Jesus, make me more like Hosea. Hosea went through so much, but in his weakness he was made strong. I know that when everything is going really well for me, I tend to lose sight of the One who is bestowing those blessings.

Even after Hosea married Gomer, she continued sleeping around with other men. But when she ran out of money and food and sold herself as a slave, Hosea still bought her back. This kind of forgiveness can only be given by You, God, the Giver of love.

After reading this, I thought of my relationship with You. I'm Gomer, the whore. I play around with the world, knowing exactly where I belong and that what I am doing is wrong. My relationship with You often becomes less of a priority to me. But when I have no other place to turn to, You are always there bidding me to come home. You have so often bought me back; You have never failed me. What is there not to trust? Please, take my pride and crush it. I want to listen to Your voice.

~ Sarah-Kate Lingerfelt

A Song in My Heart

Great have been the blessings received by men in response to songs of praise. The few words recounting an experience of the wilderness journey of Israel have a lesson worthy of our thought..."Then sang Israel this song: 'Spring up, O well; sing ye unto it: the well, which the princes digged, which the nobles of the people delved, with the scepter, and with their staves." How often in spiritual experience is this history repeated! how often by words of holy song are unsealed in the soul the springs of penitence and faith, of hope and love and joy!
- Education, pg. 162

Oh, no! Not again! Why does she have to sing every time we are together? I would always get irritated when my mom would serenade me in the car. One morning, when I was grumpy, I dared to ask her why she always sang when we were driving. "Mom, you do not even have a good voice. Besides, every time I try to review for school, I am always distracted by your chirping voice. Can you please do me a favor and stop singing!" Calmly she replied, "Honey, did you know that even famous surgeons listen to sacred music while they preform surgeries? If you have a song in your heart at all times, it gives you peace, and in your case, it will help you in your studies!" A few days later, I decided to try my mom's "annoying " practice. Every morning before I went to school, I formed the habit of keeping a song in my heart. Miraculously, it worked! It gave me such an amazing feeling of optimism, joy, and love towards others.

There are many instances in the Bible when the children of God chose to sing and praise God aloud. This not only increased their faith in Him, but also brought joy, unity, and love among them. God considered poetry and song so important for the Christian walk that He gave us a priceless treasury of Psalms. He knows that by singing at all times, we will be brought into connection with Him. Singing sacred music will give you an appetite for life, and soon your love and good attitude will become contagious like my mom's. So, cultivate the habit of having a song in your heart everywhere you go.

~ Valdis Cuvaldin

Two Sides of Music

The history of the songs of the Bible is full of suggestion as to the uses and benefits of music and song. Music is often perverted to serve purposes of evil, and it thus becomes one of the most alluring agencies of temptation. But, rightly employed, it is a precious gift of God, designed to uplift the thoughts to high and noble themes, to inspire and elevate the soul. - Education, pg. 167

Music can be such a powerful tool for good. I believe this is why Satan has worked so hard to pervert and misuse it. With six thousand years of practice, he well knows our weaknesses and tastes and has created some music to seem attractive and alluring while it is takes our minds farther and farther from heavenly things.

I well know the power and pull that Satan's music can have, but whenever I have listened to it, I have been left with a feeling of discontentment and even depression. I came to the realization that I cannot have a close relationship with God while listening to music inspired by Satan.

On the other hand, God has inspired music that lifts the soul, elevates the mind, and touches the heart. Such music can sometimes reach people when sermons and preaching cannot.

Martin Luther once said, "The devil takes flight at the sound of music, just as he does at the words of theology, and for this reason the prophets always combined theology and music, the teaching of truth and the chanting of Psalms and hymns. After theology, I give the highest place and greatest honor to music."

While traveling with the Fountainview Orchestra and Choir, I have had the privilege of seeing first hand the power of sacred music to change lives! It is truly amazing.

I love music so much now, but I look forward to hearing the music of heaven and joining in with the choir of angels! How wonderful that will be!

~ Laura Williams

Praise Him

Let there be singing in the home, of songs that are sweet and pure, and there will be fewer words of censure and more of cheerfulness and hope and joy. Let there be singing in the school, and the pupils will be drawn closer to God, to their teachers, and to one another.
- Education, pg. 168

It was another one of those days. It had been a long night, and an even longer morning, and I was NOT in a good mood. I was looking forward to the finishing the day so I could sit in my room and sulk. After class, I saw that the annoying white piece of paper announcing noon music practice had been posted. So, I gloomily stormed into practice and glowered at the director until we were finally dismissed. Rushing through lunch, I tried to avoid everyone for fear they might try to cheer me up.

Now work was next on the agenda; so I changed my clothes and headed down to the cafeteria. On a typical day, I am happy to work in the cafeteria; I just love being in the kitchen, especially because I have so much fun chatting with the other girls while we clean up. We usually talk for a while, then sing a few songs and chat some more, which makes for a relaxing work period. However, on this day I was stressed and annoyed and didn't want to talk to anyone; so I just sang quietly to myself. While I was singing to myself, I didn't feel any better, but after a while, the other girls started singing along. Singing with the other girls was so much fun! Creating harmonies and making music while working started to slowly cheer me up, and I no longer felt as bad as before. Our work supervisor came over to us and told us that while we were singing, angels were listening to us, and not just listening, but also singing along. I thought that was so cool—I mean, angels? Come on, they wouldn't care enough about our singing to come down to the cafeteria kitchen at Fountainview Academy, would they? That little experience let me know that even on the worst of days God cares about me, and He will send the right people to cheer me up. He will even put a song in my heart, as He did that day. So, if you're having a bad day, just sing a song to praise God. I can almost guarantee you'll feel better.

~ Jo Holdal

Songs of Prayer

As part of religious service, singing is as much an act of worship as is prayer. - Education, pg. 168

Singing and music are a huge part of my life, especially since I came to school here at Fountainview. Last year in my Bible class, we memorized hymns as a class. When we first started doing this, I thought it was rather pointless, but over time, as we memorized more hymns, I began to see its importance. Instead of simply reading the words off the screen as I sang, I was able to recite them from memory and focus on their meaning rather than just reading them for the sake of singing. They began to hold a place in my heart. I know in any situation, there is a song I can sing that will cheer me up and lift my thoughts heavenward. It's a way of praising God even through my trials.

Our words have power, power which we often don't even recognize. When was the last time you stopped and considered your words before speaking? If we spoke every word as a prayer, just imagine how much trouble we would avoid. Likewise, when we sing, it is even more important to recognize the importance of making our song a prayer of praise and thankfulness.

I have always loved to write poems. The last poem I wrote was for a song. It is terribly difficult to make each word fit so that the verse will have the right number of syllables and still make sense. So, as I wrote, I prayed a lot. Even though I was praying, it seemed like I didn't really know what I was doing. I wasn't even sure if any of it worked together. When I finished though, I was amazed at how well everything flowed. The words made sense, and my own writing impacted me. As I look back on that experience, I know that God was the one inspiring me. I have read many of the stories about how certain hymns were written, and I can see how God led each of the writers. Sometimes we think that hymns are old and outdated, but I encourage you to pick up a hymnal once in a while, read a few songs, and see if you are not touched. Then take those songs and turn them into a personal prayer to your Creator.

~ Danielle Schafer

Songs of Promise

How often to the soul hard-pressed and ready to despair, memory recalls some word of God's,—the long-forgotten burden of a childhood song,—and temptations lose their power, life takes on new meaning and new purpose, and courage and gladness are imparted to other souls! - Education, pg. 168

A few weeks ago, I had had a hard day and was wondering what God has in mind for my future: what college should I attend? What job will I do? Whom will I someday marry? I began to doubt that God has a plan for my life. All of a sudden, a song popped into my head, and I began to sing it to myself,

> *I am a promise,*
> *I am a possibility,*
> *I am a promise*
> *With a capital 'P'*
> *I am a great big bundle of potentiality*
> *And I am waiting*
> *to hear God's voice*
> *And I am trying*
> *to make the right choice.*
>
> *I am a promise to be*
> *anything God wants me to be.*

It just encouraged me and reminded me that God is in control of my life and He has a great plan for me.

Songs have this powerful influence on people. "There are few means more effective for fixing His words in the memory than repeating them in song" (*Education*, pg. 167). Singing can also bring back memories and cheer and uplift you when you're feeling discouraged.

Next time you feel like everything's gone wrong or your day has been especially hard, try singing to God a familiar hymn that suits the way you're wanting to feel. Songs can help uplift your attitude, so that you want to praise God with all your heart.

~ Victoria West

The Sinner's Prayer

As a part of religious service, singing is as much an act of worship as is prayer. Indeed, many a song is prayer. If the child is taught to realize this, he will think more of the meaning of the words he sings and will be more susceptible to their power. - Education, pg. 168

I can just imagine the scene when Ray Boltz wrote the song, "The Sinner's Prayer." He sits in a dark corner of his room with a small journal. Struggling long and hard with doubt and temptations, he suddenly cries out. With agonizing frustration, he falls at the feet of Jesus, weeping and whispering these words:

Jesus, I believe that You are there,
And You're listening to this sinner's prayer.
Touch this broken heart and make it new.
I believe in You.
Please forgive me for my sin,
All I've done, and all I've been.
Serving You forevermore, everyday you'll be my Lord.
Jesus, I believe that You are there,
And you're listening to this sinner's prayer.
Knowing You'll remember what You've heard,
I believe Your word.

Now, I don't know exactly what the writer's thoughts were when he wrote these words, but I know these aren't just flowery lyrics set to a tune. Sacred music, particularly vocal, is meant to be a prayer.

I know that when I'm practicing with the choir, or singing silly songs during work, I tend to forget the sanctity of music. I have to stop and think about the words I'm singing. Are they a prayer? Or are they just obnoxious utterances? Would I sing those words when I'm on my knees? It's amazing when I really listen to the words in our choir songs. The music just fills the message with so much power, and it's such a blessing!

When you play, sing, or listen to music, is your song a prayer?

~ Rachel Petrello

New Light

We have no reason to doubt God's word because we cannot understand the mysteries of His providence. In the natural world we are constantly surrounded with wonders beyond our comprehension. Should we then be surprised to find in the spiritual world also mysteries that we cannot fathom? The difficulty lies solely in the weakness and narrowness of the human mind. - Education, pg. 170

According to a recent article from the April issue of Popular Science magazine, "The more we learn, the more we realize we don't know. Radio astronomers at the University of Manchester in the UK have discovered a baffling new object in a nearby galaxy that's unlike anything we've ever seen in the Milky Way. It could be the first-ever detection of a micro-quasar, or a young supernova, or even an offshoot of the massive black hole that is believed to anchor M82. But the nature of the object has rendered each of those theories somewhat unlikely, leaving researchers casting about for answers."

For hundreds of years, the Bible has been called a book of fairy tales. It has been ridiculed as a compilation of bedtime stories and foolish imaginings of men. But if this were true, wouldn't it have been dismissed as a lie long ago? Yet, far from being forgotten, the Bible has inspired countless people to stand and give their lives for its principles. It is true that some parts of the Bible are difficult to understand. However, this fact only provides greater evidence of its divine nature. Scientists cannot comprehend the universe. They cannot even fully understand our solar system. Scientists learn new things about the universe every day. The Bible is the same way. We will never understand all of the lessons, meanings, and insights of the Bible. However, every human being can discover new truth and light if they are willing to be taught by the Divine Teacher. Ask God today to give you new light and hope as you search the scriptures for their hidden mysteries and greatest blessings.

~ Wesley Donesky

When God Allows Pain

...His word shall be ever unfolding. While "the secret things belong unto the Lord our God," "those things which are revealed belong unto us and to our children. "...The fact needs to be emphasized, and often repeated, that the mysteries of the Bible are not such because God has sought to conceal truth, but because our own weakness or ignorance makes us incapable of comprehending or appropriating truth. The limitation is not in His purpose, but in our capacity. - Education, pg. 171

On December 26, 2004, my family and I took a trip to Bali, Indonesia. What was supposed to be a non-stressful holiday turned into a very nerve-racking one. That same day, an earthquake hit southeastern Asia, with its epicenter in Sumatra, Indonesia. It was recorded as the fifth deadliest earthquake with more than 230,000 casualties. This resulted in a catastrophic tsunami. Fortunately for my family, Bali was not affected. Two days after this horrific event, I saw a headline in the news that completely messed me up for the entire trip: "Where Was God During the Tsunami?"

For several days I struggled with that question. Why would God allow so many people to die in only a few minutes? My uncle sensed my concerns, and he gave me a Bible text that answered the question I had. Deuteronomy 29:29 tells us, "The secret things belong to the LORD our God, but the things revealed belong to us and to our children forever, that we may follow all the words of this law" (NIV). Here, God clearly tells us that some things may not be revealed to us. It is not because He is trying to hide them from us, but it is because our sinful, limited minds would not understand His plans.

As Christians, we should not question God's actions. If He allows suffering and pain, He has a very good reason for doing so. It might seem hard to comprehend this, but we need to trust the Divine and accept the reality that stands before us. It should not draw us away from God, but rather drive us closer to Him. If you struggle with things you do not understand, pray that God will give you strength and power to put His judgment before your own.

~ Valdis Cuvaldin

Transformed

In its [the Bible's] power, men and women have broken the chains of sinful habit. They have renounced selfishness...Souls that have borne the likeness of Satan have been transformed into the image of God. This change is itself the miracle of miracles. - Education, pg. 172

When I was X years old (I won't say how old I was because that is kind of embarrassing), I had a very bad habit of losing my temper. The smallest things would set me off. Of course, it was mostly with family that I would display bad behavior. I'm ashamed to say it, but I would yell, slam doors, and hit people. I didn't like myself or how I acted, but when I would get angry, I wanted to let it out!

Around that same time, I was struggling to start having personal devotions. I wanted to be consistent, but it was so hard to get up in the morning! Several times I had made decisions to start, but I would always wake up tired the next morning and in no mood to actually read out of my junior devotional book. When I was talking with my mom one night, I told her that I just didn't feel like having my devotions in the morning. She replied, "Allie, just try it for one month." She told me that I needed to do it even when I didn't feel like it. So, I decided to give it another try; I could handle thirty days. The next morning though, as usual, I didn't really want to read, but by God's strength, I managed to stick with it. When the month was finished, I just kept going, and I've been having my devotions ever since.

Now, I'm not sure whether it started before or after, but around the time that I started having my devotions consistently, I began to lose my temper less frequently. God was changing me! It didn't happen overnight, and it definitely wasn't easy! But by God's power and much prayer on my part, I was gradually able to overcome.

The Bible has power—power to transform lives. If we want to be changed, we must spend that time with God every morning. Maybe it's reading a devotional book like the one you're holding or just a chapter of the Bible. Whatever way you spend it, if you take time with God, you can be changed just like I was.

~ Anneliese Wahlman

273

The Fruition of Choice

...The curse causeless shall not come. - Proverbs 26:2 KJV

My family and I were birdwatching at one of our favorite locations. As we came to the last leg of the trail heading to our car, we noticed a sign that read: "Beware of Sand-hill Cranes." It explained that it was breeding season, and this trail passed right by a nesting site. We could see the Sand-hill crane a little way ahead, sitting peacefully by the trail. Knowing that the fastest route was past the crane, we decided to try it. One by one we began to pass him on the narrow trail. He did not even look up at the first few of us, but when I went past, he chased me. Now we were stuck: some of us must pass the crane, one way or the other, if we were to stay together. Eventually, everyone got past except my dad, who was waiting until last. Dad rushed by with the crane in hot pursuit. The crane gave chase with massive strides, wings flapping and bill stabbing. Catching up, he jabbed his bill into my dad's leg. Thankfully, the crane did no real damage. Still, as I think of the fear that ran through me when I glanced back and saw the crane, I can assure you that we will never unnecessarily pass one again.

If we would have listened to the warning on the sign, we could have avoided a lot of stress. Looking back on this brings me to three points that can help you avoid adding to life's trials. First, realize that "To a great degree the experiences of life are the fruition of our own thoughts and deeds" (*Education*, pg. 146). Next, listen to God's voice so that we can make good decisions. "Be still, and know that I am God..." (Psalm 46:10 KJV). Then, no matter how God speaks to you—in your morning devotions, through His still small voice, or even by an experience during your day—follow His leading. When you use these three steps, you will make choices that honor God, and He will honor you with the peace and joy that come from good decisions.

~ Kevin Corrigan

October 2

More Than Fertilizer

In the creation it was His purpose that the earth be inhabited by beings whose existence should be a blessing to themselves and to one another, and an honor to their Creator. - Education, pg. 174

Picture this: you're taking the day off to spend time with your family at the local zoo. You've seen the leathery-skinned elephants, the penguins in their tuxedos, and the adorable otters. Then you walk by the monkey exhibit. While looking at an exceptionally hairy ape, you overhear another animal enthusiast exclaiming, "Wow! Just think, millions and millions of years ago, that is what we were! Just looking at that ape fills me with a sense of purpose! I just feel inspired knowing that is where I came from." Doesn't something sound wrong here?

So many people are wandering this earth aimlessly. They have no goals, no plans, no ideas, or dreams. They waste their lives—why? Because they have no purpose, no idea where they came from or where they are going. Think about it. If you really believed that you were created by accident and that when you died there was nothing left, then what would be the point of life? Why try to be good? What does it matter if you do wrong? Why try to get anywhere in life or do anything of worth? You're just going to die and turn into fertilizer in the end.

As Christians, we know that we are not just a coincidence. We know that we were made by an all powerful, universe-creating God. Mankind is not just a fluke of nature. God has a definite purpose for each of our lives. But do we really *know* this? If we truly believed that each of us was created by God for a specific intent, then wouldn't our lives show it? We would be spending our time and energy furthering that purpose. Our goals in life, our dreams, plans—everything would be centered in fulfilling God's purpose in our lives. We need to ask God to put that purpose into our hearts, not just our heads. It's only when we have this goal, this aim, burning within us that we can truly be what Christ wants us to be—more than fertilizer.

~ Anneliese Wahlman

I Need Delays

And not only so, but we glory in tribulations also: knowing that tribulation worketh patience; And patience, experience; and experience, hope... - Romans 5:3, 4 KJV

Impatience. I struggle with having this feeling that centers on myself instead of others. The fast-paced life that society has today teaches me to want things right away with the least possible wait. When my computer is too slow, when I have to wait longer for someone, or when my plans don't go as expected, I always sense an impatient feeling welling up inside of me. It isn't enough to look relaxed on the outside; I must also have a long-suffering spirit on the inside that is completely content to experience inconvenience. But the best way for me to learn patience is to practice it. Every inconvenience that interrupts my day is God's way of teaching me to be patient. The more my patience is tested, the more it will grow.

I also tend to be impatient in my relationship with God. When I pray, I expect an immediate answer; and when I read a verse or passage from Scripture, I want God to help me understand it right away. I desire a strong and thriving relationship with God, but that can't happen overnight. Just as in any relationship, it takes time and effort. God increases my faith and dependence upon Him when He allows me to wait for an answer. He knows that I need to experience delays because, without that test of faith, my spirituality will remain weak and shallow.

I used to dislike delays, but now I thank God for them because I know I need them. I still have so much patience to learn, but learning to praise God as I wait is a step further along the journey. "Wait on the LORD: be of good courage, and He shall strengthen thine heart: wait, I say, on the LORD" (Psalm 27:14 KJV). When impatience tries to well up inside you because you have to wait, thank God for the delay. Long-suffering patience, in its truest form, is a character trait worth having for eternity.

~ Megan Metcalf

October 4

Higher Purpose

In the creation it was His purpose that the earth be inhabited by beings whose existence should be a blessing to themselves and to one another, and an honor to their Creator. All who will may identify themselves with this purpose. - Education, pg. 174

Do you ever feel like you can't figure out what your purpose is in life? Perhaps you are moving past a milestone in your life, and you still don't know what direction to take afterwards. I will be graduating in a year, and I am not yet very sure what my plans will be. I know I want to be sure of some reason and goal to live for—something to base my life upon and work towards—and I'm sure I'm not the only one who has this desire.

Ever since I was three years old, I wanted to play the violin. I didn't start taking lessons, however, until I was six years old. But since then, music has been one of the main focuses in my life. When I became skilled enough, I played in festivals and took violin and theory exams with the Royal Conservatory of Music. For a long time now, I have been thinking of pursuing music as a career. I've been working at it with the goal and expectation that I would work to the highest level I wanted, then maybe teach violin and play in an orchestra or become a concert soloist.

Lately I have been wondering about this ambition. I've realized that I was pretty set on following my own desires and plans, even though I told myself that I would do what God wanted. But God has shown me that if I am to give my whole life to Him, then I must surrender this as well. Up until now it has been mostly a selfish purpose, and I hadn't really given much thought as to how I could serve God and others with the talent He's given me. Time is short, and I want to be sure that I am letting God work through me to bring others to Him. Even though I'm not exactly sure how God wants me to work for Him, I don't have to worry about trying to figure out my purpose in life because I have chosen to try to honor God and be a blessing in all that I do. I have decided to identify myself with His higher purpose. Will you do the same?

~ Valerie Jacobson

Faithfulness is Your Strength

For whatsoever is born of God overcometh the world: and this is the victory that overcometh the world, even our faith. - 1 John 5:4 KJV

What is true success? When I find myself going to heaven with Jesus, that will be success. "For what shall it profit a man, if he shall gain the whole world, and lose his own soul?" (Mark 8:36 KJV). This verse practically says, "The biggest success you could ever have is receiving salvation. Don't risk losing it for anything else." We also can succeed or fail in many smaller ways. Although these may not seem as important, they quickly add up to either big successes or disastrous failures. So, how do we succeed? Can success be guaranteed?

Many times we think our success is dependent upon the opportunities we have and the skills and other assets we've acquired. But the truth is that only faithfully serving God gives us the strength to succeed. In the book *Education*, I found a powerful quote that tells how to succeed: "...The strength of nations, as of individuals, is not found in the opportunities or facilities that appear to make them invincible...It is measured by the fidelity with which they fulfill God's purpose" (pg. 175). Did you catch that? Your strength is determined by how faithfully you carry out God's purpose for your life. Anyone can be faithful to God. God promises in the Bible, "I will heal their backsliding... " (Hosea 14:4 KJV). He can make you a faithful disciple. Even if you are weak, you can be strong. We are given the promise: "...My grace is sufficient for thee: for my strength is made perfect in weakness" (2 Corinthians 12:9 KJV). Your weakness isn't a hindrance to God. He can work perfectly through you.

Do you want to succeed? I guarantee that if you choose to faithfully obey God, you will overcome. Don't give up! Overcoming is a gradual process made up of many challenges. Remember that faith *is* the victory. You *have* the victory if you trust in Jesus.

~ Kevin Corrigan

Like a Child

...Verily I say unto you, Except ye be converted, and become as little children, ye shall not enter into the kingdom of heaven. - Matthew 18:3 KJV

I remember vividly my parents reading me stories from the Bible. From Abraham and Isaac to Moses and Elijah, I enjoyed every single one of them. One of the characters that fascinated me the most was Daniel. I would shout "victory" every time my mom finished reciting the story of his deliverance from the lions' den. After Daniel became my hero, I started praying like he prayed and even having the same diet as he did. The more time I spent in prayer, the deeper my connection with Jesus became. My walk with God seemed so easy. Yet, I did not realize the influence that the Bible had on my life until years later when my mom told me a story that deeply touched me.

Several years ago, she was experiencing a very hard time. Her business was not going well, and on top of that, my sister was becoming a more and more rebellious teenager. One day while I was playing, I heard my mom whimpering in her room, so it seemed normal for me to go and give her a little bit of encouragement. "Mommy, why are you crying?" I shyly said, "You seem really worried lately. Please do not be! Love and trust Jesus, and life will be much easier!" Years later, she explained to me that those simple words gave her so much courage and immensely strengthened her relationship with God.

Have you ever felt encouraged by the words of a small child? Often times, Jesus chooses to use the little ones to give us a message. Just a few words of encouragement from them can mean so much. God uses their innocent way of thinking combined with their honesty and sweetness to touch everybody they know. "Jesus said, 'Let the little children come to me, and do not hinder them, for the kingdom of heaven belongs to such as these'" (Matthew 19:14 NIV). Here, He plainly states that if we want to be in heaven, we should have the spirit of a child: optimistic, pure, loving, and having unlimited trust in God. Take time to observe a child's behavior. Children offer a great example in the way they view life. Pray that God will help you see life through a child's eyes.

~ Valdis Cuvaldin

All Things

As the wheellike complications were under the guidance of the hand beneath the wings of the cherubim, so the complicated play of human events is under divine control. - Education, pg. 178

Have you ever noticed that the happenings of life seem to have almost uncanny timing? Many times we think of these events as only coincidences, as luck or fate. However, if we pause to think of what only God could have done in our lives, we might realize how faithless and lacking this mindset is. I would not be the same person I am now—in fact I don't even want to imagine where I could have ended up—if my life hadn't been under God's control.

All throughout my life, I can remember times when God guided my paths. But when I was going through the harder experiences, I usually couldn't see that any good would come of them. Though sometimes I was scared of what would happen if I chose to let God's will be done, whenever I trusted Him to work in my life, even when my own desires screamed at me to do otherwise, I later realized that His way was best. At the exact time I needed it, He either showed me what to do or changed my life's direction. Over and over again, God has proved His knowledge of all things, His power over all things, and His loving guidance in all the affairs of my life.

When I look back at what God has done for me in the past, I am simply amazed at His wisdom and timing. I would not have it any other way. My own experience has proved this promise true: "...God causes everything to work together for the good of those who love God and are called according to his purpose for them" (Romans 8:28 NLT). Yes, there will be times when I am tempted to stop trusting God, even for just a moment, and I will face the consequences of my decisions. But God's unerring providence and timing have convinced me that He does have a calling for me. And He has a calling for you too. If you trust in God, you can rest in the knowledge that He is working in and through all things for your highest good and for His greater purpose.

~ Valerie Jacobson

October 8

A World in Agitation

Everything in our world is in agitation. Before our eyes is fulfilling the Saviour's prophecy of the events to precede His coming: "Ye shall hear of wars and rumors of wars.... Nation shall rise against nation, and kingdom against kingdom: and there shall be famines, and pestilences, and earthquakes, in divers places." - Education, pg. 179

On January 12, 2010, around five in the evening, a 7.0 earthquake hit Port-au-Prince, the capital of the small country of Haiti. Buildings crumbled as colossal cracks formed in the streets causing automobile accidents and pileups. When the quake ended, nearly a million people were homeless, and an estimated 230,000 were dead.

In the days following the quake, there were over fifty aftershocks recorded, causing more damage to the city's infrastructure. Three hundred thousand people were injured and living in the streets with hardly any medical attention or clean food and water. Roads leading out of the city were blocked by rubble, and rescue units were delayed for days.

Although the results of this earthquake were disastrous and catastrophic, countries all over the world pledged to help Haiti recover. Billions of dollars were given to help the restoration of the city, and thousands of volunteers flooded into the country in an effort to bring relief to the homeless and starving. There is hope in sight for Haiti.

But is there hope in sight for our world? As we near the end of time, more and more of these catastrophes are going to happen. "Nation shall rise against nation, and kingdom against kingdom: and there shall be famines, and pestilences, and earthquakes in divers places" (Matthew 24:6, 7 KJV). The world cannot last much longer; Jesus is coming back. Will you be ready to meet Him?

~ Wesley Mayes

Heavenly Treasure

From the rise and fall of nations as made plain in the pages of Holy Writ, they need to learn how worthless is mere outward and worldly glory. - Education, pg. 183

Babylon. The very name invokes thoughts of wealth and power. Splendid buildings, advanced civilization, proud people in need of nothing. Certainly no one ever expected it to end. Of course, there was that guy, Daniel, saying something about successive empires and a shifting kaleidoscope of new rulers, but what did he know? Babylon was strong. No danger. But in one night, it was gone. The stability, the power and magnificence—all were gone.

The rise and fall of the nations recorded in the Bible shows us that outward and worldly glory are worthless. The constant struggle for more earthly goods is blinding the human race to our need for something better, something higher. "As 'the flower of the grass,'" it will perish. "So perishes all that has not God for its foundation. Only that which is bound up with His purpose and expresses His character can endure" (*Education*, pg. 183).

As earth's history rushes onwards toward the cataclysmic end of events, we are getting just as absorbed with ourselves as did the nations before the flood. Obsessed with things we can see, and feel, and touch, we have lost sight of the unseen dimension. We say, "...I am rich, and increased with goods, and have need of nothing..." But Christ rebukes us, saying we are "wretched, and miserable, and poor, and blind, and naked..." Then He says, "...Because thou art lukewarm, and neither cold nor hot: I will spue thee out of my mouth" (Revelation 3:16, 17 KJV). "But lay up for yourselves treasures in heaven, where neither moth nor rust doth corrupt, and where thieves do not break through nor steal: For where your treasure is, there will your heart be also" (Matthew 6:20, 21 KJV).

~ Anna Fink

October 10

Make the Sacrifice

...Parents should take time daily for Bible study with their children. No doubt it will require effort and planning and some sacrifice to accomplish this; but the effort will be richly repaid. - Education, pg. 186

Many of my childhood memories are of my parents reading to me. I remember when I was about six or seven, coming into my parents' bedroom, putting on one of my dad's undershirts (stretching it out, to his annoyance), climbing up on the bed, and listening to him read me a story, usually out of *My Bible Friends* or a Dr. Seuss book. I remember when I was a little bit older having family worships. We would read the Sabbath School lesson, books on nature, and lots of stories of how God led different people through trying circumstances. My parents also bought expensive CD's of dramatized Bible stories. My sister and I would blare them in our room late into the night. Frequently my parents would have to come into our room and turn the volume down because they couldn't sleep. These memories are very precious to me, my treasures from the past. Because my parents were willing to sacrifice the time, money, and energy to implant those stories in me while I was young, they have stayed with me now that I'm older.

In this day and age, it is so important to make family time a priority. It's not uncommon for both parents to work outside the home, the older kids to go to school, and the younger ones to be sent to daycare. This lifestyle makes family time crucial and family worship indispensable. It is the only way a family can stay strong in their love for God and each other. Have you ever wondered why so many teens leave the church? Could it be that they have this mindset: what good is a religion if it's not worth practicing in your own home? Parents and children need family worships. The kids need to see that this religion means something to their parents.

You may be thinking, "Oh, that's a nice thought, but I just don't have time." Make time! Yes, it may involve sacrificing that extra thirty minutes of work at the office or folding the laundry, but it's worth it! Those precious gems of time may be the tie that holds your family together in earth's last days.

~ Anneliese Wahlman

283

Understanding

It is not enough to know what others have thought or learned about the Bible. Everyone must in the judgment give account of himself to God, and each should now learn for himself what is truth.
- Education, pg.188

I have sat through many, many sermons and agreed with a thousand things the preachers said. But when it all boils down to it, what do I personally believe? What are my thoughts and ideas? Do I really know the foundation I am standing upon?

We sometimes get the ideas of "agreeing" and "understanding" mixed up and think that agreeing with the preachers and knowing that what they have taught is correct means that we understand. But have you ever studied the Bible for yourself and seen where God desires you to stand as a Christian, personally?

We each need to take time every day for studying and learning and growing. As Christians, we need to understand truth on a personal level; we cannot just simply feed off the walk of other Christians. These people's thoughts, ideas, and beliefs are not your own until you can honestly say that you have taken the time to study them out for yourself and agree or disagree.

The more you study the Bible, the more blessed you will be. You will begin to love every moment with God, and soon, you will have a firm foundation upon which to rest your beliefs. When the judgment day comes, you will be able to give an honest account of yourself.

~ Danielle Schafer

A Knowledge of the Bible

A true knowledge of the Bible can be gained only through the aid of that Spirit by whom the word was given. And in order to gain this knowledge we must live by it. All that God's word commands, we are to obey. - Education, pg. 189

Through Christ's acquaintance with the Scriptures, He was able to obtain mental and spiritual knowledge. Throughout the ages men and women have been changed by daily reading God's Word. Knowledge of the Bible makes us responsible to perform its requirements.

In India there was a leper who was wandering in the streets. He passed by a shelter where he saw a white missionary speaking, holding an old black leather book. He was intrigued by what this preacher was saying and ended up listening to him preach for four hours. Each day he went to hear the white man preach; however, he stayed outside because of his leprosy. At the end of the Bible seminar, the leper went to the preacher and asked him to pray for him. The leper had two requests: he wanted God to give him a Bible and fingers so that he could turn the pages. The pastor was startled and doubtful, but he prayed for the leper anyway.

Soon after, the leper left town. He returned to his home village and told everyone the stories from the Bible. The people around him were astonished at his knowledge of the Bible, which he had never even read. Finally, the leper had told all he knew, but the people still wanted more. He told them that if he had a Bible, he could read and tell them more. The villagers were doubtful; they knew he was illiterate, but the leper firmly stated that he could read by the power of the God of heaven. He would need a Bible to prove it. So an old man with a few rupees bought a Bible. Miraculously, the leper was able to read, though he had never been taught. Because of this evidence, he helped convert many souls to Christ. And during this whole time, his decayed body healed until one day, the leprosy was completely gone.

God's Word healed that leper physically and spiritually, and it can do the same for us. We need to treat the Bible with reverence and share what we know, so that we may know more of God's love.

~ Bristi Waid

Promised Blessings

All that it [the Bible] promises, we may claim. - Education, pg. 189

Have you ever read the amazing blessings God promised to Israel? Those blessings were guaranteed if they obeyed Him. In Deuteronomy 28, God promised to bless their children, give them plenty of food, and establish them as a prosperous and honorable nation. On top of that, He promised to bless all their work and make them holy. Take a minute to reflect on the enormous value of these blessings. Wouldn't you like them to apply to you?

They do! Ellen White says, "The blessings thus assured to Israel are, on the same conditions and in the same degree, assured to every nation and every individual under the broad heavens" (*Education*, pg. 174). These blessings *are* for us!

So how do we claim the blessings? God promises to bless us if we "hearken diligently unto the voice of the Lord thy God, to observe and to do all his commandments which I command thee this day..." (Deuteronomy 28:1 KJV). It's simple. Listen to God when He speaks to you, claim His strength, and then obey Him. This includes searching the Bible diligently, so that you know what God asks of you. Here is a practical example of how to claim God's blessings.

A number of years ago, my family was working at a school as missionaries. One month, we had an unexpected expense that required Dad's entire paycheck. We never had very much food in the cupboard, and soon it ran out. That evening, my parents prayed, asking God for help. They claimed the promised blessing in Isaiah 33:16 that says, "...Bread shall be given him; his waters shall be sure" (KJV). The next day, the school was having a fall festival. When we arrived, we realized to our chagrin that everyone was supposed to bring some food item to fill a large basket. It was to be given as a thank-you to "someone the school appreciated." It was fortunate we hadn't known about this plan because we had nothing to give. At the end of the program, the school presented my family with the food—enough to last for a whole month! God was true to His promise! When you have a need, claim one of the Bible's promises. God *will* supply.

~ Kevin Corrigan

What's In Your Wallet?

The study of the Bible demands our most diligent effort and persevering thought. As the miner digs for the golden treasure in the earth, so earnestly, persistently, must we seek for the treasure of God's word. - Education, pg. 189

When cracks form in the crust of the earth, molten rocks and lava exit, forming mountains and volcanoes. Some molten rocks are pressurized and heated to the extent that they become diamonds and precious stones. These stones are found deep underground in large groups or veins called ore. Extracting diamonds from the ore requires long and arduous digging. Even finding possible locations for diamond ore can be difficult and dangerous. But, even though it requires skill and sacrifice, many people search diligently for possible locations of diamond ore. One of the most amazing stories of diamond mining is of a young man named Peter Tretyak, who believed that vast amounts of diamond ore lay beneath a lake that had been forsaken by miners and prospectors for decades. With no money and little hope of success, he borrowed some tools and started digging. For the next three years, he searched without results. In the fourth year he began to dig a tunnel under the lake. Finally, after more months of searching, he discovered diamond ore near the bottom of the lake. Years later, he told the story of how persistence, diligence, and hard work yielded true success.

I can personally tell you that my "treasure" (money in my wallet) doesn't seem to last long, especially when I'm hungry and Taco Bell is nearby. Even though Peter Tretyak was persistent enough to find his treasure, his true success was in learning the skills of patience and hard work. This is what Jesus meant when He said, "Lay not up for yourselves treasures upon earth, where moth and rust doth corrupt, and where thieves break through and steal: But lay up for yourselves treasures in heaven, where neither moth nor rust doth corrupt, and where thieves do not break through nor steal" (Matthew 6:19, 20 KJV). Honesty, integrity, and a joyful attitude can't be taken by thieves or destroyed by tragic circumstances. God is willing to give you a heavenly treasure that is even better than diamonds. So, what's in the "wallet" of your heart? You do have a choice. Accepting God's invaluable character requires a sacrifice of self. It can be painful, but if you are persistent, the reward is definitely worth it!

~ Wesley Donesky

287

Quality vs. Quantity

In daily study the verse-by-verse method is often most helpful. Let the student take one verse, and concentrate the mind on ascertaining the thought that God has put into that verse for him, and then dwell upon the thought until it becomes his own. - Education, pg. 189

A New Year's resolution—what a wonderful thing! I had made up my mind; I was going to read the Bible through, from cover-to-cover, in one year. As I read, I found it very interesting to see how everything happened in the Bible, and I found it easier to understand...sort of. You see, as I look back on that year, I do have regrets about how I did it. I read for quantity instead of quality. By speed-reading through the Bible, I had made a habit of reading just to reach my "quota" for the day. I did not take the time to learn what each verse meant to me, and since I didn't really understand each verse, applying it to my life was not even an option. This situation left me in a very big mess with how I looked at the Bible.

So, what have I done about it? Well, I have done a lot of praying, and God is really giving me a new understanding of the Bible. He has shown me that His Word is an infinite treasure; it is the answer key to life; it is a feast to which we have been invited, and it is something that will change our lives in ways we could never imagine. We often say, "I wish God would just tell me." He has told you in the words recorded in the Bible!

Today, I want to encourage you to search the Scriptures with prayer and let God lead you to the truth! Make it your resolution to read the Bible with the aim of discovering new meaning. Read the Bible with the focus of achieving a quality rather than a quantity message.

~ Jessica Hall

Worthy Thoughts

One of the chief causes of mental inefficiency and moral weakness is the lack of concentration for worthy ends. - Education, pg. 189

It has become a huge struggle for the people of this day and age to be completely pure in thought. We spend so much time thinking about things that have no purpose. If we looked more deeply into such thoughts, we would see their disastrous effects. We have gone so far, spending so much time thinking of ourselves, that we have completely forgotten the importance of our thoughts. We have become so embedded in the material world, that the question of where our heart is seems almost foreign to us.

We have forgotten the wise words of Paul: "Finally, brethren, whatever things are true, whatever things are noble, whatever things are just, whatever things are pure, whatever things are lovely, whatever things are of good report, if there is any virtue and if there is anything praiseworthy—meditate on these things" (Philippians 4:8 NKJV).

If we would realize that life is also a test, that each thought and action is shaping our characters and minds, we would be a lot more concerned with what goes on inside our minds.

We spend a lot of time thinking about ourselves and trying to sort out our problems, yet we should instead spend those moments of empty thought in prayer. Doing this will keep our thoughts pure and focused. Not only that, but it will give our thought purpose. God always knows what you're thinking, but He also desires to be invited into your thoughts. Talk to Him instead of racking your brains to solve your own struggles. He wants to hear from *you*. He'll listen and He'll help.

~ Danielle Schafer

Overcome Evil with Good

Let the mind be directed to high and holy ideals, let the life have a noble aim, an absorbing purpose, and evil finds little foothold.
- Education, pg. 190

When I was in the 3rd grade, a girl named Alyssa was really mean to me. She would call me names and make fun of me. The worst part is that my best friend, Emily, would fight terribly with her. They would even call each other bad names! The awful thing about that situation was that Emily was just as mean to Alyssa as Alyssa was to her. Part of the reason Alyssa disliked me was because I was friends with Emily and often stood up for her in their arguments. I would come home crying to my mom about what a bully Alyssa was to me. My mom advised me to be nice to Alyssa instead of giving her the reaction she wanted. She also said to not judge Alyssa because I didn't know what her family situation was like. Maybe she had a bad home life and just wanted to be in control of some area of her life. So I decided to repay evil with good. I started noticing Alyssa more. I saw that she didn't have any true friends, so I began reaching out to her in friendship, sitting with her at lunch, playing with her at recess, sharing things with her, and treating her like a good friend. Also, instead of hanging around whenever Emily and Alyssa would fight, I would leave.

Later, my Mom informed me that Alyssa's mom had come up to her after school one day and told her how much Alyssa appreciated me being a true friend to her and how she didn't feel like she had any other real friends. After this, I was invited over to Alyssa's house. I noticed that her older brother was mean to her; her dad was hardly ever there, and her parents had a strained relationship. She really needed a friend, and instead of letting her unkind remarks hurt my feelings, I was able to be a friend to her when she needed it most.

If we aspire to high and holy aims, seeking to bless others and look out for their best good, God will bless us, and evil won't find a foothold in our hearts. Fill your mind with so much good that evil has no place there, and you will uncover a lot more room in your heart for others.

~ Victoria West

October 18

Our Great Mission

Let the youth of today, the youth who are growing up with the Bible in their hands, become the recipients and the channels of its life-giving energy, and what streams of blessing would flow forth to the world!—influences of whose power to heal and comfort we can scarcely conceive... - Education, pg. 192

Youth, have you ever really taken the time to consider the high calling we have as Christian young people? While society has placed low expectations on young people today, God still holds us to a high standard. He has entrusted us with an important responsibility and a great privilege.

History shows that the disciples were between the ages of 17 and 25 when called to ministry. God used youth to carry the gospel to the world and begin the early Christian church, and He will use young people to help finish the work, enabling Him to return.

What an honor that the God of the universe has chosen us to work with Him to accomplish such a mission! What a privilege that the One who spoke the world's into existence wants our help to complete such a grand task!

So what are you doing about it? What are you doing to aid the cause of the gospel? Are the things of this world uppermost in your mind and heart? Are you caught up in the many distractions this world has to offer?

It is time for us to get busy—we have a world to reach! The things of this world are only temporary, while the work of salvation is everlasting. Let's not keep our Lord waiting!

~ Laura Williams

Share

The springs of heavenly peace and joy unsealed in the soul by the words of Inspiration will become a mighty river of influence to bless all who come within its reach. Let the youth of today, the youth who are growing up with the Bible in their hands, become the recipients and the channels of its life-giving energy, and what streams of blessing would flow forth to the world! - Education, pg. 192

When I read the Bible in the morning, God always teaches me something new! However, when I share what He's shown me with others, I am doubly blessed!

First of all, sharing helps me to remember what I have learned. When I repeat what God has shown me to others, it helps the lesson stick in my memory, and I'm more likely to actually apply it to my life! On the flip side, if I don't share what I learned, I've usually forgotten what I read by the time supper rolls around.

Secondly, sharing blesses others. My good friend Michael Hamel is a huge blessing to me! Whenever he reads or learns something really cool, he shares it with me. Hearing him tell what he learned in his devotions with such passion and excitement is such an encouragement to me! It brightens my day and helps me reset my focus on God. It also pushes me to share more with others and keeps me faithful in spending time with God every day.

Do you share your devotions with others? Perhaps you're thinking that you're way too shy! However, Ellen White says that "Christ and Him crucified should be the theme of contemplation, of conversation, and of our most joyful emotion" (*Steps to Christ*, pp. 103, 104). So, here is my challenge for you: though it may feel a bit awkward and intimidating, tell someone what you read this morning. Maybe you should team up with a sharing buddy to help push you out of your shell! Make it your goal to share what you read with ten people every day! Not only will it help you, but it will bless others! And the cool thing is that the more you share, the more you'll enjoy sharing!

~ Rachel Petrello

Don't Ignore Your Health, Part 1

How many a man, sacrificing health in the struggle for riches or power, has almost reached the object of his desire, only to fall helpless, while another, possessing superior physical endurance, grasped the longed-for prize! - Education, pp. 195, 196

My grandfather used to be one of the strongest men I have ever known. Born and raised on a poor ranch, he became familiar with the hardships of life at a very young age. He was always taught that working hard for his family is one of the most important things in life. He was in his thirties when his wife died, leaving him to raise three children alone. My grandpa felt responsible to offer his children the best life possible, so he started working harder than ever. But constant disregard for the laws of health led to a major stroke that left him partially paralyzed at only 60 years of age.

My grandfather definitely reached the goal he had for his children, but he did this by taking unnecessary risks, ultimately leading to a drastic consequence. Recently, I realized that I was neglecting my health by over-studying. Sleeping too little and eating poorly were the normal routine. Following my teacher's advice, I started to study one hour less every day and go for a walk instead. I also started eating properly and going to bed earlier. This whole undertaking was especially hard for me since schooling is one of my top priorities. However, I do not regret the decision I made. Since then, both my health and my academics have improved. For example, it used to take me several hours to review my daily lessons, but now that time has shortened significantly. This experience made me realize that I had been selfish with my body by abusing it. I have decided to never allow a selfish reason to dictate my health.

Have you ever sacrificed your health for a selfish reason? Sure, you might even have had a "good" one, but is it necessary to ignore your health? 1 Corinthians 6:19 says, "Do you not know that your body is a temple of the Holy Spirit..." (NIV). Decide to be temperate in everything and appreciate the health that God has blessed you with before it is too late.

~ Valdis Cuvaldin

Don't Ignore Your Health, Part 2

Anything that disorders digestion, that creates undue mental excitement, or in any way enfeebles the system, disturbing the balance of the mental and the physical powers, weakens the control of the mind over the body, and thus tends toward intemperance. - Education, pg. 203

Edith Piaf was a sweet girl with a big voice from a little French town. In her twenties, her vocal talent was discovered by one of the most acclaimed producers of the day, and in just a few months, she switched careers from a starving beggar to one of the most famous singers of her time. It might seem that life became a fabulous success for the artist, but there were a few addictions that lay hidden behind her pretty face and beautiful voice. Coming from a troubled home, Edith became familiar with the taste of alcohol and tobacco at a very young age. After she became famous, she added another "friend" to her list of sinful tendencies: drugs. In her thirties, she found herself in a big dilemma: the more success she achieved, the more dysfunctional her personal life became. She was married twice and involved in three near-fatal car accidents. She constantly neglected the advice of her doctor to take a break from singing and give up her addictions. At 47, Edith Piaf died after a long battle with liver cancer.

Edith Piaf is one of many individuals who refused to get rid of her addictions. People recall her as being a very nice person, but her love of alcohol and drugs sometimes transformed her into a monster. Even though she had huge international success and a great number of fans, when it came to temperance and her personal life, she was a failure.

Our human nature has a natural tendency towards addiction. But this includes much more than alcohol or drugs. It can mean overwork, extreme exercise, or merely a lack of motivation. It is almost impossible to get rid of these dreadful habits unless we surrender completely to God. Yes, family or rehabilitation centers may help you temporarily, but God will give you strength and motivation that nobody else can give. Take time to fall at Jesus' feet and cry out for power to overcome any addiction.

~ Valdis Cuvaldin

Sacrifice or Blessing?

Instead of marring God's handiwork, they will have an ambition to make all that is possible of themselves, in order to fulfill the Creator's glorious plan. Thus they will come to regard obedience to the laws of health, not as a matter of sacrifice or self-denial, but as it really is, an inestimable privilege and blessing. - Education, pg. 201

In November 2005, *National Geographic* featured an article entitled "The Secrets of Long Life." In this article they examined three groups of people who have the longest lifespans of any humans on earth. One team of demographers found a hot spot of longevity in mountain villages in Sardinia, Italy where men frequently reach 100 years of age. Another group is in Okinawa, Japan. These people seem to be the longest living on the planet. The third group was Seventh-day Adventists living in Loma Linda, California. They rank among America's longest-living people.

"Residents of these three places produce a high rate of centenarians, suffer a fraction of the diseases that commonly kill people in other parts of the developed world, and enjoy more healthy years of life. In sum, they offer three sets of 'best practices' to emulate" (*National Geographic*).

According to the article, all three groups don't smoke, put family first, are active every day, keep socially engaged, and eat fruits, vegetables, and whole grains.

These "best practices" are the very principles which God Himself laid out to enable us to have good health and a long life. I don't think the people found in those three groups considered their lifestyles a sacrifice. Not at all. It is a great blessing. If we will but follow God's way, we will live happy and healthy lives which we can use to serve Him to the fullest!

~ Laura Williams

Vulnerable

I will give you a new heart and put a new spirit in you; I will remove from you your heart of stone and give you a heart of flesh. - Ezekiel 36:26 NIV

A little orphan girl named Maggie was once adopted by a very rich, kindly couple. They took her home to their mansion and brought her to her new bedroom. Over the next few days, the couple noticed that Maggie hadn't unpacked her suitcase. Finally, they asked her why. She replied, "I've been to so many homes that I want to be ready, just in case I don't like it here, you don't like me, or something else goes wrong. I want to be ready to get out of here quickly!"

Though only an illustration, this story shows how human hearts can often become hardened to others when we've been hurt in previous relationships. We become scared of experiencing pain again; so we find the best solution for protecting ourselves: hardening our hearts. We become like Maggie. We're not willing to "unpack" our suitcases and allow our hearts to become attached to others. We want to be ready, just in case something goes wrong in the relationship, to leave quickly and unharmed. We become like rocks. Rocks are hard, cold, and unfeeling. You can wound, torture, and crush them—they feel nothing. If we can crystallize our hearts to the point that we are numb to others' pain and joy, we don't have to worry about getting hurt.

This mindset might provide protection, but it does not promote healing. We may be able to shield ourselves from the risk of injury, but we're also keeping ourselves from experiencing true love for anyone, even God. I myself struggle with feeling indifferent to Christ's love for me. Someone will say in worship or church, "God loves you so much! He gave His only Son to die for you!"; and it has as much meaning as, "The sky is so blue! And the grass is so green!" But God wants to give us new, vulnerable hearts—hearts of flesh—because that is the only way we can truly love Him. Truly loving people is giving them the power to hurt you, but trusting them not to. With God, we don't have to worry about Him ever hurting us! And once we trust Him with our whole hearts, we can truly love Him with abandon. And once we love Him, we can let ourselves be vulnerable to others, despite the risk of pain.

~ Anneliese Wahlman

October 24

Just Kidding!

As a madman who casteth firebrands, arrows, and death, so is the man
that deceiveth his neighbor, and saith, Am not I in sport?
- Proverbs 26:18, 19 KJV

When we were little, my brother Matthew and I were each trying to figure out our sense of humor. We went through this stage where we thought the weirdest things were funny. We would say things like, "The barn is burning!" and pause, then exclaim, "Just kidding!" and laugh our heads off, as if it were the funniest thing. At first, my mom said she thought it was harmless, but then she and my dad began to get really annoyed. She then realized that it was an issue of not telling the truth. We were really lying, then saying, "Just kidding!"

Similarly, when someone says something really hurtful, then says, "Just kidding," I wonder whether or not they really mean it, but are just trying to conceal their real feelings. Telling a lie, or saying something unkind, followed by a "just kidding," is never nice.

Ephesians 4:15 tells us that we, by "speaking the truth in love, may grow up into Him in all things, which is the head, even Christ..." (KJV). Kidding around about a lie is not speaking the truth. Kidding around about something unkind is not loving. So, "just kidding" is not "speaking the truth in love." James 3:8 tells us that the tongue "is an unruly evil, full of deadly poison" (KJV).

Think about it this way: take a pencil and a piece of paper and write down a sentence. Now, erase this sentence as much as possible. You can still read the sentence or see that there was writing there, can't you? Spoken words are like this: they cannot be erased; their mark will be there forever.

Do not speak lightly today. Do not kid around with things that need not be joked about. These things really are not funny. Remember to always "speak the truth in love."

~ Victoria West

Re-creating Yourself

There is a distinction between recreation and amusement. Recreation, when true to its name, re-creation, tends to strengthen and build up. Calling us aside from our ordinary cares and occupations, it affords refreshment for mind and body, and thus enables us to return with new vigor to the earnest work of life. Amusement, on the other hand, is sought for the sake of pleasure and is often carried to excess; it absorbs the energies that are required for useful work and thus proves a hindrance to life's true success. - Education, pg. 207

When I was younger, free time meant entertainment. Whenever I was not doing homework, I would play a video game or watch a movie. I thought this was the way a person should use their leisure time, and I liked it. But what I was not considering was the lack of spirituality in my activities. They were not only selfish, but they also did not develop me in any way. One Sabbath morning, on my church bulletin board, there was a big announcement: "Recreational activity: visiting a nursing home!" To my own surprise, I ran to my mom and expressed my desire to join the activity. She made the necessary arrangements, and that afternoon, I joined the group from my church. Looking back, I realize that an activity which appeared boring actually helped me to relax and grow spiritually, something that no video game or movie could ever do.

God gives us plenty of recreational activities that do not absorb energies or weaken our spiritual health, but rather refresh and develop our bodies and minds in amazing ways. Gardening, jogging, surfing, drawing, and hiking are just a few examples of re-creating activities. Involving competition and entertainment in your active life will stimulate the pleasure of winning, of gaining more power. This can create addictions and ultimately destroy lives. Do you find pleasure in entertainment? Make a goal to spend your time in activities that will develop your character, rather than destroying it.

~ Valdis Cuvaldin

Teachers at Recess

The true teacher can impart to his pupils few gifts so valuable as the gift of his own companionship. - Education, pg. 212

When I was in the 3rd and 4th grades, I had the best teacher ever. His name was Mr. Kakazu, or Mr. K. He was Hawaiian and had a mustache and a goatee. He also had a ukelele which he used to accompany the class in the Scripture songs he wrote. We did a lot of interactive things in his class: acting and drawing, poetry, songs, and writing. We had to use our creative side to demonstrate the concepts we were learning. Mr. K. also had this bell that he would ring to get the class's attention; then we would all say "Aloha!" clapping out each syllable of the word. That was how he would turn our attention to whatever announcement he had. But the most memorable times we had with Mr. K. were when he would play with us at recess. We would play dodge ball, and Mr. K. was the best. He was better than all the other guys. Also, Mr. K. would jump rope with us. He could jump really fast too. He spent time with us, not only in the classroom, but also during our recreation periods. This is what makes him stand out to me as my favorite teacher.

Teachers should be companions for their students. They should spend time with them not only in the classroom, but also outdoors in the students' recreation time, or at recess. Parents also should seek to do outdoor activities with their children. Gardening, biking, hiking, canoeing, running, exploring, and other outdoor activities are excellent forms of recreation for parents to enjoy with their kids. Parents, these experiences will be cemented into your children's memories and draw you closer as a family, as well as closer to your Creator. What greater gift can you give than the gift of your companionship?

~ Victoria West

Thrift is a Gift

The lessons of economy, industry, self-denial, practical business management, and steadfastness of purpose, thus mastered, would prove a most important part of their equipment for the battle of life.
- Education, pg. 221

It would be very hard to find someone as thrifty and good at bargain-hunting as my mom. She has ways of finding deals that even a frequent flea-marketeer couldn't match. We have never had an abundance of money; so she always taught my sister and me that every penny counts. She buys food in bulk and spends time shopping around to find the lowest prices. We have fun finding brand new clothes in thrift stores and making decisions on how to spend money wisely. It is important to my mom to find little ways of saving money, like keeping my dad's business receipts for tax returns and hanging out laundry to save electricity. And no matter how little money we have, she is faithful in returning our tithes and offerings. She puts God first, and He rewards her, making our money stretch further than I'll ever understand. Our money belongs to God and using it carefully is her way of honoring Him.

Every penny in my possession is a blessing from God so that I can bless others. Learning to spend money wisely is difficult, but very important. God expects me to be a good steward of the money He has given me. I'm making it a habit to ask myself, "Is it worth buying this? Could this money be better used to help someone else?" On that final day, when I must give an account to God for what I have spent, I want to make sure that it was used for God's work and for the glory of His name. How sad it would be to find that I had squandered it away on worthless items. "But lay up for yourselves treasures in heaven, where neither moth nor rust doth corrupt, and where thieves do not break through nor steal: For where your treasure is, there will your heart be also" (Matthew 6:20, 21 KJV). Do you know where your heart is? Join me and place your heart, your possessions, and your money in The Place that will last for eternity.

~ Megan Metcalf

Truly Educated

True education does not ignore the value of scientific knowledge or literary acquirements; but above information it values power; above power, goodness; above intellectual acquirements, character. The world does not so much need men of great intellect as of noble character. It needs men in whom ability is controlled by steadfast principle. - Education, pg. 225

I have been a student for the past 12 years of my life. Ever since I first started kindergarten, I have loved school. I loved it so much that at 7 years old, when my grandparents asked me if I wanted to go to Disneyland, I said that I didn't want to go because I'd miss school! The reason for my love of school, I suppose, was the fact that I did well and enjoyed learning. I also liked being with my friends and having fun, but the intellectual aspect was quite important to me even as a young child.

All throughout the years of my schooling, I got good grades, and learning was easy for me. Academics, along with my musical studies, became almost the biggest focus of my young life. I still enjoy school and work hard to do well in that area. But lately I've realized that God's desire for me is higher and more inclusive than just getting a good education, earning scholarships, going to college so I can earn money, and being proud of all the knowledge and work I will have gained and accomplished. If I learn all there is to know and become the smartest person in the world, but do not have God living in me—if I do not have a character that will enable me to use whatever knowledge and intellect I've gained for God's purposes and His glory—then I have not received true education.

See what has happened to our world: the majority of people use education for the sole purpose of fulfilling pride and the desire for selfish gain. Intelligent people with corrupt characters walk all over each other in their quest for power and money. It is our duty and calling to put a stop to this trend and to develop noble characters, so that we can use the minds God has given us to make a real difference in this world. Only the greatest Teacher can do this work in us, when we allow ourselves to be truly educated by Him.

~ Valerie Jacobson

301

Conflict

...Never was any previous generation called to meet issues so momentous; never before were young men and young women confronted by perils so great as confront them today. - Education, pg. 225

Imagine with me that you're in a battle. Maybe you're in a desert, a lush jungle, a deserted town, or on a beach. Bullets whizzing past, wounded men moaning, gunshots cracking, and the sounds of men running for cover fill your ears. You look around and come face to face with the enemy. Locking eyes, you both freeze. In an instant you call out to God for protection, and the soldier turns around and runs off.

Now, you may not realize it, but you are in a battle. And you look the enemy in the eyes many times throughout the day. However, instead of calling for protection and help from God, you often succumb to the enemy and become a prisoner. You're not the first or the only one in this battle though. Down through the ages, every generation has been part of this conflict. Maybe they were not conscious of this fight, but they still made a choice. Christians throughout time have had to make the choice to follow God or to go along with society, and today we have the same decision to make.

There have been some very dark periods of history for the Christian church, when its members went through terrible persecution. Yet even those terrible events are going to be surpassed in the future. Right now we have comparative freedom: we can still worship openly, at least in the Western world, and we aren't facing widespread oppression yet. However, our battle is almost worse, I believe. We are called to war against our minds and our very natures. We must guard ourselves from any form of evil, evil that is being made increasingly easy to get access to. With the click of a mouse or the push of a button, you can unlock the very stores of wickedness. Satan has made sin so easy to get to, and he mixes a little bit of good in with the bad so as to make it harder to discern. Still we must rely on God to help us and to protect us. Though there will be a time when we will be victimized, we can rest secure in the knowledge that, no matter what the conflict, Christ can take us through it safely.

~ Jo Holdal

Better Than Gold

True education does not ignore the value of scientific knowledge or literary acquirements; but above information it values power; above power, goodness; above intellectual acquirements, character. The world does not so much need men of great intellect as of noble character. It needs men in whom ability is controlled by steadfast principle. - Education, pg. 225

Not too long ago, a racquetball player named Reuben Gonzolas was in the final match of his first professional racquetball tournament. He was playing in the perennial championship for his first shot at a victory on the pro circuit. At match point in the fifth and final game, Gonzolas made a "kill shot" into the front corner to win the tournament. The referee and one of the linemen confirmed the shot was a winner. But after a moment of hesitation, Gonzolas turned and declared that his shot had hit the floor first. As a result, the serve went to his opponent, who went on to win the match. Everyone was stunned as Reuben Gonzolas calmly walked off the court. That week, a leading racquetball magazine featured Gonzolas. The lead editor searched for an explanation of the first-ever occurrence of a contestant in a professional racquetball game disqualifying himself when everything was officially in his favor. Who could ever imagine it in any sport or endeavor? When asked why he did it, Gonzolas replied, "It was the only thing I could do to maintain my integrity."

Integrity is defined as the quality of being honest and having strong moral principles; moral uprightness. But what does the word integrity mean to you personally? The Bible says, "Better is the poor that walketh in his integrity, than he that is perverse in his lips, and is a fool" (Proverbs 19:1 KJV). You will encounter situations that require a choice to either stand firm or compromise. You may say that integrity is right and will bring happiness, but do you really believe it? Reuben Gonzolas's example is evidence that integrity makes us healthy, wealthy, and wise. Just knowing that you are able to maintain integrity and honesty will give you a better feeling than all the racquetball trophies in the world. Start with small things, and soon God will give you the strength to preserve your integrity in the harshest circumstances.

~ Wesley Donesky

Character

The world does not so much need men of great intellect as of noble character. It needs men in whom ability is controlled by steadfast principle. - Education, pg. 225

"Character: moral or ethical quality: a man of fine, honorable character" (Dictionary.com). Our character is who we are; our likes and dislikes, who we hang out with, our demeanor, and our general outlook on life define our character. Our influence on others also stems from our character, and it is how we build our character that determines our eternal destiny.

So, how do we build our character? The book *Education* says: "In every generation and in every land the true foundation and pattern for character building have been the same. The divine law, 'Thou shalt love the Lord thy God with all thy heart;...and thy neighbor as thyself'" (pg. 228). However, there is a difference between human love and God's love. Human love is based on our feelings, our impulses, or whether or not another person fills a need or gratifies our personal pleasure. But God's love is unselfish and does not depend on feeling or impulse; God's love is for everyone. He does not wait for us to give Him something in return; He loves us because we are His children.

So, how do we get God's love into our hearts? First of all, we have to love God. His unselfish love cannot be gained by our own seemingly good deeds or actions; it must come from a relationship with Him. We can compare it to a mirror and a flashlight. If I am holding the flashlight in my hand, and the light is reflecting off the mirror some distance away, then as I walk towards the mirror with the flashlight, the reflected beam grows stronger and stronger. It's the same in our walk with Jesus. As we grow closer to Him, our love for others will also become stronger. As a result of this love, our character will be shaped to become one with Christ's.

"Love is patient, love is kind. It does not envy, it does not boast, it is not proud. It is not rude, it is not self-seeking, it is not easily angered, it keeps no record of wrongs. Love does not delight in evil but rejoices with the truth. It always protects, always trusts, always hopes, always perseveres" (1 Corinthians 13:4-7 NIV).

~ Wesley Mayes

November 1

Turn Up the Heat

Behold, I have refined thee, but not with silver; I have chosen thee in the furnace of affliction. - Isaiah 48:10 KJV

This message is not for those of you who only want to feel warm and fuzzy inside. It is not meant to make you feel comfortable; rather, it is bound to make you uncomfortable. Then why would you even want to go on and read this? I don't know, but I will say that this is a message from the heart, from my own experience, and I feel no need to apologize if it causes you discomfort.

A few months ago, the Sabbath sermon during Week of Prayer really spoke to me. It was about the "refiner's fire," and the speaker encouraged us to ask God to uncover all the dross in our lives—selfishness, pride, impatience, to name some examples—and to take it away, so that what was valuable in us would more fully reflect God's perfect character. He warned that when you ask God to burn away the dross, your flaws will not be fixed overnight; in fact, life will only seem to get worse. But we can trust in the God who is controlling the fire.

Knowing that I probably had some hidden character defects, I decided to ask God to turn up the heat. After that, it seemed that my life turned upside-down—more than once. I can't put into a few words all the struggles I went through physically, emotionally, mentally, and spiritually, but I know that I am not the only one to have experienced similar trials. I began to see characteristics in myself that I had known were wrong in my mind, but hadn't fully realized in my heart, and these discouraged me. Still I prayed, cried, searched God's Word, and prayed some more. And from each trial He brought me through with a stronger faith and a truer character.

Looking back, I can see that God has done a great work in me, but I am still far from perfect. After all I've endured, my number one flaw still keeps rearing its ugly head: selfishness. I challenge you to ask God to show you inside yourself. Tell Him to turn up the heat, so that He can refine your character and bring you closer to Himself. It will be scary, and it will be hard. Is this a risk you are willing to take?

~ Valerie Jacobson

What a Nerd!

True education does not ignore the value of scientific knowledge or literary acquirements; but above information it values power; above power, goodness; above intellectual acquirements, character. The world does not so much need men of great intellect as of noble character. - Education, pg. 225

During my first few grades of school, I was the biggest nerd you could ever meet! I am serious! The only thing that mattered to me was getting good grades! I did not have any friends; I never helped my classmates with their assignments! I thought that every school had a smart kid that everybody teases; so the nickname "nerd" did not bother me. I was very proud of my achievements. But something happened that made me realize that my values were not on the right track. Every year my city hosts a regional math contest which involves teamwork. For months in advance, I prepared for this event, hoping that I would be part of the team representing my school. After a thorough evaluation from a special committee, a final decision was reached. To my surprise and disappointment, I was not selected. Why was I left out? Later I received a tap on my shoulder. "You are a very smart kiddo, but character is more important than intellectual achievements," my teacher told me. Years later, I was able to understand what she meant. I needed to realize that there is more to life than getting good grades.

People are naturally more attracted to a person who is humble and easy-going, rather than a person who possesses great intellect, but lacks genuine kindness. Developing these social abilities is part of cultivating our characters. Do you struggle with the same problems I had? Ask God to guide you whenever you are tempted to put knowledge above character. Our characters are the only things we are going to take with us to heaven; there is nothing more important than developing them!

~ Valdis Cuvaldin

November 3

Truth Comes Out

Here is the only safeguard for individual integrity, for the purity of the home, the well-being of society, or the stability of the nation. Amidst all life's perplexities and dangers and conflicting claims the one safe and sure rule is to do what God says. "The statutes of the Lord are right," and "he that doeth these things shall never be moved."
- Education, pg. 229

The truth is always found out, no matter how much you may try to hide it. In the end it's as transparent as glass. A little nine-year-old girl, named Shema, used to work for a wealthy family in Bangladesh. Early before the sun rose, she would gather wood for a fire and cook rice for her master's family. Every day she worked diligently washing clothes and taking care of her master's children, even though she herself was only a child. Shema cleaned the house from top to bottom and scrubbed the floors on her hands and knees. Then she went about a mile down to the river to gather water for cooking and washing. Often, after preparing a large meal for her master's family, not much was left for her. Many nights she would go to bed without even as much as a piece of bread to eat. Then one afternoon, her mistress went into town for two days and forgot to take her purse with all her money in it. After her mistress left for town, Shema found the purse. She knew that if she were to take some money out of the purse, her mistress would never know because she had so much money that she never thought twice about how much she kept in her purse. Shema was so tempted to steal a few dollars so that she could buy herself a nice new dress, but she restrained herself and brought her struggles to the Lord.

"For there is nothing hidden that will not be disclosed, and nothing concealed that will not be known or brought out into the open" (Luke 8:17 NIV). You know, it's the small things in life that matter. If, with God's help, we are faithful in that which is least, then we will be faithful in that which is great. Just like Shema, we can have peace in our souls when we are true and honest. One day, each one of us will be faced with an open book filled with the accounts of our lives. It is up to you to determine what will be written on those pages, whether they will be filled with happiness and peace, or with regret and remorse.

~ Bristi Waid

Go Fish, Part 1

Christ discerned the possibilities in every human being. He was not turned aside by an unpromising exterior or by unfavorable surroundings. He called Matthew from the tolbooth, and Peter and his brethren from the fishing boat, to learn of Him. - Education, pg. 232

Once there was a group called "The Fishermen's Fellowship." They were surrounded by streams and lakes full of very hungry fish. They met regularly to discuss their call to fish and loved talking about the thrill of catching fish! Soon someone suggested that they should make a philosophy of fishing. They carefully defined and redefined fishing and the purpose of fishing, until they had developed a complete set of methods and tactics. Then one day they realized that they were going about it the wrong way. They had been approaching fishing from the viewpoint of the fisherman instead of looking at it from the fish's point of view. How do fish view the world? How do the fishermen appear to the fish? What do fish eat and when? They decided that once they knew things like this they would be able to master fishing. After all, these are good things to know. So, with this in mind, they set off to do research, attending conferences on fishing and traveling to far off countries to study different kinds of fish. Although some fishermen got Ph.D.'s in "Fishology," still no one had actually gone fishing.

This part of the parable really applies to me. So often I get caught up in the the theory of "fishing," or witnessing, that I'm not practical. I do a lot more thinking about how I could witness than actually going out and witnessing. Now, I'm not saying that going to conferences and learning about witnessing is bad, but God is doing a work in us, and because He is working in us, we need to "workout." He has given me the ability to fish; so I need to get up off my lawn chair and join the fishing derby!

~ Jessica Hall

Go Fish, Part 2

Then He said to them, "The harvest truly is great, but the laborers are few; therefore pray the Lord of the harvest to send out laborers into His harvest." - Luke 10:2 NKJV

When we left "The Fishermen's Fellowship," no one had gone fishing, and a committee was formed to send out fishermen. Seeing that the fishing places outnumbered the fishermen, the committee decided they needed to determine their priorities. A priority of fishing places was posted on bulletin boards in all of the fellowship halls, but still no one went fishing. A survey was launched to find out why no one was fishing; most did not answer the survey. But, from those who did, it was discovered that some felt called to study fish, a few to furnish fishing equipment, and several to go around encouraging the fishermen. Now with conferences and seminars to attend, the members of "The Fishermen's Fellowship" simply didn't have time to fish.

One day a newcomer, named Jake, joined "The Fishermen's Fellowship." After Jake went to one meeting, he got his Fishing Bible and went fishing. He tried a couple of techniques and soon got the hang of it, catching a choice fish. At the following meeting, Jake got up and told his story about how he caught his fish. Everyone at the meeting was blessed by what Jake had to share, and soon he was scheduled to speak at all the Fellowship chapters and share how he did it. Unfortunately, because of all the speaking invitations and his election to the board of directors, Jake no longer had time to fish. He soon started to feel restless and longed to feel the tug of the line once again. He quit speaking, resigned from the board, and said to a friend, "Let's go fishing." They did, and they caught fish.

The members of "The Fishermen's Fellowship" were many, the fish were plentiful, but the fishers were few. There is a call, a call to get into your boat and go fishing. Why not listen to the call and go fish?

~ Jessica Hall

The Cost of Enlightenment

...How wonderfully we are bound together in the great brotherhood of society and nations, and to how great an extent the oppression or degradation of one member means loss to all. - Education, pg. 238

Tonight I wrote a letter of sympathy and encouragement to Yang Rongli, a pastor in Shanxi Province, China. After holding a prayer rally, Pastor Rongli's church was demolished, and he was accused of disturbing the peace. He was then taken to prison, where he has been held since November 2009.

After writing Pastor Rongli, the pain and suffering which so many Christians in restricted nations are experiencing became more real to me. Every day, thousands of Christians take a stand for Jesus, because they know that His words are true: "And do not fear those who kill the body but cannot kill the soul" (Matthew 10:28 NKJV). Taking a stand for Christ is something in which persecuted Christians find joy.

How about you? Do you find joy in sharing Christ's love in a post-modern culture, a culture that thinks it is becoming more enlightened by the comprehension of a whole spectrum of worldly philosophies? What such a culture really needs to hear is the philosophy of one Man: Jesus Christ. The gospel may be simple by the world's standards, but it is the only enlightenment that will bring lasting fulfillment.

"Remember the prisoners as if chained with them—those who are mistreated—since you yourselves are in the body also" (Hebrews 13:3 NKJV). I tend to try to push out of my mind the reality of people dying for Christ's sake, but I am called to remember them and pray for them and to rejoice that so many people are willing to lose their lives to win the Great Controversy.

~ Sarah-Kate Lingerfelt

He'll Put a Smile on Your Face!

All may possess a cheerful countenance... - Education, pg. 240

Jesus makes everything pleasant. When He was on earth, He left every home and town happier than before He visited. If you let Him, He can make your life happier too. The challenge is to not dwell on the things that are keeping you down. The challenge is to smile at life. As you read the following account of how Jesus lifted my attitude, don't forget, with Jesus, anything is possible!

One morning a few years ago, everything seemed to be going terribly wrong. I did not want to get in trouble, but I had no desire to obey my mom either. I went around the house doing my chores, being sure not to be kinder than necessary to anyone. As always happens, I ended up treating someone outright unkindly. Soon I was disputing with Mom over the correction I had received. Mom asked God for guidance and sent me on a walk around our field to give me a chance to calm down. As I carried out my forced exercise, I grumbled in my heart. Then, by God's mercy, something distracted me. I found a pair of killdeer and their nest holding three eggs. I raced back to the house to share the discovery with my family. On the way back, even without me realizing it, God cleared my mind and helped me to have a new attitude. I could see why I had been reprimanded, and I was ready to do my best to get along with the rest of my family.

Only God can change a mindset. Only He can help you when you feel hopelessly stuck in miry gloom. God promises, "A new heart also will I give you, and a new spirit will I put within you: and I will take away the stony heart out of your flesh, and I will give you an heart of flesh" (Ezekiel 36:26 KJV). In this text God promises to give you a new heart *and* spirit. What a promise! The next time you are struggling to be positive and agreeable, ask for His help and choose to be cheerful. God has amazing ways to put a smile on your face!

~ Kevin Corrigan

311

An Audience with the King

True reverence for God is inspired by a sense of His infinite greatness and a realization of His presence. - Education, pg. 242

Imagine that you are standing outside a large portal. It is the entrance to a great throne room. Slowly the gate swings open, and you step inside. Immediately, you are overwhelmed with the magnitude, beauty, and pure glory of the place. A brilliant light flows through the room, reflecting off the walls studded with gold, silver, and precious stones. Huge marble pillars line the way to the throne. You look down and discover you are standing on pure transparent gold.

As you approach the throne, you see the Source of the light. You are now standing in the very presence of the Creator of the universe, the King of Kings, the One who gives you life. Overcome with a sense of awe, you fall to your knees, unable to look at Him. You feel so sinful and small. Suddenly He rises and comes to your side. As He puts His arm around your shoulder, you look at the nail prints in His hands. Gratitude and peace fill your heart as you look into the smiling face of the One who gave His life for you. "Tell me about your day," He says as He takes a seat next to you.

This is how I like to think of prayer. When I started to see it like this, it completely changed the way I prayed. Prayer is entering into the presence of God. It is a private audience with the King of the universe. Heavenly angels veil their faces at the mention of His name. How much more should we, sinful human beings, show Him reverence? If we continuously keep this in our minds, how different would our prayers be?

~ Laura Williams

November 9

The Fence or the Ambulance

Beloved, I wish above all things that thou mayest prosper and be in health, even as thy soul prospereth. - 3 John 2 KJV

A dangerous cliff spread its shadow over the quaint little town. It was not unusual for people to walk quite near the edge in order to see the view. The terrible thing was how many people slipped and fell to the rocks below. Everyone agreed that something must be done—but what? Some said that a fence must be made. Many others wanted an ambulance to take care of the people who would fall. Soon the cry for an ambulance won out. When the city folks heard of the unfortunate people that had fallen over the cliff, great and small pitched in with real concern to buy an ambulance. Day after day the ambulance rushed up the road leading to the bottom of the cliff, doing its duty as best it could. Finally, one day, an old man remarked, "It's surprising that so many people work hard to repair damages, and so few give attention to preventing the cause. If we had a fence, people would not slip over the edge in the first place." However, others replied, "It's landing at the bottom where people get hurt. The slipping at the top doesn't do so much damage" (Story adapted from a poem by Joseph Malines).

Likely, you see the obvious need for a fence in this allegory. Although the ambulance was a blessing, it could only do so much. Yet we often make the same mistake. We try to fix the result of a problem, without addressing the cause. This is strikingly true when you examine most people's way of dealing with their health. We will go anywhere and do anything to get well once we are sick. Indeed, many donate money for hospitals, special equipment, and scientific research that is looking for a cure. Although we must help the sick, think what pain and loss could be avoided if they never became ill in the first place.

No one needs to be unaware of how to *stay* healthy. Many helpful chapters in the Spirit of Prophecy tell clearly the principles that sustain good health. Have you read *Counsels on Diet and Foods*? If you haven't, it is God's gift to you. The instruction it contains will keep you healthy and happy your entire life. If you're like me, you already know much of the instruction. Do you follow it? Health is a treasure that will make your life happy and useful. You will never regret good health!

~ Kevin Corrigan

Come Back to Reverence

*True reverence for God is inspired by a sense of His infinite greatness
and a realization of His presence. - Education, pg. 242*

Reverence for God has always been important in my life. Since the
day I was born, I was taught to be a quiet, attentive listener to the
church service. God's presence was in the sanctuary, and the holy
angels were seated with us on the pews. The sanctuary was treated
with respect and solemn awe because the Lord of the universe dwelt
there. In Biblical times, the sanctuary had such sacredness that only
the priests could enter. As they carried out the daily ordinances, they
searched their souls to make sure no sin remained in their hearts as
they entered God's presence. With head bowed and a prayer in their
hearts, they silently brought the offerings and prayers for forgiveness
to God on behalf of the people. Unfortunately, this kind of reverence
for God is almost extinct. Church is treated lightly, almost as a social
gathering; people talk and laugh as they wait for the service to begin,
giving little thought to preparing their hearts for the message God
wants them to hear. Cell phones ring and children sing, while others
constantly walk in and out. As the sermon draws to a close, the
congregation makes an immediate escape for the door, rushing to
bake their casserole for dinner. Did they forget the real reason for
going to church? They would quickly change their demeanor if they
could see the holy angels recording every whisper and every act in the
books of heaven.

It's a sad scene, but oh, so true. If anyone is guilty of this, I am.
When I was young, I didn't fully grasp the significance of who God
really is. I didn't understand the reason why I should reverence His
house. But as I grow older and mature in my relationship with God, I
am filled with wonder and respect for Him. I don't want to leave His
presence. I want to linger just a moment longer, instead of rushing out
after the church service. God's character never changes, He still
desires us to savor every spare minute with Him. In the final days
there will be a people who will come back to primitive Godliness, to a
simple reverence that reflects the reverence they will have when, in
heaven, they bow with the angels at the foot of the throne of God. God
is calling both you and me to come back to reverence. Will you choose
to respond?

~ Megan Metcalf

November 11

Fashion Parade?

Even the day and the services of worship are not exempt from fashion's domination. Rather they afford opportunity for the greater display of her power. The church is made a parade ground, and the fashions are studied more than the sermon. - Education, pg. 247

One day as I was sitting in church, I witnessed one of the most disturbing scenes I have ever encountered. While listening to the sermon, I heard two ladies whispering behind me.

"Look at her dress! Where did she get it from? Second hand store or something?" one asked.

"I feel so sorry for her! I wonder how she dared to come to church like that. I mean...even my dog is better dressed!" the other one replied.

The culture I was raised in tends to wear very extravagant clothes to church. It is considered a sign of reverence toward God to be dressed in a sophisticated manner, but from personal experience, I have observed that the more people show off, the more proud and judgmental they become. As soon as they see someone dressed simply, people start gossiping as if the person committed a crime. They are not only judging the individual, but rejecting him socially as well. Are we starting to treat church as a fashion parade? Shouldn't our purpose be to praise and worship God and accept each other in love?

Do you like shopping? I do. In fact, writing this devotional was very uncomfortable for me since clothes are a big part of my life. But, I always ask myself before purchasing a garment, "Is this modest? Does it honor God?" Do not judge people by the way they dress—that is not the purpose of coming to church. Oftentimes, fashion brings division among the attendees. At the end of the day, people would rather recall what a certain person wore than the main theme of the sermon. Because of their gossip, other Christians are afraid to attend the service. Is there any benefit in harshly judging people for the way they appear? Think twice about the consequences when you are tempted to talk about someone's outfit behind their back.

~ Valdis Cuvaldin

What is Faith?

Faith is trusting God—believing that He loves us and knows best what is for our good. - Education, pg. 253

One Sabbath, I was having a "cloudy" day. Just before the sermon, as the speaker was giving the opening prayer, I thought, "God, it would be cool if he preached on that chapter in the book *Education* that encouraged me the other day...what was it? Faith and... Something?" I hadn't even really prayed; I just thought it would be cool if that happened, but knew it wouldn't. The speaker had already picked the sermon, and it wouldn't have anything to do with my chapter. After prayer, I thought, "Just watch...He won't preach on it; I know it." Just then, the speaker said, "The chapter I am going to preach on is 'Faith and Prayer.'" I sat bolt upright! And for the rest of the sermon, I couldn't help but smile. God had heard my prayer!

So many times, when hard situations come my way, I feel like God is not there, that he isn't working in my life. But when I look back at all the things He has done for me in the past, I take courage and have faith that He will do what is best for me in my life. A couple weeks ago, I went to a youth conference. I was so blessed! It was amazing to see how God had planned the meetings and seminars to perfectly fit my needs! One of the things I learned was to praise God more often and to write down the things God has done for me. Then, if I am feeling down, I can look back in my "Blessings Book" and see all the things that God has done for me in the past.

When I remember what God has done for me, I can see that whenever I felt He wasn't active in my life, He was. He was working with me, leading me through trials to test my character and drawing me closer to Himself. I realize that looking to the past should make my faith in Him even more solid. But sometimes it's really hard to have faith in God and what He can do for me. Then I have to remember that even though I may not feel Him, He is there. No matter what the circumstances may tell me, Jesus will always be by my side to guide me through. My part is to trust in Him and rest in the faith that He loves me and will do what is best for me to grow closer to Him.

~ Yannika Stafford

November 13

Our Weakness is His Strength

Faith is...believing that He loves us and knows best what is for our good. Thus, instead of our own, it leads us to choose His way. In place of our ignorance, it accepts His wisdom; in place of our weakness, His strength; in place of our sinfulness, His righteousness.
- Education, pg. 253

In December of 2009, my school went on a two-week music tour in California. Each day we performed at least one concert, sometimes two. I had two solos to sing at each concert, and after about a week, I began to get sick and eventually lost my voice. Every evening just before the concert, completely unable to talk, I would earnestly pray that God would give me my voice to be able to sing for His honor alone, in the hopes that someone in the audience would be blessed. Each night, my voice would return just as I began to sing. When the concert was over, it promptly went away again.

As this process continued each day, my faith was strengthened, and I had to learn to completely depend on God. He taught me that I could not do it in my own strength, but that He was there to help me. My faith in the power of prayer was also strengthened.

Now, whenever I am in another situation where I am struggling with completely trusting God, He reminds me of that tour and how He answered my prayers each night, and I know I can trust Him again.

Paul says in Philippians 4:13, "I can do all things through Christ which strengtheneth me" (KJV). So, whenever you feel like you don't know what to do, or you are afraid, trust in God because He will never let you down.

~ Laura Williams

A Living Faith

Faith is trusting God—believing that He loves us and knows best what is for our good. Thus, instead of our own, it leads us to choose His way. - Education, pg. 253

I didn't want to be sick any longer. I had been for a few weeks already, and I wanted to be well. It was the winter of 08-09, and I had whooping cough. I began asking God why He had allowed me to become sick. Soon I got my answer. He told me I was living my life in such a hurry that I could not hear Him telling me what to do. It was true. I remembered asking God for guidance, and now I had the time to listen. I quietly spent the next few weeks getting God's opinion on what really counts and redirecting my life.

While I was sick, I watched a live Seventh-day Adventist youth conference over the Internet. As I listened each evening, I heard God asking me, "Does your life reflect faith that is real enough to obey Me? Will you follow Me when it goes against your inclinations? How about when everyone says what you're doing is okay, and I say it's not?" Right then and there, I chose to obey God no matter what He asked of me. Sometimes what He asks is uncomfortable, but obeying God gives me peace and satisfaction. He is the happiest one in the universe, and I can't help feeling just the same when I serve Him.

Jesus already did the most difficult thing that could be done. He died the second death on the cross for you and me. Although it's unbelievable what He chose to go through to accomplish it, think of what He has gained: He will have all eternity with anyone who chooses to be saved, and sin will be eternally eradicated. The hard things we do now are nothing compared to what we'll gain. The Bible promises, "For our light affliction, which is but for a moment, worketh for us a far more exceeding and eternal weight of glory..." (2 Corinthians 4:17 KJV). Does your life reflect a faith that is real enough to obey God? Choose a living faith. Eternity waits for you.

~ Kevin Corrigan

'Tis a Gift

If we receive the promise, we have the gift. - Education, pg. 253

It was a cold January morning. A man dressed in blue jeans and a baseball cap positioned himself against a wall at the Metro Plaza Station in Washington, D.C. In his hand was a violin on which he proceeded to play some most elegant music.

It was a crisp, clear night, when a baby's cries split the air. A few chickens clucked and fluttered their wings while cows lazily stamped their feet. All of a sudden, shepherds from the nearby fields rushed through the threshold of the barn to see this Baby, now peacefully asleep. With an air of reverence, the shepherds knelt one by one around the manger.

The man in blue jeans was rather nondescript by worldly standards. Yet as he began to play, it was clear that he was no ordinary musician. In the midst of the busy rush hour, his fiddle jumped and sang. The musician was none other than Joshua Bell, the world-class musician. Yet Mr. Bell, whose concerts are packed— seats selling for over a hundred dollars—earned a scant $32.17. Even though Mr. Bell freely shared his music, people were too busy to listen to a "common street musician."

When Christ entered our world, no one recognized Him for the King He was. A simply dressed carpenter, Christ traveled through the countryside sharing words of life with all who would listen. Too busy searching for a worldly king, a general who would defeat the Romans and set up a worldly empire of pomp and grandeur, the Jews did not recognize God's own Son, the Messiah sent to rescue them from the clutches of Satan.

Mr. Bell gave his gift of music, but people were too busy to stop and listen. Today, God freely presents a gift far more precious—the promise of His love. Are you too busy to recognize His gift? As you go through this day, take the time to thank God for His love and to open your eyes, so that you will not miss the blessings He has for you.

~ Sarah Chang

Who Strengthens Me?

Faith is trusting God—believing that He loves us and knows best what is for our good. - Education, pg. 253

When you think of great people of faith, who comes to mind? Maybe you think of Noah, who had to trust God when He said, "Build a boat"; or David, a shepherd who trusted God so much that he went and killed a giant with only a sling and stone. Esther trusted that God put her in the king's court for a reason, and in the end, she was able to save a whole nation. You could think of Daniel in the lions' den—now that was trust! He had faith that God would protect him from the hungry lions, and God did! And what about the people who were not in the Bible? There were Wycliffe and Huss, Jerome and Luther, Tyndale and Knox, Zinzendorf and Wesley, and multitudes of others. All these people had something in common: they had a true faith in God.

Now, what do you think we have in common with these people? I know that my life has not included being thrown in a lions' den, or building an ark. Nevertheless, I need to have just as much faith as all of these people. "Faith is needed in the smaller no less than in the greater affairs of life. In all our daily interests and occupations the sustaining strength of God becomes real to us through an abiding trust" (*Education*, pg. 255).

Hebrews 11:1 gives us a beautiful definition of faith: "Now faith is being sure of what we hope for and certain of what we do not see" (NIV). Though our lives may not seem to demand a lot of faith, we need to continually lean on the everlasting arms of our God. This is the only way we can have assurance, and the only way we will know Who strengthens us.

~ Jessica Hall

Our Great Gift

*Faith that enables us to receive God's gifts is itself a gift, of which
some measure is imparted to every human being. It grows as exercised
in appropriating the word of God. In order to strengthen faith, we
must often bring it in contact with the word. - Education, pp. 253, 254*

The air hangs heavily in the invalid's room. The labored breathing
of the man on the bed pierces the silence and seems to add a sense
of finality to the grim situation. The man is John Wycliffe, fearless
reformer and preacher. His endless work, coupled with the constant
pressure from his opponents, has taken its toll on his health, and he is
slowly becoming weaker and weaker. As the dim light of dusk fades
into the blackness of night, candles cast eerie shadows on the walls.

Suddenly, the door squeaks noisily on its hinges and is thrown
heavily against the wall. Eight men hastily make their way into the sick
man's room. They are civil officers and representatives of four
religious sects and are confidant that, in his feeble condition, Wycliffe
will recant all of the things that he has said and done against them.
"'You have death on your lips,' they said; 'be touched by your faults,
and retract in our presence all that you have said to our injury'" (*The
Great Controversy*, pp. 87, 88). Wycliffe motions for his attendant to
prop him up in bed and looks steadily at the men. "'I shall not die, but
live; and again declare the evil deeds of the friars'" (Ibid.). He speaks
in a voice untainted by disease or sickness. The listening men draw
themselves up in shocked silence and shuffle out of the room.

Wycliffe's prophecy came true. He recovered and was able to
accomplish his task of translating the Bible into English so that even
the simplest family could understand it. We have a great gift in the
Bible. Many individuals have given their lives for the opportunity that
we have, and yet, we so often take it for granted. God wants to get to
know each one of us personally, and the best way for us to gain a
relationship with Him is through His written Word. Spend some time in
it today!

~ Wesley Mayes

When We Need It Most

As surely as the oak is in the acorn, so surely is the gift of God in His promise. If we receive the promise, we have the gift...We may go about our work assured that what God has promised He is able to perform, and that the gift, which we already possess, will be realized when we need it most. - Education, pp. 253, 258

Have you ever wanted something so much that you found yourself thinking of it almost all the time? Perhaps it was a Christmas or birthday present that you really wished someone would give you. Or maybe it was a goal you were aiming for, and you worked hard every day to reach it. On a deeper level, many of us have wanted peace of mind, rest from stress, and answers to life's hard questions. Whether good or bad, I know that all of us have had serious wants and desires at some point in our lives.

Lately I've been wanting a number of things in my life, and I find myself worrying about them a lot. I've prayed for them, though at the same time, I've asked that God's will be done. Sometimes it's been hard waiting to see what God will do, wondering exactly what the result of my shaky faith will be, scared that I might not like the way things turn out. This promise in the Bible, however, has really spoken to me: "Delight yourself in the LORD and he will give you the desires of your heart" (Psalm 37:4 NIV). First, I need to find joy in a life of serving, loving, and knowing God. As I get closer to Him, what I want will become more like what God wants. Then He will give me the desires of my heart because they will be in accordance with His will.

When God promises me something, it's like He's given me a gift certificate. In essence, a gift certificate is money, but it hasn't been cashed into tangible bills and coins. I already have what God has promised in the sense that it belongs to me, but I don't necessarily have it in reality yet. God is going to cash in the certificate for me at the right time. Though I'm still learning to delight myself in God, I will constantly cling to the promise He's given me. When you and I surrender our wills to God and trust that He can do absolutely anything we ask, He will give us all that is best when we need it most.

~ Valerie Jacobson

Come Up Higher

...Enoch, pure in heart, holy in life, holding fast his faith in the triumph of righteousness against a corrupt and scoffing generation... - Education, pg. 254

Enoch was different. Amidst the thriving wickedness of the antediluvian world, Enoch lived a pure and holy life. He went against the mainstream in order to reach God's standards. And in our world today, God is calling Christians to come up higher, just like Enoch did.

"An elevated standard is presented before the youth, and God is inviting them to come into real service for Him...You are to be men who will walk humbly with God, who will stand before Him...free from impurity, free from all contamination from the sensuality that is corrupting this age. You must be men who will despise all falsity and wickedness, who will dare to be true and brave..." (*Messages to Young People*, pg. 24).

God is calling for a group that will rise above the standards the world has set. God is calling for a group who dare to be responsible, excel in school, respect their parents, dress modestly, and live to bless others. God is calling for a group who will give the warning message about Christ's soon return, just as Enoch helped proclaim the message of God's love to the world before the flood. God is calling for a group who dares to walk with God and serve Him alone.

I want to be a part of that group, don't you? They have the privilege and responsibility to rise above mediocre Christianity and show the world what living for Jesus really means!

"Young men, press to the front, and identify yourselves as laborers together with Christ, taking up the work where He left it, to carry it on to its completion" (Ibid., pg. 25). As a Christian, you are called to come up higher, and it's my hope that you'll answer the call.

~ Rachel Petrello

Faith

Faith is needed in the smaller no less than in the greater affairs of life. In all our daily interests and occupations the sustaining strength of God becomes real to us through an abiding trust. - Education, pg. 255

As the first light of dawn streaks across the horizon, two men creep noiselessly through the shadows of a nearby cliff. One is Jonathan, the son of the king of Israel, and the other is his armor-bearer. The two young men pick their way through a rocky gorge until the camp of the Philistines comes into view. The camp is guarded on one side by a seemingly impassible cliff and heavily garrisoned on the remaining three sides. The two men walk into the open and are instantly spotted by the guard stationed on top of the cliff. "...Behold," he laughs tauntingly, "the Hebrews come forth out of the holes where they had hid themselves...Come up to us, and we will shew you a thing" (1 Samuel 14:11, 12 KJV).

As soon as they hear the Philistine's words, the two duck out of sight once again. They scramble quietly to the cliff base and begin to pick their way up the rocky face. Halfway up the cliff, Jonathan disappears into a jagged crack that is completely hidden by hanging vines, and his armor-bearer follows suit. Now, totally out of sight, the pair finish their difficult ascent and draw their swords.

Because the cliff is thought to be impassible, the few guards stationed on top have grown careless and are quickly overpowered. The scuffle with the guards attracts the attention of the other soldiers and a full-fledged battle ensues. Outnumbered a hundred to one, Jonathan and his armor-bearer struggle for their lives and their nation. Unbelievably, in the confusion their adversaries begin to turn on each other. The commotion attracts the attention of the Israelites, and they come to the rescue. The Israelites were able to vanquish their enemies because of the faith of two men. They trusted that God would be able to protect them, and in that confidence, they were victorious.

If I will but put my faith in Christ, He will never fail to guide and protect in my life. And although I may not be fighting against Philistines, His love and grace will always be there to help me battle against sin.

~ Wesley Mayes

November 21

The Children of Israel

Enoch....Noah...the children of Israel...David...Shadrach and his companions...Daniel...Jesus...Paul ...These are the world's true nobility. This is its royal line. In this line the youth of today are called to take their places. - Education, pp. 254, 255

In my devotions one morning, I read the chapter entitled "Faith and Prayer" in the book *Education*. The list in the above quote caught my attention. I was astonished to see that the children of Israel were listed along with some of the most famous men of the Bible as the world's true nobility!

The Israelites were far from what would be considered a noble lot! Even though they had seen countless miracles, heard the very voice of God, and were fed with manna day by day, they continuously forgot God's blessings and complained of their inconveniences! "...They were ready to faint at every obstacle encountered" (*Patriarchs and Prophets*, pg. 292). Why would this group be listed among the greatest men of faith this world has ever seen?

Then I suddenly realized that spiritually I am just like the children of Israel. I don't show appreciation for the blessings God gives me, and even if I do, I forget them. Then, when the blessings disappear and life gets tough, I start complaining and doubt God's promises! I'm exactly like the rebellious, stubborn children of Israel, with a serious lack of faith and trust.

What a promise this quote is to me! Having a righteous character and faith like the men mentioned above often seems utterly impossible. I'm in such a pitiful spiritual condition! But if a group like the Israelites can make it, then there's hope for me too! There's a place reserved for me in the royal line beside the children of Israel, and there's a place there for you too.

~ Rachel Petrello

The Secret Place

To live thus by the word of God means the surrender to Him of the whole life. There will be felt a continual sense of need and dependence, a drawing out of the heart after God. Prayer is a necessity; for it is the life of the soul...It is secret communion with God that sustains the soul life. - Education, pg. 258

Think for a moment about all the people you depend on. For those of us who like to think of ourselves as independent, the list may be short, but I know that each of us has at least a few people in our lives that we really couldn't live without. We depend on our family to care for us and give us security. We depend on our friends to keep up a healthy social life and make us feel loved. We depend on our fellow workers and supervisors to accomplish tasks. We depend on higher authorities to run our governments, organizations, schools and so on. But when these fail us, who will we have to depend on?

These past couple of months I've been through many internal struggles. At first I had so many questions; nothing made sense. I wrestled on my knees with God, asking why, wanting answers, wanting peace. He reminded me that I had to give everything to Him, though I thought I already had. The struggle made me realize that I really hadn't given it all to God. Night after night the dean who checked me in at night would find me still on my knees beside my bed long after my light was out. I finally made it to the point where I truly let go and let God take over. It was then that God filled me with peace.

Since then, I've noticed that Satan tends to throw discouragement and troubles at me whenever life starts becoming normal again. I am no longer afraid to face these, though, because I learned from that encounter with God on my knees. Now I know I can't live without that time I spend in secret communion with God. He sustains me through the easy times, and when trials come I am ready to continue to trust in Him. Every morning, every night, every minute of the day, I've realized my utter dependence on God. When there is nothing left to trust, no one to confide in, He will meet you in the secret place of prayer and satisfy your innermost longing.

~ Valerie Jacobson

Promise

...We may go about our work assured that what God has promised...will be realized when we need it most. - Education, pg. 258

I was having a very emotional night. A best friend had just told me something that made me very upset, and I didn't know what to do or how to handle it. I was sobbing on my bed and wishing I could do something or tell someone. Then I thought of one of my good friends whose sibling was going through the exact same thing. It was late at night, and I didn't really want to bother her with my problems when she had her own to deal with. But she had told me before that if I ever needed something, to just come and ask.

Finally, I couldn't stand the pain any longer. I went to her room, knocked on the door, and proceeded to enter. When she asked what was wrong, I started bawling. The whole time, she just sat next to me and let me cry. She was there for me, hugging and supporting me, never pressing me to tell her anything. She had told me in good times that she would be there anytime, but I didn't realize that completely until I desperately needed her.

You know, God is just like my friend. He has made promises to me in His word: promises to protect, love, guide, and comfort me. Sometimes, when the sun is shining on our lives, we look at God's promises and claim them, but we don't feel them right away. It's when we are in our deepest sorrow, our darkest hour, that His promises shine like a beautiful light, reminding us of His love and care. So don't think that, because you don't feel God's promises being fulfilled in your life right now, they can't be trusted. No, He is always there to love and provide for you. You just have to claim His promises and believe that when you need them most, they will be realized.

~ Yannika Stafford

I Come in Color

It is because so many parents and teachers profess to believe the word of God while their lives deny its power, that the teaching of Scripture has no greater effect upon the youth. - Education, pg. 259
They hear what you say, but they don't act on it! - Ezekiel 33:32 NLT

Stop. Breathe deeply. I want you to picture this: the setting is black and white, and models are posing. However, their features aren't distinct, for the blacks, grays, and whites blend together, and nothing in particular grabs your eye. But wait! You are in that picture, but you can barely recognize yourself or distinguish that it's really you.

As a Christian, do you "talk the talk," but choose not to "walk the walk"? Do you blend in, or stand out? So often, people will compromise their values in order to do the popular thing, to fit in and not be the "weirdo."

When I am performing regular day to day tasks such as shopping at the mall, studying in school, waiting for my piano lesson, or checking out at the grocery line, I wonder if I stand out. Do I stand out with courteousness, helpfulness, laughter, and cheery smiles? Or am I a stumbling block that causes people to whisper, "Man, that Sarah girl. She claims to love God, but I saw her doing such and such."

If we profess to follow Christ, then that profession will be reflected in everything we do. As a Christian, you are not called to party like the world, look like the world, dress like the world, and talk like the world. Rather, you ought to arrive in color and radiate so much vibrance that people can't help but wonder what it is that you possess—something that they lack, yet realize they need. Believe what you say, do it, and share it!

Stop. Breathe deeply. I want you to picture this: the setting is black and white, and models are posing. Yet, amongst the collage of faces, one face comes in color. A face so vivid, so bright, and so colorful that you can't help but take notice. I hope that person is you!

~ Sarah Chang

November 25

Take Time

Many, even in their seasons of devotion, fail of receiving the blessing of real communion with God. They are in too great haste. With hurried steps they press through the circle of Christ's loving presence, pausing perhaps a moment within the sacred precincts, but not waiting for counsel. They have no time to remain with the divine Teacher. With their burdens they return to their work. - Education, pg. 260

Recently, I went through a period when I was not spending as much time with God in the morning as I should. I would get up late, then try to prepare for the day before having my devotions. But I would always end up starting late and not getting as much from my time with Jesus as I could because I was hurrying. So, one night as I lay in bed, I was talking to God, and I asked Him to wake me up sometime between 5:00 and 5:30. When I opened my eyes in the morning, I looked at my clock, and it read 5:13. I was so happy, that I just lay there and praised God for a few moments before rising. I was able to start my devotions much earlier and have a good, fulfilling time with God. Let me tell you, I had much more strength to endure the day than I'd had in a long time!

"Be still, and know that I am God..." (Psalm 46:10 KJV). God calls us to spend that time with Him in the morning. Think of it as the manna that He sent for the Israelites. Every morning they went out and collected just enough for that day. It didn't just magically appear in the containers in their tents; they actually had to go, kneel down, and pick it up. It's the same in our time with God. Every morning He gives us just enough strength for the day. We are not promised strength for the week or for the year, just for the day. However, it doesn't just spontaneously generate within us. We need to be kneeling at the feet of Jesus every morning to pick it up. At the table of God, we are fed the Living Bread and can drink deeply from the Fountain of Life. But only if we take the time to arrive for breakfast. Eating too quickly can cause indigestion; so slow down, enjoy the spiritual food, and gain your strength for the day. Jesus has invited you. Will you come?

~ Carmen Hartwell

Time?

Not a pause for a moment in His presence, but personal contact with Christ, to sit down in companionship with Him—this is our need.
- Education, pg. 261

Slam! I came rushing into the house. "Okay, Jesus!" I panted. "Sorry I'm fifteen minutes late, but I had to make sure the laundry was in the dryer, my friend got last night's homework, and my school stuff was packed."

"But," replied Jesus, "we only have 30 minutes assigned to be together every day, and now we only have half of that time left. You're too busy to spend any other time with me."

"Yeah, I know. But I am here now. So let's start...What should I read this morning?" Five minutes later... "Okay, I'll share that in worship. Now I've got to pray and get going. Dear Jesus, Be with me... I'm busy today, so help me have a good day... Amen."

"But..."

"Sorry Jesus, I have to run now!"

"We didn't talk..."

"Yeah. So sorry about that. I need to run to breakfast now, and before that I have to finish the grocery list. Maybe we can talk tomorrow." Slam!

How often have you done that to God? Think about it. We need to be spending quality time with Him to get to know Him. You can't love someone you don't care about. You can't care about someone you don't know. And you can't know someone who you don't spend time with. So why don't you spend some time getting to know Jesus today?

~ Yannika Stafford

November 27

Higher Ground

Success in any line demands a definite aim. He who would achieve true success in life must keep steadily in view the aim worthy of his endeavor. - Education, pg. 262

Do you have a set of goals that you would liked accomplished before your life is over? Maybe a list of them on your refrigerator door, in your notes on your iPod Touch, or in your personal journal? It's a very constructive practice to sit down and write out some goals for the life ahead of you.

From the 6th to the 8th grade, I was involved in a cross country running team. And whenever we had a race, I had a goal to try to beat my previous best time. Often my goal was achieved; sometimes it wasn't, but it was always my definite aim. Whatever the outcome, there was one thing that was very encouraging to me during those days of running. It was a passage from the Bible, which was printed on the backs of our running shirts: "I press toward the goal for the prize of the upward call of God in Christ Jesus" (Philippians 3:14 NKJV).

Now I have more than one goal. In fact, I have about twenty big dreams that I would like to accomplish before I die, and the number is still growing every time I think of something awesome I would love to do in the future. But, the thing we mustn't forget is that there is an even higher goal than the goals that we can set here on earth. Heaven should be my ultimate aspiration. It should be the ultimate aspiration of all the believers in Christ Jesus. "But lay up for yourselves treasures in heaven, where neither moth nor rust doth corrupt, and where thieves do not break through nor steal..." (Matthew 6:20 KJV). May the words from the old hymn "Higher Ground" be your ambition:

My heart has no desire to stay
Where doubts arise and fears dismay;
Though some may dwell where these abound,
My prayer, my aim, is higher ground.

~ Cyrus Guccione

Christ the Construction Worker

From Him the whole body, joined and held together by every
supporting ligament, grows and builds itself up in love, as each part
does its work. - Ephesians 4:16 NIV

It takes a master artist to select a raw piece of material and create something so beautiful that it impacts all who see it. This is exactly what Christ did. He took a group of twelve men—raw material, nothing extraordinary—many of whom were among the lowly of society, and joined them together in His love, creating a masterpiece that would change the course of human history.

Peter was much like some of us. Bold, self-confident, and quick to perceive faults, he needed a lot of work. Yet Christ looked past Peter's idiosyncrasies and beheld a faithful, loving servant. Jesus taught Peter humility. Like a baby, Peter had to go through the routine of falling and getting back up again before he learned to "walk." But through the grace of God, he became spiritually strong.

Then there was John the Beloved. John was, by nature, an ambitious, self-seeking, proud young man. Jesus rebuked John's self-centered focus and developed in him a character that reflected His own. Jesus brought to light a sincere, loving human being whose true longing was to be like his Master.

These are just two disciples, and there are still ten more who had their own issues. But these men were put into the best refinery. They went in as raw ore and came out pure steel, constructed into a city placed on a hill that couldn't be hidden. When Christ is our focus, we become one, and through Him we can do amazing things.

~ Sarah-Kate Lingerfelt

Take the Risk

Success in any line demands a definite aim. - Education, pg. 262

For as long as I can remember, my family wanted to move to the country. We met more than once with a real estate agent who showed us all the houses that were for sale. There were a few houses that we really liked, but none of them ever worked out for us. We prayed and prayed about it. "Lord," we said, "please give us a house. We are saving up money, and we know that it is good to live in the country. Please, show us the house You want us to have."

My parents held onto their definite aim of living in the country. They saved up money and prayed. They had the goal, and God was up to helping them achieve that goal. Mind you, they were thinking, *We can just have a little fixer-upper house, and we'll be happy, even if it is not very far into the country.* Well, God took that prayer, trust, faith, and planning and worked wonders. Not until He saw the right time for us to go to the country was there any way we were going to move.

Through different experiences, God started to show us where we should live. So, now that we had a location, we were thrilled. However, there were no houses available. Then one day, my mom was talking to a good friend and mentioned that we wanted to move, but there was no house for us to buy. Her friend said, "I think I might know of a place, but I will have to get back to you." She talked to the owners of the house and found that the renter was getting married and moving out; so they were looking to sell. Before my parents got the call telling the price, they prayed about it and set their own price. They asked for a sign: if God wanted us to have that house, then the asking price would have to be the same as the price that my parents had set.

Well, now we live in that five-year-old house out in the country. We are able to open up our curtains and see God's beautiful creation with the sun rising on the mountains.

God has so much to offer you. He wants you to set your aim high. He also wants you to make that aim definite. Trust Him and take the risk. Be specific in what you pray for and let Him guide your path.

~ Jessica Hall

333

A Purpose

He who would achieve true success in life must keep steadily in view the aim worthy of his endeavor. - Education, pg. 262

There was once an extremely successful London merchant named Malcolm who was engaged in Mediterranean commerce. Since he was getting older, he decided that it was about time for him to retire. So, he sold his business and resolved to buy himself a large mansion in the country.

After months of searching, Malcolm decided on one surrounded by immaculate gardens and overlooking a shimmering river. He had all the modern conveniences that anyone would ever want: servants, the newest carriages and coaches, splendid horses, and even a large library. But Malcolm was not content. He felt that he no longer had any purpose or aim. His life had been tied up in his business, and when his business ended, so did his life. As time went on, Malcolm became more and more depressed. He believed his life wasn't worth living. So, early one morning, he set out on his last mission: he would jump off the nearby bridge into the river. As Malcolm walked through the predawn mist, his feet echoing hollowly on the cobblestones, he thought of the life that he should have lived. Nearing the bridge, the sound of footsteps broke into his thoughts. "Who could be up at this hour?" Malcolm wondered. An emaciated young man emerged from the fog and jumped at the sight of Malcolm.

"Wh-what are you doing here?" Malcolm stuttered nervously.

The man sniffed, "I'm here to end my life. My family is being put into the street today because we can't pay our rent, and I cannot live with the shame."

"I can help you," Malcolm replied. And forgetting about his suicide, he left and paid the family's debt. He found his life in helping others.

Malcolm didn't have an aim in his life. He thought he would enjoy a life of selfish ease, but in the end, all he had was emptiness. God wants to be the aim in our lives. He wants to lead us to fulfillment through Him. Malcolm discovered his aim in helping others and, eventually, gave his life to Christ. Place your life in Jesus' hands, and the aim that He gives will bring you eternity.

~ Wesley Mayes

December 1

Long-term Success

Success in any line demands a definite aim. He who would achieve true success in life must keep steadily in view the aim worthy of his endeavor. Such an aim is set before the youth of today. - Education, pg. 262

Why do we endure suffering? Why do we choose to withstand the pain of everyday life? It is simply because we have a goal to achieve and an object to accomplish. Our belief that the future will be better than the past keeps us pressing forward. We achieve success by setting future goals and then accomplishing them.

A recent study at a prestigious college revealed that the 3% of students who had written down their dreams and goals achieved better financial results than the other 97% of students combined. There are many people who have accomplished their dreams by keeping their goals in front of them. Thomas Edison, for example, believed in the impossible. The idea of a practical electric light seemed outrageous to everyone but him. Even after failing two thousand times, he claimed that he had not failed, but had merely discovered two thousand ways in which not to make a light bulb. Even when no one believed in him, he kept trying, and now his invention is used all over the world. Henry Ford had the idea of creating a gas-driven wagon that we now call the car. His dream also seemed impossible. Yet he achieved it by setting a goal and persistently trying to accomplish it.

What is your dream? Perhaps you want to seek a certain profession or serve mankind through some special task. Whatever it is, if you keep your goal in sight and ask God to help you, you will succeed. The journey of a thousand miles begins with the first step. Keep walking. Keep dreaming. Keep believing.

~ Wesley Donesky

This is the Time

The heaven-appointed purpose of giving the gospel to the world in this generation is the noblest that can appeal to any human being...Those who think of the result of hastening or hindering the gospel think of it in relation to themselves and to the world. Few think of its relation to God. Few give thought to the suffering that sin has caused our Creator. - Education, pp. 262, 263

"Go ye therefore, and teach all nations..." (Matthew 28:19 KJV). Christ spoke these words as He departed from us physically on the Mount of Olives. They are a challenge for each of us to face. Many of us feel, however, that this command was given just to the missionaries overseas or the powerful evangelists that are popular today. We are scared, weak, unwilling, unconsecrated, and unholy, and we try to wash our hands of the whole affair. It's always about us and the reason we don't want to share our faith. But have we considered the awful pain and sorrow this brings to God? He has given us a priceless gift, and He wants us to share it. But too often we accept it for ourselves and refuse to share it with others because we are afraid of what they might think of us.

God commanded us to "teach *all* nations..." (emphasis added). This doesn't just mean the poor man in India or the starving child in Africa, but the next-door neighbor, our co-workers, the cashier at the grocery store. We rarely think of the duties that lie nearest to us. We sit placidly in church singing, "I love to tell the story..."; so why aren't we telling it?

This is the time in history when we are being called to take a firm stand. This is the time that we need to unite in efforts to spread the gospel through an accurate representation of Christ. This is the time when we most need to look at the cross and the suffering that our sin and apathy have been causing God. This is the time to be bold for the sake of truth. This is the time. The call has gone out. Will you answer?

~ Anna Fink

December 3

Quenching Thirst

Ethiopia is stretching out her hands unto God. From Japan and China and India, from the still-darkened lands of our own continent, from every quarter of this world of ours, comes the cry of sin-stricken hearts for a knowledge of the God of love. - Education, pp. 262, 263

In my devotions, I have been reading through the book of Jeremiah, and it has shown me a wonderful side of God. It's the part of Him that longs for His children, that cries out, "Come to Me...and I will give you rest" (Matthew 11:28 NKJV). "'Return, O backsliding children,' says the LORD; 'for I am married to you. I will take you, one from a city, and two from a family, and I will bring you to Zion. And I will give you shepherds according to My heart, who will feed you with knowledge and understanding'" (Jeremiah 3:14, 15 NJKV).

People all around this world are in need of God. So many know there is a Higher Power, Something above themselves, but too few actually have a true understanding of God. They are led astray to false religions, worshiping idols, and giving themselves to the lifeless gods of this world.

Are we what is keeping these people from meeting the Savior? As Christians, we have a priceless opportunity to share the gospel with these people. They are so thirsty, each one waiting for a drink. And here we are with full wells for ourselves, drinking enough to live, yet not willing to share the Living Water with those who are begging for just one drink.

God longs to reach out and bless these sin-sick souls, and He wants to use *you* to reach them. Reading through the Scriptures, you can just hear the pain in God's voice, the longing to take His children home, away from this awful world. He needs willing souls to stand up and recognize the task before them. People all around the world need to hear about our God. Are you ready to go tell them?

~ Danielle Schafer

The Princess and the Bee

The cross is a revelation to our dull senses of the pain that, from its very inception, sin has brought to the heart of God. - Education, pg. 263

It was a spring day in Northern California. Underneath a canopy of oak trees drove a red Ford Explorer. In it were a three-year-old girl named Emily and her daddy. They were on their way to get some ice cream at the corner store. Emily suddenly let out a loud scream! Her daddy quickly slammed on his brakes and pulled off to the shoulder.

"What's wrong, Emily?" he quickly asked.
"Bee, Daddy, bee!" Emily exclaimed.
"Don't worry, Princess. I'll get it." Her daddy reached for the bee, knowing the inevitable result. He winced as the bee drove it's little stinger into his hand. And as he opened his hand, the bee flew out the window. Daddy started driving again, and Emily began to cry.
"Oh Daddy, the bee stung you," she sobbed, tears running down her chubby little cheeks.
"I know, Emily, it did; but it's gone now, and you don't have to worry about it anymore," he assured her as he wiped the tears away with his free hand.
"But Daddy, didn't it hurt?" she sniffled.
"Yes it did, but it was worth it because I did it for you."

When they arrived at the store, he turned off the car and turned to look at Emily, who was still weeping in the back seat.
"Emily, look at my hand. Do you see the little stinger?"
"Yes, Daddy."
"Because I love you so much, I made sure that the bee didn't sting you, even though I knew that it would sting me. I took care of it."
"Yes, Daddy, that is why I love you even more."

So often we encounter trials and temptations, but we do not have to fear facing them on our own. Our Daddy, our Heavenly Father, is sitting right next to us each and every moment of our lives. He is there to take the sting and help us with anything that may harm us. All we have to do is ask. Daddy is ready to say, "I'll take care of it."

~ Jessica Hall

December 5

Ambassadors to a Dying World

...From every quarter of this world of ours, comes the cry of sin-stricken hearts for a knowledge of the God of love. Millions upon millions have never so much as heard of God or of His love revealed in Christ...They have an equal claim with us in the Saviour's mercy. And it rests with us who have received the knowledge...to answer their cry..."Who knoweth whether thou art come to the kingdom for such a time as this?" - Education, pp. 262, 263

When the above quote was written, literally "millions upon millions" had not heard of Christ. But that was over 100 years ago. Why then is this statement still very relevant today? You could say that rapid population growth in the last century means that many more people in the world need to hear the gospel. On the other hand, there ought to be many more Christians now than in the early 1900s.

I have been hearing "Jesus is coming soon" for my whole life. Time has been "short" for a long time now. Why are we still on Earth? Christ told us, "And this gospel of the kingdom will be preached in all the world as a witness to all the nations, and then the end will come" (Matthew 24:14 NKJV). So the end hasn't come because the gospel hasn't been preached to every person on the planet. Every single Christian who has the knowledge of God and His love is an heir of God's kingdom. So shouldn't every Christian share the "gospel of the kingdom"? Don't let only professional preachers answer the world's cry. You are called to reach people. They may be next door or somewhere in Africa. Especially now, when sin will soon reach its worst point in history, millions need to hear of a loving God, a risen Savior, and a soon-coming King. Wherever God calls me, I want to be willing to go tell others about my King. Are you willing to be His ambassador to a dying world?

~ Valerie Jacobson

Put Out the Power!

Many do not become what they might, because they do not put forth the power that is in them. They do not, as they might, lay hold on divine strength. - Education, pg. 267

Teens today are a group of highly stereotyped people. Adults have certain expectations of us: we will be disrespectful, lazy, into drugs and alcohol, and will do the least amount of work necessary to get by. But, God has called the youth of our generation to do something different—something of eternal worth. He does not expect us to go and do something great just so we can say we did it, but He asks us to consider our talents, get God-given direction and counsel, and then start working for Him with passion!

When I was younger, I was terrified of playing soccer. It looked like a lot of fun, but I just didn't want to look stupid because I didn't know how to play very well. Finally, my dad convinced me to give it a try. It was hard at first, but I eventually grew to love it, and even though I still am not good, I have lots of fun just playing backyard soccer with my friends.

There might be something hard to do in your life, whether it's trying something new, giving up a bad habit, talking to your non-Christian friends about God, or choosing a life career. Whatever it is, lay hold on Jesus' strength, use the power that God has given you, and go for it!

~ Anna Fink

The Beak of a Bird

The specific place appointed us in life is determined by our capabilities. Not all reach the same development or do with equal efficiency the same work...But each should aim just as high as the union of human with divine power makes it possible for him to reach.
- Education, pg. 267

There is a variety of birds, each having the specific uniqueness and capabilities to suit his needs for survival. Every type of bird is different in size and shape, color and characteristics. The humming bird is equipped with a small, lightweight body and wings that allow it to fly from flower to flower. Its long, delicate beak is just perfect for slipping into the center of the flower to extract the sweet nectar. In contrast to the humming bird is the wood pecker with its strong, solid body and short, sturdy beak. It is built for the sole purpose of drilling holes into the sides of trees to find bugs and worms hidden beneath the surface. The beak of a humming bird would never be able to take on the task of drilling into a tree. And the beak of a wood pecker would never be able to reach far into the stem of a small flower to draw out the nectar. Each bird is given the exact tools it needs to be able to feed itself in the way that God designed.

Lately, God has been working on my heart and revealing a weakness I have. Many times I am tempted to compare myself to others, or to wish I was able to do something as well as they can. God wants me to be content with the abilities He has given me because He wants me to know that I am perfect for my purpose in life.

I no longer need to compare myself with those around me. I'm still pressing toward higher goals through God's power, but I know for certain that I am designed, like the birds, to fulfill the purpose I was created for.

~ Megan Metcalf

Excellence without Excuse

But each should aim just as high as the union of human with divine power makes it possible for him to reach. - Education, pg. 267

"I hate him with all my heart! I really do! Nothing that I do makes him happy. He is so blunt and mean with me! I feel I will never be good enough!" Tears were running down my cheeks as I sat in front of the mirror. I had just spent seven and a half hours on my math assignment, and my uncle was still not satisfied. I had just finished solving 47 problems, and he thought I could have done better. Why couldn't he just tell me that I did a good job? I immediately categorized him as one of those ruthless, tyrannical people that, no matter what you do, will never appreciate your efforts. So I started avoiding him as much as possible.

Years after this incident, I realized the impact that my uncle had on my life. I finally saw what he had been trying to teach me. The reason he had not verbalized his appreciation was not because he wanted to make me feel bad, but rather to give me a reality check about life. For example, in my elementary school, I would often be over-praised for the grades I received, but in high school, my teachers would always expect more from me. My uncle successfully taught me to aim as high as I could—to aspire to excellence without excuse.

Have you ever found yourself not giving your best? If you do not use the talents God has blessed you with at a superlative level, it is a waste. Do not be afraid to set high standards for yourself. It will motivate you to do everything proficiently. Ultimately, God wants us to achieve excellence without excuse. Ask God to show you how to aim higher, and you will experience His flow of blessings poured out upon your life.

~ Valdis Cuvaldin

December 9

One More Step

For a just man falleth seven times, and riseth up again: but the wicked shall fall into mischief. - Proverbs 24:16 KJV

I felt like crying. Pain pulsed through my legs, and my shoulders were sore. I panted and gasped for air, struggling to propel one foot forward. It was a warm weekend in May, and as part of Socials 10 class, we were required to backpack to Stryne Cabin. The two miles of steep uphill walking made my muscles groan. When I was informed of our "assignment," I didn't even know what backpacking was! Nevertheless, I was excited to see someplace new. Hiking the trail was a constant struggle. But most encouraging was when Mr. Lemon would repeat, "Just one more step. You can do it, just one more step. You'll be there before you know it."

A motto that I have recently been trying to incorporate into my life is "Failure is not an option." If you train yourself to realize that success is the only way to go, then failure will not be a part of the picture. There will be times when we feel like we are complete failures, but then we need to pick ourselves back up again and determine to do better next time. I know it's hard—I've been in the "You're a failure" zone many times. When we feel tired, discouraged, and weak, and tell God, "I hate this. I want to quit," God patiently tells us to take a step, even if it's a small one.

In Japan, they have little Daruma dolls that are weighted at the bottom. No matter how hard you try, you can't knock them over. "Seven times down, eight times up," is a phrase that every Japanese child knows. God blessed you with special gifts and abilities. It is your duty to use everything you have to bring others to God. Don't give up!

~ Sarah Chang

343

The Sabbath Keepers

...Let the pupils study the lives of such men as the apostle Paul and Martin Luther, as Moffat and Livingstone and Carey, and the present daily-unfolding history of missionary effort. - Education, pg. 269

Today, any of the European peoples of antiquity who spoke a Celtic language are called Celts. The historical Celts were a diverse group of tribal societies whose history and origins may be traced all the way back to Noah leaving the ark.

Patrick (c.387-493), one of the best known Celtic missionaries, was born in Roman Britain. His father and grandfather were workers for the gospel. When Patrick was about sixteen, he was captured and taken to Ireland as a slave. He worked as a herdsman in captivity for six years. But he wrote that "his faith grew in captivity, and that he prayed daily." At a very young age, he continued his father's and grandfather's work by preaching the gospel to the Irish.

Another famous Celtic missionary was Brendan of Clonfert (c.484-577), often called "The Voyager." It has been said that he once sailed from Ireland to Iceland and Newfoundland in a small leather Currach, a type of Irish boat with a wooden frame over which animal skins were stretched. In Iceland he met a man named Pol. Brendan thought Pol was such a fine Christian that he named the island Is(s)u-land. Is(s)u is the Celtic/Gaelic name for Jesus. The original name of Iceland may have been Isu-land, or The Land of Jesus. But when the heathen Vikings arrived in the late 9th century, they gradually dominated the culture in Iceland and changed the name to Island (English: Iceland), because they did not want anything to do with Jesus, whom they called the "White-Christ."

The Celtic Church practiced baptism by immersion, foot washing as part of the Lord's Supper, and some members were vegetarians. In the 12th century, Celtic Christians were accused of adhering to the Jewish faith because they kept the seventh-day Sabbath. Therefore, the first Icelanders were most likely Celtic Sabbath-keepers. I think it is very encouraging to learn about people throughout history who preserved the truth and kept the true Sabbath.

~ Elísa Elíasdóttir

Becoming a Moses

...He sees the height to which they may attain. Although human beings have abused their mercies, wasted their talents, and lost the dignity of godlike manhood, the Creator is to be glorified in their redemption.
- Education, pg. 270

When I read the story of Moses, I see God's tender mercy. God rescued Moses from a decree to kill all the infant boys in Egypt. God had a plan for Moses. After living among royalty, Moses began to have compassion for his own kin, realizing the brutal treatment they were receiving from their Egyptian masters. One day, Moses saw an Egyptian beating a Hebrew. Enraged, he killed the Egyptian on the spot. When Pharaoh got wind of this, he was incensed. He sentenced Moses to death, but the Lord showed mercy and provided a safe haven for Moses in the wilderness. Moses could have become a great leader in Egypt, but he turned down this opportunity. God took him out of a worldly metropolis and placed him in a quiet, scenic place where nature could speak. His character and habits had been molded by some of the mysticism and idol worship in Egypt. Therefore, God took Moses into the wilderness to unlearn these falsehoods. God saw the heights Moses could reach and brought him into His divine presence so that he could realize the power of Omnipotence. But when God called Moses, he was afraid. He complained that he wasn't a good speaker, but still God bade him to stand before Pharaoh, and Moses consented.

In this story of one of the meekest of men, the Creator is glorified. The rescued child of God became the rescuer of God's children who were still ensnared in bondage. Christ Jesus will do the same with you and me, if we will let him.

~ Sarah-Kate Lingerfelt

Remodeling Your Heart

He [God] sees on every hand souls in darkness, bowed down with sin and sorrow and pain. But He sees also their possibilities; He sees the height to which they may attain. Although human beings have abused their mercies, wasted their talents, and lost the dignity of godlike manhood, the Creator is to be glorified in their redemption.
- Education, pg. 270

Nothing can test the patience and skill of a builder more than a good fixer-upper—the kind that needs more than just a new coat of paint or some extra nails. Imagine a small house that's barely recognizable; everyone but you would think that it's an abandoned shack. Parts of the roof and walls have fallen in, and the floor is dangerous to walk on because it could collapse any second. But you see something that no one else sees in this dilapidated old pile of sticks. You see potential. You know that you can turn this house into a beautiful mansion with an indoor swimming pool and tennis court and everything you've ever wanted in your home. The only problem is that you don't have the tools or the money to complete the project. You could start painting a wall here, or patching up the roof there, but you simply cannot complete the project with the tools or supplies you currently have. You need the help of a carpenter who has what it takes to completely remodel the house.

God sees on every hand souls that are bowed down with the mold and rot of sin. But, He also sees their possibilities. He sees the beautiful home that He can create in each of their hearts. Although human beings have wasted their talents and become old empty shacks, the Creator is to be glorified in their remodeling. Sound familiar? Read the top of the page again. It's amazing to think that God wants to live in my heart and in your heart. He said in Revelation 3:20, "Here I am! I stand at the door and knock. If anyone hears my voice and opens the door, I will come in and eat with him, and he with me" (NIV). We are all fixer-uppers. And we all have the same potential of becoming a beautiful home for God. If you turn the keys of your heart over to Him, I guarantee, you will like the results.

~ Wesley Donesky

December 13

Revelation

This is the secret of power...Reflect Him. - Education, pg. 282

Power. What is it about that word that makes millions of people worldwide go crazy? Maybe it is because we feel controlled, because we wish we could control, that we all desire to have our piece of the power pie. But most of us, if given power, would misuse it. We all have the power to govern ourselves, but I know that my judgement has failed me numerous times because Satan has a formidable ally: self. He uses you to get you to fall; he uses your own sinful desires to distort your judgement and reasoning, causing you to hurt yourself and others. So if you had power over others, what makes you think that you would do the right thing, if you know you're being influenced by Satan and your sinful self?

Ever wondered why so many dictators go wrong? Can one person be trusted to have ultimate, unchallenged authority over an entire nation's people and resources? Something is wrong with that concept. But there is good news! Each of us has power to fight back, the power called choice. Choice has the greatest influence over your life, and you control it.

When you're driving a remote controlled car, it doesn't have any choice concerning where it wants to go or what it wants to do; it is completely at your mercy. That car represents your will; you are in control. But you can't be trusted with that control because you have been infected with the "self" virus. So you have to make a choice to give up that control to one of two beings. You could give your will to Satan, to be used to his advantage without a thought about your well-being. And once your battery dies, Satan will simply discard you. Or you could choose to give your will over to God. When you do that, you will have happiness, and your battery will never run dry. Only by giving your control over to God will you be able to reflect Him, and when you reflect Him, you will stay charged. Each day will be a further revelation of His power in your life and will radiate that power to those around you. I want that; don't you?

~ Jo Holdal

Little Helpers

Let fathers and mothers take time to teach their children, let them show that they value their help, desire their confidence, and enjoy their companionship, and the children will not be slow to respond.
- Education, pg. 285

Ever since I was little, my dad always let my sister and me go to work with him to help with various jobs. Since he is an electrician, he taught us how to put light fixtures and paddle fans together, how to use several tools and pieces of equipment, and how to wire electrical outlets. We loved helping him and felt important because we were able to do "big people" work. We would ride with him in his big diesel truck, leaping out the door with our work clothes on, hammers and screw drivers in our pockets. My relationship with my dad is strong because he spent time with me, teaching me to work just like he did.

Jesus also worked alongside His earthly father, Joseph, learning a useful skill in the carpenter's shop. He helped Joseph throughout His life until God called Him to ministry. His years of service to His family demonstrates the importance of children learning skills under their parents' supervision. This time should be enjoyable, side-by-side work, so that there is a positive bond formed between the parents and children. The children will feel important and wanted, giving them motivation to learn and grow in maturity. They will love the feeling of accomplishing a project with their parents, and trust will be strengthened that will last throughout their lives.

~ Megan Metcalf

December 15

Jumping to Conclusions

In our efforts to correct evil, we should guard against a tendency to faultfinding or censure. - Education, pg. 291

There once was a pastor who was organizing an evangelistic campaign in his small town. He had reserved an auditorium in the local Adventist high school to hold his meetings. One day, shortly before the series was to begin, the principal of the high school called him, saying, "I am so sorry to inform you that the rain storm last night caused some serious damage. The use of the auditorium is out of the question for at least two weeks." Now the poor pastor really had a problem. Where were they to hold the meetings? While he was brainstorming, he suddenly remembered that the local theater only ran movies on Saturdays and Sundays because the town was so small. Since it was Sunday, he decided to drive over and speak to the manager. After two intense hours of negotiating, they finally reached an agreement. Sabbath morning the pastor walked into church and was greeted by ugly stares from his church members. He asked his head elder what was wrong. The elder said, "Don't act like you don't know. We all know where you were and what you were doing last Sunday." The pastor smiled and got up to preach. He said, "I have an important announcement to make. We have had to change the location of the evangelistic meetings due to the storm damage at the high school. Last Sunday I spent about two hours with the theater manager making arrangements to hold our evangelistic meetings there." The church members gasped. Some of them had seen the pastor go into the theater. They thought they knew why he had gone there, when in actuality he had been doing the Lord's work.

Instead of jumping to conclusions, we should let God do the judging. Often things are not as they appear, and we are too quick to judge before we have all the facts. Like the Bible says, "Judge not that ye be not judged. For with what judgment ye judge, ye shall be judged: and with what measure ye mete, it shall be measured to you again" (Matthew 7:1, 2 KJV). God is the only righteous judge.

~ Daniel Glassford

Persistent Love

The divine Teacher bears with the erring through all their perversity. His love does not grow cold; His efforts to win them do not cease. With outstretched arms He waits to welcome again and again the erring, the rebellious, and even the apostate. - Education, pg. 294

Unconditional love is rarely experienced. Yet it has the ability to change people's lives in a way that nothing else can. In a letter to the Corinthians, Paul said, "And now these three remain: faith, hope and love. But the greatest of these is love" (1 Corinthians 13:13 NIV). Counselors have observed that people who engage in addictive, self-abusive behaviors such as using drugs or cutting themselves will rarely try to stop the negative behaviors when they are told that the behaviors themselves are harmful. However, if the people who are receiving counseling can think of one person that will love and accept them no matter what they have done, a large portion of them will discontinue the addictive, self-abusive behaviors without further counseling.

Jesus was the greatest counselor of all time. He said, "...I will never leave thee, nor forsake thee" (Hebrews 13:5 KJV). God will never give up on His children. And those who are struggling against sin are the special objects of His love. "For all have sinned and fall short of the glory of God, and are justified freely by His grace through the redemption that came by Christ Jesus" (Romans 3:23, 24 NIV). All people have their battles with sin and temptation. Whatever you are struggling with, just remember that you are not forgotten. God's love can win a victory over sin in your life today. Trust Him and remember that He will never stop loving you or calling you to a place that is higher than anything this world offers.

~ Wesley Donesky

A Battlefield

...This world is not a parade ground, but a battlefield...The true way of dealing with trial is not by seeking to escape it, but by transforming it.
- Education, pg. 295

God allows trials in our lives to test our faith, to show us that good things can come from seemingly bad experiences.

My family and I decided to go on a mission trip to India when I was around 12 years old. My mom and dad preached a campaign to people from five villages, and every night I would set up the computer and projector for the sermon. Each night the Indian people were captivated by the graphics on the screen and for the first time they learned of a God who loved them unconditionally. Everything seemed to be going as planned until one night, when Satan decided that things were going too well.

It was a Friday night and millions of bugs filled the evening air. The bugs were attracted to the brilliant white light of the projector, and inevitably a few bugs made their way inside. Kaaa-boooom! There was a sudden explosion followed by the sound of tinkling glass. Everyone gasped because smoke was pouring out of the projector. My dad hustled over to the machine, a scowl across his face. There was no mistaking it: the projector bulb had exploded. Then my mom, who was preaching, shouted through the half-dead microphone, "The God of heaven can do anything, so we are going to pray to God and ask Him to make the projector work again." As my Mom prayed, 900 Indian people reverently bowed their heads, and when my Mom had finished praying, they opened their eyes. The projector was back on! It was a miracle! Later that week, over 500 people gave their hearts to a God who is more powerful than all their gods combined.

I learned that day that this world is most definitely a battlefield. But our God is able to defeat the enemy and create something good out of an apparent disaster. He will stop at nothing to bring others to a knowledge of His great love for them.

~ Daniel Glassford

Call to Arms

All are called to endure hardness, as good soldiers. They are to be strong and quit themselves like men. Let them be taught that the true test of character is found in the willingness to bear burdens, to take the hard place, to do the work that needs to be done, though it bring no earthly recognition or reward. - Education, pg. 295

Have you ever imagined yourself as a soldier? The smart uniforms, ordered ranks, and precision marching are enough to impress anyone. But this is not the purpose of the army. Its purpose is to take ordinary men and women and make them stronger, more focused, and willing to work harder. Soldiers are put through gruelling physical training and mental stress to condition their minds and bodies and prepare them for battle. They must be prepared to endure and overcome the worst circumstances and to implicitly follow every order, because their lives and the lives of their comrades may depend on their utter obedience and willingness to face danger.

This mental image is so intense and hard to relate to. But then, it's only in our imagination, right? No. Life is a battlefield. The trials and struggles we face are not much different from the hardships a soldier must go through. In this sin-sick world, troubles and perplexities are inevitable. Now that we've come to this realization, don't panic! It's not all just a pointless fight. It's not our part to give up because we see how hard life can be. Trials can make us stronger, more prepared to handle bigger troubles, and more willing to do the necessary tasks of life, no matter how hard or thankless they may be.

God, our Commander, is waiting for us to be willing to face the hard times of life with hope and determination. He wants us to follow Him with the knowledge that our Leader has already suffered the most and died a heroic death to save us. The battle is already won; the plan is almost complete. All God asks of us is to be brave for a little while longer, to trust in Him, and to go through anything for His glory. Will you answer the call?

~ Valerie Jacobson

Friends

A man that hath friends must shew himself friendly: and there is a friend that sticketh closer than a brother. - Proverbs 18:24 KJV

<u>Recipe for Friendship</u>

1 Cup Loyalty		1 ½ Cups Oatmeal
1 Cup Trust		1 ½ Cups Flour
2 Cups Fun		¾ Cup Brown Sugar
¾ Cup Encouragement		½ Cup Oil or Margarine
1 tsp. Spontaneity	OR	1 tsp. Baking Powder
A pinch of Sunny Days		2 tsp. Salt
½ Cup Sweet Things		½ Cup Carob Chips
A kaleidoscope of memories		Nuts or Raisins
		1 tsp. Vanilla
		½ Cup Milk

1) Mix and place on greased cookie sheet using a small scoop or spoon. OR
   Tell all your friends you love and appreciate them.

2) Bake at 350° for 12-15 minutes or until golden brown. OR
   Write cards for elderly people in your local nursing home. Visit them, and make new friends!

3) Remove cookies from cookie sheet and place on a cooling rack. Makes twenty cookies. OR
   Perform a chore for a neighbor to be the best friend that you can be. And bake cookies to share!

   Friends are wonderful. They laugh with you, cry with you, and will lend a listening ear when you need it. When you spend time with your friends here on earth, remember your other Friend who watches and guides you and will be there for you when others have forsaken you. In order to have friends, be a friend!

~ Sarah Chang

Battlefield!

...The children and the youth...should be taught that this world is not a parade ground, but a battlefield. All are called to endure hardness, as good soldiers. They are to be strong and quit themselves like men. Let them be taught that the true test of character is found in the willingness to bear burdens, to take the hard place, to do the work that needs to be done, though it bring no earthly recognition or reward.
- Education, pg. 295

It was April 12, 1861, and the American Civil War began when shots were fired on Fort Sumter. Both sides sent out calls to gather troops for an army. Men of all ages began pouring into the recruiting stations, excited about the prospect of riding forth to victory. They admired the uniforms and swelled with pride under the flags that brightly snapped in the breeze. No one expected the war to last long, and not much time was spent training. Then the first battle began with heavy casualties, and people began to realize that it would be a long, hard struggle.

This world can seem bright and enticing, luring us to sin with its sights and sounds. We flock to places where the temptation is heavy and trade our salvation in order to "look good" to others.

But this world is not a parade. It is a long, hard battle, fought both in the seen and the unseen realms. We are admonished to "take unto you the whole armour of God, that ye may be able to withstand in the evil day..." (Ephesians 6:13 KJV). This is a battle, but "God hath not given us the spirit of fear; but of power, and of love, and of a sound mind" (2 Timothy 1:7 KJV).

~ Anna Fink

December 21

What Are You Holding Onto?

The exchange we make in the denial of selfish desires and inclinations is an exchange of the worthless and transitory for the precious and enduring. This is not sacrifice, but infinite gain...Whatever Christ asks us to renounce, He offers in its stead something better. - Education, pg. 296

When I was a baby, I was always getting into mischief. One day, while my mom was on the phone, I saw a shiny silver knife lying on the table. With much effort, I climbed on top of the table. My mom came back into the room just in time to see me running my itty-bitty baby fingers over the blade. I giggled as I noticed my distorted reflection in the metal. Mom reached to take the knife, but I grasped it more tightly, pulling the blade toward my tummy. My mom asked me to give her the knife, but I stubbornly shook my blond peach-fuzz hair as I said, "No! Mine!" I was convinced that Mom just wanted to take away my fun. She looked at me with a terrified expression on her face, not wanting to think about what would happen if I toppled over. As soon as all my fingers were firmly around the handle, and not the blade, Mom made a mad grab and took the knife away. I burst into tears! Mom had taken away my coolest toy ever! Mom picked me up and carried me to the kitchen. She showed me how sharp the knife was as she whacked a carrot in half, but I was unimpressed. She offered me a beautiful shinny rattle, but I tossed it on the floor.

How often are we just like that? God comes to us and says, "Please, hand over that relationship in your life that is bringing you down. Stop spending time on those things which have no eternal value." But we shake our heads stubbornly and say, "No! It's mine!"

Is there something in your life that you need to give to God? Don't be scared to hand it over. God never takes away anything that is for your good. Besides, once those things are out of your life, you will have time to notice the wonderful replacements He has sent, and which will bring you true joy and fulfillment.

~ Daniel Glassford

355

Aim High

Let the child and the youth be taught that every mistake, every fault, every difficulty, conquered, becomes a stepping-stone to better and higher things. It is through such experiences that all who have ever made life worth the living have achieved success. - Education, pg. 296

Hold onto God's hand.
In times of trouble
God will always guide you.
Hope for the future
Even when storm clouds pour.
Rainbows glimmer at the end of every storm.

When times are rough
And trouble comes our way,
Always remember that God's love is here to stay.
And when all hope seems lost
Shout "Ever higher! We will prevail!"
Pressing onward, marching forward
Straight through the stormy gale.
Do your best to meet and pass the test,
And God will truly smile, indeed.
To discover all that we can do...
To help others along the way...
To try new things...
And be a friend to everyone...
As the years drift by, I want to look back
And rest assured that I held myself to a higher standard.
That I chose right over wrong—stood up for what I believe.
I will lead by example and never take the easy way out.
View each problem, whether great or small
As a stepping stone to success.
Yes, higher is our goal,
And for God, let us strive to do our best!

~ Sarah Chang

God's Gravity

When once the gaze is fixed upon Him, the life finds its center. The enthusiasm, the generous devotion, the passionate ardor, of the youth find here their true object...To honor Christ, to become like Him, to work for Him, is the life's highest ambition and its greatest joy.
- Education, pg. 297

Gravity: the unseen force that holds all things in their proper places. It causes the moon to revolve around the earth, the earth around the sun, and the sun around the center of the Milky Way. These cosmic bodies naturally follow the laws of gravity. They don't have to think, "Shall I choose to let gravity guide my course today? But a human perspective of life shows a whole different story.

Sometimes I feel like I'm just floating through life, being pushed and pulled by everything around me. I try to go forward, doing what's required of me and reaching for goals I've set, but all the outside circumstances influencing me make it hard. I can remember times in my life when my aims and focus were fickle and easily changed. I usually ended up confused as to what I was truly focusing on.

It's at these times that I must remember where my focus should be. I need to look up at Christ, not at myself and my confusions and inadequacies. When I allow Christ to take His rightful place in my life, my energies, focus, needs, and wants—every aspect of my life—will become secondary to Him. At the same time, these will also find their purpose in Him. God has the power over everything in life that pushes and pulls me. I need to center my life in Christ and let it revolve around Him, so that in serving, honoring, and becoming like Him, I will have a sure purpose and direction. My decision is to fix my gaze on Christ and let His gravity take hold on my life. Will you choose the same?

~ Valerie Jacobson

Imagine Heaven

Heaven is a school; its field of study, the universe; its teacher, the Infinite One. A branch of this school was established in Eden; and, the plan of redemption accomplished, education will again be taken up in the Eden school. "Eye hath not seen, nor ear heard, neither have entered into the heart of man, the things which God hath prepared for them that love Him." Only through His word can a knowledge of these things be gained; and even this affords but a partial revelation.
- Education, pg. 301

Close your eyes for a moment. Imagine a place where you can have the house of your dreams, and where there is no time to worry. Imagine a place where people are not jealous, mean, or hypocritical, where all live in harmony with each other. Imagine a place where there is no more pain or sorrow, and where doctors will be out of jobs. Imagine a place so big that you can explore it forever. Imagine a place where lions and lambs play together, and where famous people will talk with the underdogs. Imagine a place where you will not fail anymore, and no one will care how much "weight you gained lately." Imagine a place where there will be no racism. Imagine a place where there will be no more natural calamities. Imagine a place where everybody is your best friend, and where nobody will say goodbye again. Imagine a place where there will be no more death or separation. Imagine a place where you will be eternally with God. Imagine...heaven.

Would you like to be in a place like that? God clearly tells us that heaven is far better than anything we could ever imagine. Isn't it amazing that a loving God longs for us to one day be with Him in such a wonderful place? Missing out on heaven is really hard to do. Think about it! You have God and all the angels on your side. What do you have to worry about? Heaven is cheap enough that anybody can afford it; Jesus paid the price with His blood when He was crucified. This is what I call the ultimate blessing! Do you want to go to heaven? If you do, place all your problems in God's hands and make the decision today to follow Him at all times!

~ Valdis Cuvaldin

Invisible Protection, Part 1

Celestial beings have taken an active part in the affairs of men. They have appeared in garments that shone as the lightning; they have come as men, in the garb of wayfarers. They have accepted the hospitalities of human homes; they have acted as guides to benighted travelers. - Education, pp. 304, 305

From the window, John and Sarah could see the snow softly falling around their family's cabin in the mountains. Their parents had left early that morning to acquire supplies for the winter, when the roads would be blocked by the severe winter storms. As they watched the snow slowly float down and settle into drifts, they couldn't help but think about the day's events...

After an early breakfast, their parents started up the old truck and began the several hour journey to the nearest town for supplies. Later that morning John and Sarah worked on their homework, enjoyed a ping-pong match, and made some fudge. That evening, after cleaning up the supper dishes, they prayed and read from the Bible. Then they prepared for bed. As they were just about to turn in for the night, they heard a knock on the door. John opened the door and there, standing in the doorway, was a dark, burly man who quickly asked, "Are your parents home?"

John answered, "I'm sorry, but they're not home right now. If you'd like, you can call…"

"Well then, I guess I'll just take over here," the man interrupted in a sly voice. John noticed a small, black metal object inside the man's coat and he knew instinctively that the man was an armed criminal or an escaped convict of some kind. After demanding food and money, the man lay down on their couch for a nap and said, as he patted the object in his coat pocket, that if they tried anything funny, he wouldn't hesitate to use his "little friend." John and Sarah quietly walked over to the kitchen and decided to pray. Almost before they had finished their prayer, they heard another knock on the front door.

~ Wesley Donesky

Invisible Protection, Part 2

Celestial beings...have thwarted the spoiler's purpose and turned aside the stroke of the destroyer. - Education, pp. 304, 305

This time when John opened the door, he was met by a tall, friendly-looking man who appeared very hungry and cold. John immediately invited him to get warm. The man walked in and sat down across from the man who was reclining on the couch. After the two men had talked for a while, the robber began to get nervous. He knew that sooner or later the taller man would figure out who he really was. Just as he was about to pull out his gun, the taller man suddenly stood up and dashed across the room. With one hand, the tall man picked up the robber; then he walked across the room and opened the door with the other hand. In one toss, the tall stranger threw the robber out of the house and warned him never to come back again. The robber quickly got up and ran away into the forest. John and Sarah thanked the man, but instead of receiving the credit for saving them, the man told them to thank God for His protection. Then he asked, "Would it be all right if I stayed for the night?"

"Of course," said John, and Sarah showed him to the guest room.

When breakfast was ready the next morning, John went to wake the man. But when he opened the door to his room, there was no one inside. And the bed looked like it hadn't been touched. As he looked around the room, he noticed a small note on the dresser. It said, "Be not forgetful to entertain strangers. For by entertaining strangers, some have entertained angels."

God's protection has often come through angels in human form. "The angel of the LORD encampeth round about them that fear Him, and delivereth them" (Psalm 34:7 KJV). When you trust God and believe that He is always there for you, help will come. You might even be saved by an angel.

~ Wesley Donesky

December 27

Zoom Out

Every redeemed one will understand the ministry of angels in his own life...All the perplexities of life's experience will then be made plain.
- Education, pg. 305

Do you like to travel? I sure do! It's so exciting to go to new places and learn about other cultures. I love immersing myself in a different culture and learning what the lives of others are really like. I sometimes wish I never had to stop traveling, and guess what? I don't!

You and I are on a journey. Our map is the Bible; our goal, Heaven. How do we get there? By reading only one part of the map? By taking only a few verses and basing all our decisions on those texts? I'd rather read the whole map and be prepared. Even better, we can ask our Guide, Christ, for directions, and He'll get us there because He has already blazed the trail for all to follow.

Have you ever wanted to meet your guardian angel? I have, ever since I was a little girl. It's so fascinating to think how many times I may have seen mine and not known it. I can't wait for Heaven, when I can finally meet my guardian angel and find out all the close calls I have had without even realizing it. So often I want to just zoom in and focus on my little life right now—all my issues and joys; but what I really need to do is zoom out. When we zoom out, we see the big picture, and it's a lot easier to understand where we're going and how to get there.

When we get to Heaven, we'll be greeted by our guardian angels. Won't that be exciting? We'll have the opportunity to learn of all the mysteries that were so perplexing on Earth, and our mishaps will be explained. We will zoom out and see the big picture. We will finally understand exactly why things turned out the way they did. I can hardly wait for that day!

~ Jo Holdal

361

You'll Not Be Forgotten

All of the perplexities of life's experience will then be made plain.
Where to us have appeared only confusion and disappointment,
broken purposes and thwarted plans, will be seen a grand, overruling,
victorious purpose, a divine harmony. - Education, pg. 305

There was once an old missionary who was returning to his homeland after many years of service. Years before, he and his wife had buried their only children who had died during a cholera epidemic. After 60 years of marriage, the old missionary had had to say goodbye to his dear wife as she went to rest in a shallow grave in Africa. Bent over with arthritis, he walked up the gangplank onto the ocean liner that would take him home.

It just so happened that a U.S. President was on board that same ship, coming back from a hunting expedition in Africa. When they arrived at the port in San Francisco, no one was allowed to get off the ship until the President and his entourage had received their welcoming ceremonies. Bands played and the red carpet was rolled out. Finally, after an hour of celebration, the ship was allowed to unload cargo and passengers. Since the missionary was slow, he waited till the last. By the time he got off the ship, darkness had fallen. Cold fog wrapped around his thin shoulders. No one was there to greet him. Struggling to carry his one suitcase, he stumbled through the streets until he found an inexpensive hotel. Heaving his suitcase into the small room, he sunk to his knees beside his bed and began to weep. "Lord," he cried, "is this the way a poor old missionary is to be treated? I know I am not famous like the President. I don't need bands to play for me, but to have no one greet me when I come home is just too much!" After sobbing for a few more minutes, he heard the Lord say to him, "But son, you aren't home yet!"

Do you feel like you are insignificant? All the work we do on earth in His name will not be forgotten. When we get to heaven, we will be glad we chose our higher course to serve God. Our reward will be eternal life with those we influenced for heaven.

~ Daniel Glassford

December 29

No More Disappointments

There the loves and sympathies that God has planted in the soul will find truest and sweetest exercise. The pure communion with holy beings, the harmonious social life with the blessed angels and with the faithful ones of all ages, the sacred fellowship that binds together "the whole family in heaven and earth"—all are among the experiences of the hereafter. - Education, pg. 306

Do you look forward to heaven and the new earth? I can't wait to take in all the wonders of creation that I can't experience here on earth. I will explore the farthest reaches of space, the deepest depths of the ocean, and the densest forests, without fear of suffocating, drowning, or getting lost. It will be so cool to play with huge lions, to eat delicious fruit like I've never imagined, and to pick never-fading flowers bursting with colors I've never seen before. But, there is more to the new earth than all these wonderful interactions with nature.

Here on this earth I've discovered that friendships can be tiring. They don't just happen. Friendships take hard work, and often our efforts bring only disappointment. It is so easy to damage or ruin friendships because of our selfish natures. God gave us an instinctive desire to love and to be loved, and while we can have good friendships here in this world, in the new earth we will have the fullest measure of God's love flowing through us. This is one of the main reasons that I am excited for the new earth. There, I'll be able to see my old friends and make many more new ones, without having to worry that my selfish motives will mar any of my friendships.

I can't wait to discover all the natural wonders of heaven and the new earth. I'm even more excited to finally be able to have friendships that will be the "truest and sweetest." However, the one thing I look forward to the most is spending time with Jesus, the One who has given me that disposition for love, and who will love me no matter what, even when I mess up in my relationship with Him. I don't want to disappoint Him anymore; I choose to accept His love, friendship, and salvation. He who never fails nor disappoints longs to spend eternity with you too. Will you choose to be there?

~ Valerie Jacobson

More Than the Angels

The redeemed only, of all created beings, have in their own experience known the actual conflict with sin; they have wrought with Christ, and, as even the angels could not do, have entered into the fellowship of His sufferings... - Education, pg. 308

Have you ever wanted to be an angel? To be sent by God Himself to rescue a person on earth from death, to proclaim an important message for God, or even to stop the attack of an intruder? Angels have exciting lives in service for heaven. Aside from being in contact with God, they have also been able to watch earth's history unfold since creation 6,000 years ago.

Even though angels have incredible roles to play, we as humans have something they don't have: the testimony of living on a sinful planet, suffering with Christ for His name's sake, and gaining victory over sin by His power. Yes, the angels had to make a choice between good and evil when Lucifer rebelled in heaven, but we have a special story that no other created being can tell.

Because you are daily overcoming sin by the blood of the Lamb, you will one day stand before God in your pure, white robe of Christ's righteousness with a crown of glory upon your head, proclaiming that God is faithful and true. You are a human being, and Jesus became a human being and died for the human race. It amazes me to think that the scars in the nail-pierced hands of Christ are for us and us alone. Out of every being God created in the universe, we will be the dearest and the closet to God—we are the ones He gave His life to save. The heavenly choirs of angels will sing triumphant songs of the redeemed. What a joyful day that will be when Christ, the Bridegroom, can finally be reunited with His bride. How glorious it will be when He comes on the clouds of heaven to take us home for eternity! With that special position I have with Christ, I wouldn't want to miss that reunion for the world.

~ Megan Metcalf

364

December 31

Finally, You're Home!

Then, in the results of His work, Christ will behold its recompense. In that great multitude which no man could number, presented "faultless before the presence of His glory with exceeding joy," He whose blood has redeemed and whose life has taught us, "shall see of the travail of His soul, and shall be satisfied." - Education, pg. 309

A few months ago, the senior class went on a mission trip to Malaysia. The night they were arriving back at Fountainview, I was so excited I could hardly stand it! I was literally pacing the room, jumping on the bed, sighing, and constantly looking out the window for bus headlights! My poor roommate thought I had gone completely crazy! My best friends were on that bus! They had been gone for three whole weeks, and I couldn't wait to see them! I grabbed my journal and started writing furiously:

"Oh! I wish they would just get here! The seniors are coming back tonight! Their estimated time of arrival was somewhere between 7:30-9:00 pm, and right now it's 8:43!!! I am so excited!...Ah! More headlights! I hope this is it! OH THIS IS TORTURE!!!"

Have you ever felt that same anxious, excited feeling when you're about to see someone you love? Did you know that is exactly how God feels about you? Have you ever imagined God running back and forth, butterflies bouncing up and down inside His stomach, constantly checking His eternity clock and counting the milliseconds to when He'll be able to see you? His heart is aching with intense, excited longing to finally see you face to face, throw His arms around you, and take you home!

Just like when the seniors finally arrived, and I ran out eagerly to meet them, someday God will run out to meet you. The anxiety of waiting will be over, and He'll swoop you up into His arms, holding you close to His chest, and amidst laughter and tears of joy He'll shout, "Finally! You're home!"

~ Rachel Petrello